Developing Better Readers and Writers Using Caldecott Books

Kathryn I. Matthew

Neal-Schuman Publishers, Inc.

New York   London

Published by Neal-Schuman Publishers, Inc.
100 William St., Suite 2004
New York, NY 10038

Printed and bound in the United States of America.

The paper used in this publication meets the minimum requirements of American National Standard for Information Sciences—Permanence of Paper for Printed Library Materials, ANSI Z39.48-1992.

Library of Congress Cataloging-in-Publication Data

Matthew, Kathryn I.
    Developing better readers and writers using Caldecott books / Kathryn I. Matthew.
      p.   cm.
    Includes bibliographical references and index.
    ISBN 1–55570–557–X (alk. paper)
   1. Language arts (Elementary)—United States. 2. Caldecott Medal. 3. Illustrated children's books—Study and teaching—United States. I. Title.
    LB1576.M3934 2006
     372.6—dc22   2006005974

For Madelyn Koehl

CONTENTS

LIST OF FIGURES

PREFACE

When librarians and teachers collaborate they form a powerful partnership: the librarian brings an extensive knowledge of children's literature and the teacher brings knowledge of students' unique interests and abilities. This combination is most often brought together to develop literacy skills, but it can also be used to improve valuable writing skills. *Developing Better Readers and Writers Using Caldecott Books* provides easy-to-follow lessons that librarians and teachers can use to build literacy and writing skills simultaneously.

Librarians are naturals for teaching writing. They recognize the best writing in the best books from the best authors. By proactively partnering with teachers—communicating, attending planning sessions, and participating in curriculum development—they can make a world of difference in the school environment and in students' lives. Collaboration emphasizes strengths, repairs weaknesses, and builds strong interpersonal skills among faculty.

❖ ───────────────

Thomason and York (2000) contend that the best way to prepare students for standardized writing achievement tests is to ensure that they are fluent writers. Fluent writers have a variety of writing models in their heads and they are accustomed to writing, so they do not become flustered on standardized tests. These students are competent, confident writers.

───────────────── ❖

❖ ───────────────

The Caldecott award honors Randolph J. Caldecott, a noted nineteenth-century English illustrator. The picture books of this self-taught artist showed that with just the right drawings to move the story along, only a few lines of text were needed to tell the story (Marcus, 2001). In 1938, the American Library Association created the award, giving the first prize to the citizen of the United States who created the most distinguished picture book published the previous year. In addition to the medal winner, runner ups—designated as honor books—are also singled out as being of a very high quality.

───────────────── ❖

READING BOOKS AND WRITING WELL

Even before they learn to read, children are able to appreciate picture books by listening to the story, looking at the pictures, and absorbing the message. Children immersed in quality literature assimilate the structure, sound, and patterns of language. Once they begin to read, picture books can provide models, inspire topics, and help students understand the craft of writing (Johnson and Giorgis, 1999). Throughout these formative years, they can build a storehouse of resources to draw upon when they write.

Caldecott award and honor books are excellent choices for children because they are of literary merit; they engage readers of different ages, interests, and cultures; they come from a variety of genres; and they include different literary elements. For librarians, they are easy to promote and teach with because they are readily available and appeal to a variety of reading levels (Chamberlain and Leal, 1999).

VISUAL LITERACY AND CALDECOTT WINNERS

Illustrated books help children build valuable visual literacy skills. This visual literacy helps readers gain a deeper understanding of the text and informs students' understanding of the storytelling process. In addition, studies show that offering repeated opportunities to examine and study the illustrations in picture books not only aids in their understanding of the story but also helps students develop an appreciation of art (Giorgis and Johnson, 1999). Visual literacy skills improve when educators suggest a variety of options for responding to literature and give students more time to find ideas for their writing and more time to compose texts. Offering writing lessons based on well-illustrated, well-written books will launch your students into new levels of creative and complex writing.

❖ The Power of Illustrations

The text of *The Stray Dog* (Simont, 2001) simply says that family spent the week thinking about the lost dog they left behind at the picnic grounds. The illustrations—Dad overfills his coffee cup, Mom burns dinner, the daughter trips spilling her drink, and the son stands on the baseball field oblivious to the ball landing near him—reveal the depth of their concern for the dog as these mishaps fill their daily lives.

When Sophie Gets Angry—Really, Really Angry . . . (Bang, 1999) uses colors to enhance the action: vibrant reds and oranges depict explosions of anger, cool blues and green dominate as the child calms down.

Duke Ellington: The Piano Prince and His Orchestra (Pinkney, 1998) draws swirling colorful lines emanating from the instruments to make the readers feel the rhythmic, pulsating music.

❖

❖

A reluctant writer maintained interest in his writing when he had multiple opportunities to read a book and saw books other students had written based on the book. These experiences gave him the confidence to write as an expert (Graham, 2001).

Reluctant writers benefit from having books read aloud to them, mini-lessons showing them how the authors use different strategies, and collaborative writing experiences to help them gain confidence in their writing abilities (Robb, 1995).

Second grade students' literary borrowing included borrowing characters, plot devices, setting, conflict, and language patterns from familiar books as well as borrowing ideas from their classmates. These second graders immersed in a literature-rich environment made connections between the books they read and their writing as they developed their own writing style (Lancia, 1997).

❖

THE READING AND WRITING CONNECTION

Reading helps students build vocabulary, gain knowledge of grammar, and master spelling. In fact, Krashen (2004) notes that research strongly concludes that the only way to become a good reader and writer is to read. Children who hear books read aloud and then read and reread books on their own internalize the grammatical features and develop an appreciation of writing. As they examine the text in familiar picture books, they begin to comprehend how writers incorporate literary elements and use grammatical concepts.

Are students' writing skills in need of help? Study after study seems to indicate that they are.

The Neglected "R": The Need for a Writing Revolution, a report issued by the National Commission on Writing in America's Schools and Colleges, recognized a national need to develop students' writing proficiency. Their recommendation included doubling the amount of time students spend writing; concentrating on fair and authentic writing assessments; and providing teachers with professional development skills and resources to teach writing.

The Nation's Report Card: Writing 2002, based on the National Assessment of Educational Progress (NAEP) measurement of writing proficiency, showed that overall, two-thirds of the students tested in grades four, eight, and twelve, scored below the proficient level of writing. (National Center for Educational Statistics, 2002). Their test required children to write narrative, informative, and persuasive pieces using a variety of stimulus materials.

Developing Better Readers and Writers Using Caldecott Books discusses a variety of writing styles and diverse literary tools. It builds on children's reading habits and emphasizes creative writing projects that get students started early.

BOOK ORGANIZATION

Developing Better Readers and Writers Using Caldecott Books is divided into eight chapters, each focusing on a different genre: realistic fiction; historical fiction; traditional literature; memoirs, autobiographies, and biographies; poetry; fantasy; information; and letters and diaries. Each genre is introduced with a brief overview, followed by information about authors who write in it, and ways librarians and teachers can use it with students.

LESSON ORGANIZATION

Each chapter includes lessons that encourage both reading and writing centered around an appropriate Caldecott book. Lessons are divided into the core elements of reading and writing.

Reading

The reading process features three distinct parts: before reading, during reading, and after reading.

- Before reading contains the story summary and activities to activate students' prior knowledge.

- During reading suggests interesting points for the librarian or teacher to highlight during the actual reading.
- After reading features questions and materials for discussion before writing.

Writing

This process has four components: mini-lesson, modeling, writing assignments, and a conference.

- The mini-lesson exposes children to a particular literary element found in the book that typifies the genre.
- Modeling has the librarian demonstrate for the children how to incorporate the literary element into a writing assignment.
- The writing activity provides children with an opportunity to use the literary element in their own writing.
- The conference is a formal or informal individual discussion about the writing activity. This discussion can include the adult and the child, the adult and a small group of children, two students, or a small group of students.

For example, in the Fantasy genre, after reading and discussing *Kitten's First Full Moon* (Henkes, 2004), the mini-lesson focuses on how the repeated refrain creates a familiar, rhythmic pattern to the book. During modeling the librarian demonstrates how to write about Kitten's attempts to reach the bowl of milk in the sky, followed by the book's refrain of "Poor Kitten! Still there was a little bowl of milk, just waiting." Very young students can be given a sheet of paper with the refrain written at the bottom and they can draw pictures of ways Kitten can try to get to her bowl of milk in the sky. Beginning writers may write a sentence describing Kitten's attempt. Older students use a cause-and-effect chart to organize their writing about Kitten's attempts to reach the milk. As they write about Kitten's attempts they use the repeated refrain from the book or create their own phrase.

Each book features informative sidebars that apply benchmarks from the *Information Literacy Standards for Student Learning* from the American Association of School Librarians and the Association for Educational Communications Technology Information Literacy (1998); benchmarks from the *Standards for the English Language Arts* sponsored by the National Council of Teachers of English (NCTE) and the International Reading Association (IRA); grade-level recommendations; lesson objectives; and author and illustrator information.

Each chapter concludes with resources for librarians and teachers, resources for students, and ideas for parents and caregivers.

Note: Read about the process in greater detail in Source A: "The Key Components of a Writing Workshop," on page 205. Other sources include blackline masters for use with the activities and cross-reference indices of Caldecott books by author, illustrator, and title. A subject index completes the book.

CHAPTER DESCRIPTIONS

Chapter 1, "Realistic Fiction," lets students discover the world around them within the pages of books. Lessons are based on:

- *Officer Buckle and Gloria* (Rathmann, 1995),
- *Owl Moon* (Yolen, 1987),

- *Knuffle Bunny: A Cautionary Tale* (Willems, 2004),
- *Ella Sarah Gets Dressed* (Chodos-Irvine, 2003),
- *The Stray Dog* (Simont, 2001),
- *When Sophie Gets Angry—Really, Really Angry . . .* (Bang, 1999), and
- *A Chair for My Mother* (Williams, 1982).

Chapter 2, "Historical Fiction," travels through time and cultures and incorporates:

- *The Man Who Walked Between the Towers* (Gerstein, 2003),
- *Smoky Night* (Bunting, 1994),
- *Mirette on the High Wire* (McCully, 1992),
- *Coming on Home Soon* (Woodson, 2004),
- *Peppe the Lamplighter* (Bartone, 1993), and
- *Tar Beach* (Ringgold, 1991).

Chapter 3, "Traditional Literature," includes folktales, tall tales, fables, and fairy tales. Students explore and learn with:

- *The Three Pigs* (Wiesner, 2001),
- *Joseph Had a Little Overcoat* (Taback, 1999),
- *Rapunzel* (Zelinsky, 1997),
- *Lon Po Po: A Red-Riding Hood Story from China* (Young, 1989),
- *Fables* (Lobel, 1980),
- *John Henry* (Lester, 1994),
- *The Stinky Cheese Man and Other Fairly Stupid Tales* (Scieszka, 1992), and
- *Frederick* (Lionni, 1967).

Chapter 4, "Memoirs, Autobiographies, and Biographies," explores personal life stories and the life stories of others. Books in this chapter include:

- *Snowflake Bentley* (Martin, 1998),
- *Song and Dance Man* (Ackerman, 1988),
- *The Glorious Flight: Across the Channel with Louis Blériot* (Provensen and Provensen, 1983),
- *Duke Ellington: The Piano Prince and His Orchestra* (Pinkney, 1998),
- *Working Cotton* (Williams, 1992),
- *Bill Peet: An Autobiography* (Peet, 1989), and
- *When I Was Young in the Mountains* (Rylant, 1982).

Chapter 5, "Poetry," immerses students in verse and gives them models to use to write their own poems. It engages students in reading poetry with books such as:

- *Noah's Ark* (Spier, 1977),
- *Time of Wonder* (McCloskey, 1957),
- *A Tree Is Nice* (Udry, 1956),
- *The Spider and the Fly* (Howitt, 2002),
- *A Child's Calendar* (Updike, 1999),
- *Harlem: A Poem* (Myers, 1997),
- *Zin! Zin! Zin! A Violin!* (Moss, 1995), and
- *A Visit to William Blake's Inn: Poems for Innocent and Experienced Travelers* (Willard, 1981).

Chapter 6, "Fantasy," introduces titles that skew reality and imagine other possibilities. Titles featured include:

- *Kitten's First Full Moon* (Henkes, 2004),
- *My Friend Rabbit* (Rohmann, 2002),
- *Tuesday* (Wiesner, 1991),
- *The Polar Express* (Van Allsburg, 1985),
- *Jumanji* (Van Allsburg, 1981),
- *Where the Wild Things Are* (Sendak, 1963), and
- *McElligot's Pool* (Seuss, 1947).

Chapter 7, "Information," helps students explore their environments and develop an understanding of their world. This chapter features:

- *So You Want to Be President?* (St. George, 2000),
- *White Snow, Bright Snow* (Tresselt, 1947),
- *What Do You Do with a Tail Like This?* (Jenkins and Page, 2003),
- *In the Small, Small Pond* (Fleming, 1993),
- *Freight Train* (Crews, 1978), and
- *The Desert Is Theirs* (Baylor, 1975).

Chapter 8, "Letters and Diaries," helps students understand this more personal and practical form of writing. They learn from:

- *Click, Clack, Moo: Cows That Type* (Cronin, 2000),
- *Tibet: Through the Red Box* (Sís, 1998), and
- *The Gardener* (Stewart, 1997).

Examining the literary elements in the Caldecott Medal and Honor books provides children with interesting and challenging models to incorporate in their own writing. I hope librarians and teachers continue to forge the partnerships that will inspire the creativity and imagination of their students. I hope all three groups discover or rediscover the joys of reading and writing!

REFERENCES

American Association of School Librarians and Association for Educational Communications and Technology. 1998. *Information Power: Building Partnerships for Learning.* Chicago: American Library Association.

Chamberlain, Julia, and Dorothy Leal. 1999. "Caldecott Medal Books and Readability Levels: Not Just 'Picture' Books." *The Reading Teacher* 52, no. 8 (May): 898–893.

Giorgis, Cyndi, and Nancy J. Johnson. 1999. "Children's Books: Visual Literacy." *The Reading Teacher* 53, no. 2 (October): 146–153.

Graham, Lynda. 2001. "From Tyrannosaurus to Pokemon: Autonomy in the Teaching of Writing." *Reading* 37, no. 1 (April): 18–26.

Johnson, Nancy J., and Cyndi Giorgis. 1999. "Literature and Writing." *The Reading Teacher* 53, no. 3 (November): 234–244.

Krashen, Stephen D. 2004. *The Power of Reading: Insights from Research*, 2nd ed. Westport, CT: Libraries Unlimited.

Lancia, Peter J. 1997. "Literary Borrowing: The Effects of Literature on Children's Writing." *The Reading Teacher* 50, no. 6 (November): 470–475.

Marcus, Leonard. 2001. "Medal Man: Randolph Caldecott and the Art of the Picture Book." *Horn Book Magazine* 77, no. 2 (March/April): 155–171.

National Center for Educational Statistics. 2002. *Nation's Report Card: Writing 2002*. [Online] Available: http://nces.ed.gov/nationsreportcard/writing/results2002/ [cited 11 February 2004].

National Commission on Writing in America's Schools and Colleges. 2003. *The Neglected "R": The Need for a Writing Revolution*. [Online] Available: http://www.writingcommission.org/ [cited 11 February 2004].

Robb, Laura. 1995. "A Workshop for Reluctant Writers." *Education Digest* 61, no. 4 (December): 65–68.

Thomason, Tommy, and Carol York. 2000. *Write on Target: Preparing Young Writers to Succeed on State Writing Achievement Tests*. Norwood, MA: Christopher-Gordon.

CALDECOTT MEDAL AND HONOR BOOKS FEATURED IN THE LESSONS

Ackerman, Karen. 1988. *Song and Dance Man*. Illustrated by Stephen Gammell. New York: Knopf.

Bang, Molly. 1999. *When Sophie Gets Angry—Really, Really Angry*. New York: Blue Sky.

Bartone, Elisa. 1993. *Peppe the Lamplighter*. Illustrated by Ted Lewin. New York: Lothrop.

Baylor, Byrd. 1975. *The Desert Is Theirs*. Illustrated by Peter Parnall. New York: Scribner.

Bunting, Eve. 1994. *Smoky Night*. Illustrated by David Diaz. San Diego, CA: Harcourt Brace.

Chodos-Irvine, Margaret. 2003. *Ella Sarah Gets Dressed*. San Diego, CA: Harcourt.

Crews, Donald. 1978. *Freight Train*. New York: Greenwillow.

Cronin, Doreen. 2000. *Click, Clack, Moo: Cows that Type*. New York: Simon & Schuster.

Fleming, Denise. 1993. *In the Small, Small Pond*. New York: Henry Holt.

Gerstein, Mordicai. 2003. *The Man Who Walked Between the Towers*. Brookfield, CT: Roaring Brook.

Henkes, Kevin. 2004. *Kitten's First Full Moon*. New York: Greenwillow.

Howitt, Mary Botham. 2002. *The Spider and the Fly*. Illustrated by Tony DiTerlizzi. New York: Simon & Schuster.

Jenkins, Steve, and Robin Page. 2003. *What Do You Do with a Tail Like This?* Boston: Houghton Mifflin.

Lester, Julius. 1994. *John Henry*. Illustrated by Jerry Pinkney. New York: Dial.

Lionni, Leo. 1967. *Frederick*. New York: Pantheon.

Lobel, Arnold. 1980. *Fables*. New York: Harper.

Martin, Jacqueline Briggs. 1998. *Snowflake Bentley*. Illustrated by Mary Azarian. Boston: Houghton Mifflin.

McCloskey, Robert. 1957. *Time of Wonder*. New York: Viking.

McCully, Emily Arnold. 1992. *Mirette on the High Wire*. New York: Putnam.

Moss, Lloyd. 1995. *Zin! Zin! Zin! A Violin!* Illustrated by Marjorie Priceman. New York: Simon & Schuster.

Myers, Walter Dean. 1997. *Harlem: A Poem*. Illustrated by Christopher Myers. New York: Scholastic.

Peet, Bill. 1989. *Bill Peet: An Autobiography*. Boston: Houghton Mifflin.

Pinkney, Andrea Davis. 1998. *Duke Ellington: The Piano Prince and His Orchestra.* Illustrated by Brian Pinkney. New York: Hyperion.

Provensen, Alice, and Martin Provensen. 1983. *The Glorious Flight: Across the Channel with Louis Blériot.* New York: Penguin.

Rathmann, Peggy. 1995. *Officer Buckle and Gloria.* New York: Putnam.

Ringgold, Faith. 1991. *Tar Beach.* New York: Crown.

Rohmann, Eric. 2002. *My Friend Rabbit.* Brookfield, CT: Roaring Brook.

Rylant, Cynthia. 1982. *When I Was Young in the Mountains.* Illustrated by Diane Goode. New York: Dutton.

Scieszka, Jon. 1992. *The Stinky Cheese Man and Other Fairly Stupid Tales.* Illustrated by Lane Smith. New York: Viking.

Sendak, Maurice. 1963. *Where the Wild Things Are.* New York: HarperCollins.

Seuss, Dr., pseud. (Theodor Seuss Geisel). 1947. *McElligot's Pool.* New York: Random House.

Simont, Marc. 2001. *The Stray Dog.* New York: HarperCollins.

Sís, Peter. 1998. *Tibet: Through the Red Box.* New York: Farrar Straus Giroux.

Spier, Peter. 1977. *Noah's Ark.* Garden City, NY: Doubleday.

St. George, Judith. 2000. *So You Want to Be President?* Illustrated by David Small. New York: Philomel.

Stewart, Sarah. 1997. *The Gardener.* Illustrated by David Small. New York: Farrar Straus Giroux.

Taback, Simms. 1999. *Joseph Had a Little Overcoat.* New York: Viking.

Tresselt, Alvin. 1947. *White Snow, Bright Snow.* Illustrated by Roger Duvoisin. New York: Lothrop.

Udry, Janice May. 1956. *A Tree Is Nice.* Illustrated by Marc Simont. New York: HarperCollins.

Updike, John. 1999. *A Child's Calendar.* Illustrated by Trina Schart Hyman. New York: Holiday House.

Van Allsburg, Chris. 1981. *Jumanji.* Boston: Houghton Mifflin.

———. 1985. *The Polar Express.* Boston: Houghton Mifflin.

Wiesner, David. 1991. *Tuesday.* Boston: Houghton Mifflin.

———. 2001. *The Three Pigs.* Boston: Houghton Mifflin.

Willard, Nancy. 1981. *A Visit to William Blake's Inn: Poems for Innocent and Experienced Travelers.* Illustrated by Alice and Martin Provensen. New York: Harcourt Brace.

Willems, Mo. 2004. *Knuffle Bunny: A Cautionary Tale.* New York: Hyperion.

Williams, Sherley Anne. 1992. *Working Cotton.* Illustrated by Carole Byard. New York: Harcourt Brace.

Williams, Vera B. 1982. *A Chair for My Mother.* New York: Greenwillow.

Woodson, Jacqueline. 2004. *Coming on Home Soon.* Illustrated by E. B. Lewis. New York: Putnam.

Yolen, Jane. 1987. *Owl Moon.* Illustrated by John Schoenherr. New York: Philomel.

Young, Ed. 1989. *Lon Po Po: A Red-Riding Hood Story from China.* New York: Philomel.

Zelinsky, Paul O. 1997. *Rapunzel.* New York: Dutton.

THE STANDARDS FOR THE ENGLISH LANGUAGE ARTS

The *Standards for the English Language Arts* (1996), sponsored by the National Council of Teachers of English (NCTE) and the International Reading Association (IRA), are the models for many states' standards. Evident in these standards is the connection between reading and writing.

Standard 1.

Students read a wide range of print and nonprint texts to build an understanding of texts, of themselves, and of the cultures of the United States and the world; to acquire new information; to respond to the needs and demands of society and the workplace; and for personal fulfillment. Among these texts are fiction and nonfiction, classic and contemporary works.

Standard 2.

Students read a wide range of literature from many periods in many genres to build an understanding of the many dimensions (e.g., philosophical, ethical, aesthetic) of human experience.

Standard 3.

Students apply a wide range of strategies to comprehend, interpret, evaluate, and appreciate texts. They draw on their prior experience, their interactions with other readers and writers, their knowledge of word meaning and of other texts, their word identification strategies, and their understanding of textual features (e.g., sound-letter correspondence, sentence structure, context, graphics).

Standard 4.

Students adjust their use of spoken, written, and visual language (e.g., conventions, style, vocabulary) to communicate effectively with a variety of audiences and for different purposes.

Standard 5.

Students employ a wide range of strategies as they write and use different writing process elements appropriately to communicate with different audiences for a variety of purposes.

Standard 6.

Students apply knowledge of language structure, language conventions (e.g., spelling and punctuation), media techniques, figurative language, and genre to create, critique, and discuss print and nonprint texts.

Standard 7.

Students conduct research on issues and interests by generating ideas and questions, and by posing problems. They gather, evaluate, and synthesize data from a variety of sources (e.g., print and nonprint texts, artifacts, people) to communicate their discoveries in ways that suit their purpose and audience.

Standard 8.

Students use a variety of technological and information resources (e.g., libraries, databases, computer networks, video) to gather and synthesize information and to create and communicate knowledge.

Standard 9.

Students develop an understanding of and respect for diversity in language use, patterns, and dialects across cultures, ethnic groups, geographic regions, and social roles.

Standard 10.

Students whose first language is not English make use of their first language to develop competency in the English language arts and to develop understanding of content across the curriculum.

Standard 11.

Students participate as knowledgeable, reflective, creative, and critical members of a variety of literacy communities.

Standard 12.

Students use spoken, written, and visual language to accomplish their own purposes (e.g., for learning, enjoyment, persuasion, and the exchange of information).

INFORMATION LITERACY STANDARDS FOR STUDENT LEARNING

National standards offer teacher librarians guidance as they collaborate with teachers to teach writing. The *Information Literacy Standards for Student Learning* from the American Association of School Librarians and the Association for Educational Communications Technology Information Literacy (1998) provide guidance to library media specialists as they develop programs to assure that students become competent users of ideas and information. These nine standards are:

Standard 1:

> The student who is information literate accesses information efficiently and effectively.

Standard 2:

> The student who is information literate evaluates information critically and competently.

Standard 3:

> The student who is information literate uses information accurately and creatively.

INDEPENDENT LEARNING

Standard 4:

> The student who is an independent learner is information literate and pursues information related to personal interests.

Standard 5:

> The student who is an independent learner is information literate and appreciates literature and other creative expressions of information.

Standard 6:

> The student who is an independent learner is information literate and strives for excellence in information seeking and knowledge generation.

SOCIAL RESPONSIBILITY

Standard 7:

> The student who contributes positively to the learning community and to society is information literate and recognizes the importance of information to a democratic society.

Standard 8:

> The student who contributes positively to the learning community and to society is information literate and practices ethical behavior in regard to information and information technology.

Standard 9:

> The student who contributes positively to the learning community and to society is information literate and participates effectively in groups to pursue and generate information.

1 ❖ REALISTIC FICTION

In realistic fiction, children find characters who have problems and experiences similar to their own. They find characters much like themselves, who see things through their eyes. The characters mirror the children's emotions, feelings, experiences, interests, and problems, which helps children discover ideas for dealing with their own problems and develop empathy for others' perspectives. In realistic fiction, children discover that life does not give easy answers but it gives possibilities (Rochelle, 1991) and it gives hope (Yolen, 1999).

Children want realistic fiction that reflects their particular reality (Rochelle, 1991). Tyson's (1999) research on sharing culturally diverse books with fifth-grade African-American males demonstrates the importance of sharing realistic fiction that relates to children's lives. When the boys found characters like themselves, they responded emotionally to the story. When the characters' lives did not reflect the boys' lives, they were reluctant to read and respond to the books. By collaborating with teachers, librarians assure that students find their lives reflected in the books they read; books to meet their diverse interests, backgrounds, and experiences. This collaboration increases students' opportunities to become readers who apply what they read to their own lives (Bishop and Larimer, 1999).

The authors of the realistic fiction presented in this chapter drew upon their personal life experiences for their manuscripts. They selected incidents from their own lives or from the lives of their family members. They based the books on their family stories, but they are written in such a way that readers know they could also be their own family stories. When watching a family video, Peggy Rathmann's family was surprised to discover their dog licking a platter of poached eggs just before they ate the eggs. Rathmann uses the dog's surreptitious antics to create a surprising video revelation in *Officer Buckle and Gloria*.

❖ ──────────────

Recommended Grade Levels

3–6

Standards for the English Language Arts

3, 4, 5, 6, 7, 11, 12

Information Literacy Standards for Student Learning

3, 4, 5

Objectives

The students will:

- Practice persuasive writing by creating a commercial to convince their audience of the importance of following a safety tip.

──────────────── ❖

Officer Buckle and Gloria

by Peggy Rathmann
Caldecott Medal Winner, 1996

READING

Before Reading

Story Summary
None of the school children listen to Officer Buckle's boring recitation of safety tips until Gloria the police dog accompanies him to his presentations. Just out of Officer Buckle's line of vision, Gloria is performing her slapstick renditions of what happens

❖ ──────────────

Author

At the suggestion of a published writer, Peggy Rathmann signed up for a children's book writing and illustration class. The class assignments turned into published children's books, including this award winner. In the writing classes, Peggy learned by listening to the other students read their stories, by observing their reactions to her stories, and from the teacher's sensitive, personal critiques (Peck and Hendershot, 1997). On the advice of her writing teacher Rathmann creates characters that share embarrassing traits that mimic her own. Like Officer Buckle, she is obsessed with safety and no one listens to her safety tips either. Some of the 101 safety tips that cover the endpapers and are tacked to the bulletin boards throughout the book come from nieces, a nephew, and other youngsters. When she had difficulty thinking up safety tips she paid the children $25.00 for every safety tip they wrote that her editor selected for the book. Additional information about Peggy Rathmann and her books can be found on her Web site at http://peggyrathmann.com.

────────────── ❖

when you fail to follow the safety rules. When Officer Buckle discovers Gloria's antics, he stops making his safety speeches. A colossal accident at the school, a stack of letters from the children with drawings of the accident, and a big kiss from Gloria persuade Officer Buckle to return to the stage. After all, the best safety tip is "Always stick with your buddy!" Bright watercolor and ink illustrations featuring a rainbow of colors explore the persuasive power of humor. This book is available on DVD with narration by John Lithgow. It is also available on videocassette and audiocassette.

Activating Prior Knowledge

To introduce students to this book, ask them about safety rules they follow at home and at school. Then, ask the students "What happens when you do not follow the safety rules?" Give each student a blank white paper star to write and to illustrate a safety tip. Post their safety tips on school bulletin boards in the hallways, in the library, or in their classrooms.

During Reading

As you read, share the illustrations with the students as they are integral to understanding the story. Whereas Officer Buckle may not be able to figure out why the students are suddenly paying attention to his safety tips, your students will quickly observe that Gloria's animated demonstrations of the dire consequences of ignoring the safety tips are the reason for the attention. When you finish reading the book put it in a prominent place so the students can read the safety tips scattered throughout the illustrations.

After Reading

Use questions such as these to begin a discussion of the book:

- Why did the students ignore Officer Buckle when he appeared without Gloria?
- Why did the students listen when Gloria appeared with Officer Buckle?
- How did Officer Buckle learn about Gloria's antics?
- Why did Officer Buckle decide not to give any more safety talks?
- Why did the students fall asleep when Gloria appeared without Officer Buckle?
- What persuaded Officer Buckle to start giving his safety talks again?
- Why was the story interesting?
- Did the story persuade you that safety is important? Why or why not?
- What is your favorite safety tip?

WRITING

Mini-lesson—Persuasive Writing

- Explain to the students that authors use persuasive writing to convince people to think the way they think or to convince people to buy their products.
- Tell the students that commercials and advertisements often include humor, demonstrations, and catchy slogans such as "Got milk?" to persuade us to buy products.
- Ask the students to think about commercials that they have recently watched. "Was the commercial funny?" "Did it show people using the product?"

- Tell the students that in this story Rathmann shows how humor and demonstrations can persuade people to do something.
- Explain to the students that Officer Buckle's dry, boring recitation of safety tips could not persuade the students to be safe, but Gloria's comic antics depicting what happens when you do not follow the safety tips persuaded the students that it was important to be safe.

Modeling

- Tell the students that commercials get the point across in thirty seconds using no more than sixty-five words (Gourley, 1999).
- Explain to the students that they are going to write a commercial to persuade an audience that a safety tip is important.
- To model how to organize the commercial begin by selecting a safety tip.
- Project a blank diagram such as the one shown in Figure 1-1.
- Write the safety tip as a clearly stated opinion in the first part of the diagram.
- Ask the students to help you create a list of persuasive facts stating why the safety tip is important.
- Write the students' responses on the board so they can all see them and have them narrow the list to the three most important facts.
- Then, have the students help you rewrite the facts to include lively words, colorful adjectives, and strong verbs.
- Ask the students to help you organize the reasons in order of importance.
- Write the persuasive facts in the chart placing the most important reason first to catch the audience's attention.
- Have the students help you write a catchy slogan to end the commercial.

Writing Activity

- Divide the students into groups of three or four.
- Provide each group with a diagram such as the one in Figure 1-1 to help them stay focused and organize their writing. There is a blank diagram in the appendix.
- Have the students decide on a safety tip and write the safety tip as a clearly stated opinion in the first part of the diagram.
- Have the students work together to generate a list of persuasive facts stating why the safety tip is important.
- Tell the students to narrow their list down to the three most important facts and organize the facts in order of importance.
- Have the students check to see that they have used lively words, colorful adjectives, and strong verbs.

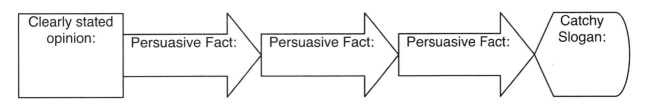

Figure 1-1. Commercial Diagram

- Tell the students to write persuasive facts in the chart, placing the most important reason first to catch the audience's attention.
- In the last space on the diagram, have the students write a catchy slogan to end the commercial.
- Using the diagram, the students then write a script for their commercial.
- Allow the students time to rehearse their commercials and perform them for their classmates.
- If a video camera is available tape the commercials to share with other classes or at a parents' night.

Conferencing

- Meet with the groups and ask them to read their script aloud.
- Have the students work together to edit their commercials to thirty seconds, using no more than sixty-five words.

Owl Moon

by Jane Yolen
Illustrated by John Schoenherr
Caldecott Medal Winner, 1988

READING

Before Reading

Story Summary
A father and his daughter make their way through the cold, snowy woods under the light of the moon listening and watching for an owl. Their quiet trek through the woods is rewarded by a few precious moments with an owl. Soft, watercolor illustrations beautifully depict the poetic text and describe a very special father–daughter adventure. This book is available on audiocassette and videocassette.

Activating Prior Knowledge
Read aloud the author's and the illustrator's dedications at the beginning of the book. Write the word "owling" on the board and point out the root word "owl." Then, ask the students what they think "owling" means?

During Reading

Read the book in a calm, soothing tone. As you read, pause to let the students linger over the beautiful watercolor illustrations depicting the quiet, frozen walk in the moonlit woods.

After Reading

Yolen describes the setting in this book using descriptive phrases and vivid details. Ask the students to close their eyes and to let the words paint pictures in their minds as

❖ ———————————

Recommended Grade Levels

2–8

Standards for the English Language Arts

2, 5, 6, 9, 11, 12

Information Literacy Standards for Student Learning

5, 9

Objectives

The students will:

- Examine examples of descriptive phrases, and
- Write descriptive paragraphs about objects in pictures.

———————————— ❖

you read some of the descriptive phrases in the book. Read "little gray footprints followed us." Ask the students to describe the picture that they drew in their minds as you read. Then, read "whiter than the milk in a cereal bowl." Ask the students to describe the picture that they drew in their minds as you read.

WRITING

Mini-lesson—Writing Descriptions

- To describe an object, writers often look at ordinary things in unusual ways.
- Return to the phrase "little gray footprints followed us."
- Ask the students to tell about a time that they left tracks behind them as they walked in the sand or snow.
- Point out to the students that Yolen took an ordinary occurrence and described it in an unusual way by describing the footprints as following the characters. Yolen wrote "little gray footprints followed us" to paint a vivid picture in readers' minds.
- Return to her description of the snow as "whiter than the milk in a cereal bowl." Readers familiar with the milk left in a cereal bowl can easily picture the scene in their minds.
- Point out to the students that in this phrase she is comparing two unlike things, a metaphor.

Modeling

- Project a picture that you are going to describe so that all of the students can see the picture. For example, Figure 1-2 is a picture of a flowerbed.
- As the students examine the picture, ask them, "What words describe what you see in the picture?"
- Write their words on the board and incorporate some of them into your description.
- Begin writing your description, which might look something like this:

  The smooth, mottled, gray rocks felt cool to my touch. Nestled within the gaps between the rocks were brittle, brown leaves. Rising from beneath the dead, decaying leaves small green plants offered up delicate, pink blooms.

- As you write, ask the students to help you think up descriptive phrases.
- Call the students' attention to phrases you used to describe things in unusual ways, such as "offered up delicate, pink blooms."
- After you have written a few sentences of your descriptive paragraph, have the students begin their writing.

Writing Activity

Younger Students
- Provide each student with a picture to describe.
- Give the students time to talk about their pictures with a partner.
- As the students talk about their pictures, circulate around the room and encourage them to brainstorm a list of words to use to describe the objects in their pictures.

Author

Jane Yolen is a prolific author who shares her talent with others through writing workshops and presentations. Her writing spans genres and generations. Her father wrote books and radio scripts and her mother wrote short stories. Many of her stories reflect experiences from her life and those of her family members. *Owl Moon* (Yolen, 1987) is based on the owling excursions her husband took their children on and her Web site contains pictures of her husband, daughter, and granddaughter with owls. *The Emperor and the Kite* (Yolen, 1967), illustrated by Ed Young, was a Caldecott Honor book. Additional information about Jane Yolen, pictures of her family, and information on her books can be found at http://www.janeyolen.com.

Illustrator

John Schoenherr is a wildlife artist whose works are exhibited nationwide. He has illustrated picture books and science fiction book covers. He has also written and illustrated his own books. His rural home in New Jersey and his travels provide him with opportunities to observe and paint wildlife in their natural habitats. His mother was from Hungary and his father from Germany. At home, they spoke German and when he ventured outside to play, he discovered his playmates spoke Chinese and Italian. He drew pictures to communicate with his playmates and he learned English by reading comic strips.

Figure 1-2. Flowers and Rocks

- Have the students begin writing their descriptions.
- As the students write their descriptions, remind them to refer back to their list of descriptive words.
- As the students write, return to your paragraph and continue writing.

Older Students
- Provide each student with a picture to describe.
- Give the students time to talk about their pictures with a partner.
- As the students talk about their pictures circulate around the room and ask them what they might hear, or smell, or feel if they were standing in the picture.
- Have the students write down words that describe what they see, hear, smell, feel, or taste as they look at the picture.
- Then, tell the students to incorporate their descriptive words in their writing.
- As the students write, return to your paragraph and continue writing.

Conferencing
- After the students have been writing for about fifteen minutes, circulate around the room and check their progress.
- Ask students who are struggling with their writing to join you for a small group conference.
- Return to Yolen's text and have the students reread some of her descriptive phrases.
- Share one of the students' pictures with the group and work with the group to write descriptive sentences about the picture.

- At the end of the writing activity invite some of the students to read their descriptions to their classmates.
- At the end of their writing time remind the students to put their writing in their folders to finish during another writing session.

Knuffle Bunny: A Cautionary Tale

by Mo Willems
Caldecott Honor Book, 2005

READING

Before Reading

Story Summary
A simple trip through the neighborhood to the laundromat leads to disaster when the beloved Knuffle Bunny is left behind at the laundromat. On the way home Trixie realizes that Knuffle Bunny is missing. When her attempts at speech go unrecognized, she begins to bawl and her body goes "boneless." Her bewildered dad realizes the source of Trixie's distress when they arrive home and her mom asks, "Where's Knuffle Bunny?" A frantic trip back to the laundromat results in Dad rescuing Knuffle Bunny from the washing machine. Willems used a computer to blend digital photographs and hand-drawn ink sketches to create the book's illustrations.

Activating Prior Knowledge
In this story, Trixie the baby cries and goes limp as she tries to get her dad to understand her problem. Trixie talks in gibberish and her dad does not understand what she is saying. Ask the students if they have younger siblings who speak in gibberish or if they have ever been in a situation where people did not understand what they were trying to say.

During Reading

The large print text with only a few words on each page and cartoon-like illustrations superimposed over the photographs make it easy to point out Trixie's gibberish as you read. The students enjoy repeating the gibberish as you read.

After Reading

Use these questions to start a discussion of the book.

- What clues did you find in the illustrations to let you, the reader, in on the secret that Dad does not know?
- Could this story have really happened? Why or why not?
- Why do you think Dad put Knuffle Bunny in the washing machine?
- What do you think will happen the next time Dad and Trixie go to the laundromat?
- How would you describe Dad?
- How would you describe Trixie?

Recommended Grade Levels

1–4

Standards for the English Language Arts

3, 4, 5, 6, 8, 12

Information Literacy Standards for Student Learning

3, 5, 8

Objectives

The students will:

- Create a story map with a beginning, a middle, and an end to organize their writing, and
- Use the story map to write a narrative.

Author

Mo Willems grew up in New Orleans. He worked as a scriptwriter and animator for Sesame Street. He writes for shows on Nickelodeon and Cartoon Network. His work has garnered six Emmy awards and two Caldecott Honors. He also received a Caldecott Honor for his book *Don't Let the Pigeon Drive the Bus!* (Willems, 2003). Additional information about Mo Willems and his work is at http://www.mowillems.com.

- Why do you think the author titles this story "a cautionary tale?"
- How do you go about finding things you lose?

WRITING

Mini-lesson—Story Mapping

- Tell the students that stories have a beginning, a middle, and an end. A story map is one way to diagram the parts of the story.
- Describe to the students how the beginning sets the stage for the action, the middle reveals the problem, and the end presents the solution to the problem.
- Explain to the students that a story map is one way to organize their thoughts before they begin writing.
- With *Inspiration* concept mapping software projected on a large screen, have the students help you create a story map such as the one in Figure 1-3. The story map can also be drawn on the chalkboard or overhead transparency.
- For older students add details to the story map such as in Figure 1-4.

Modeling

- Ask yourself these questions out loud so that the students can hear your thought processes, and to get them thinking about ideas for their own stories. "Was there ever a time when someone did not understand what I was saying? What did I do to get them to understand me? What happened the last time I lost something? Was there a time when my favorite toy or blanket ended up in the washing machine?"
- Lost keys are a familiar household occurrence and children can usually relate to experiences about searching for lost keys or being locked out of the house.

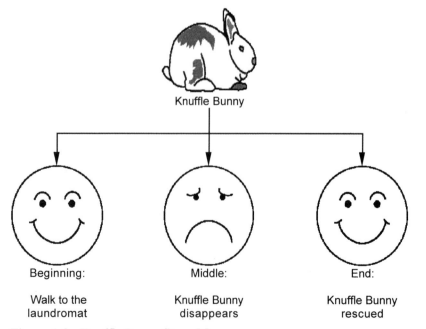

Figure 1-3. *Knuffle Bunny* Story Map

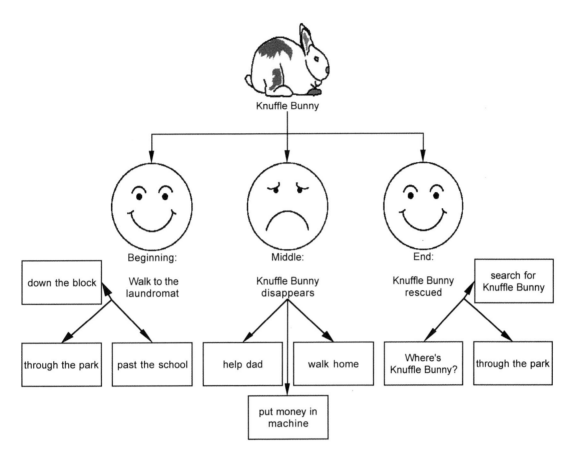

Figure 1-4. *Knuffle Bunny* Story Map with Details

- Once you have an idea in mind create a story map such as the one in Figure 1-5.
- After you create the story map, look at it carefully and decide if you need to make revisions.
- Once you have the story map created, you can add graphics.

Writing Activity

- If *Inspiration* software is not available provide the students with a paper template such as the one in the appendix, or simply have them draw three boxes on blank paper and label the boxes beginning, middle, and end.
- If *Inspiration* software is available to the students, tell them to begin with simple boxes to hold their text and later add symbols to match their stories.
- Tell the students to create links to add details to the beginning, middle, and end of their stories.
- Have the students export their story maps to a word processing software and begin writing their stories.
- Students who are not using the software program can write their stories with paper and pencil.
- Once the students begin writing their stories use your story map to write your story.

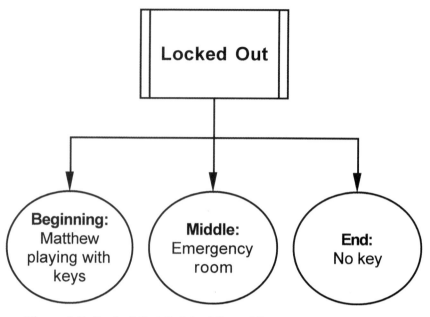

Figure 1-5. Locked Out Original Story Map

Conferencing

- Have the students show you their story maps.
- Ask them to point out where in the story they included the details listed in their story maps.
- Share your story map and writing with the students to show them how you incorporated the details from your story map into your writing.

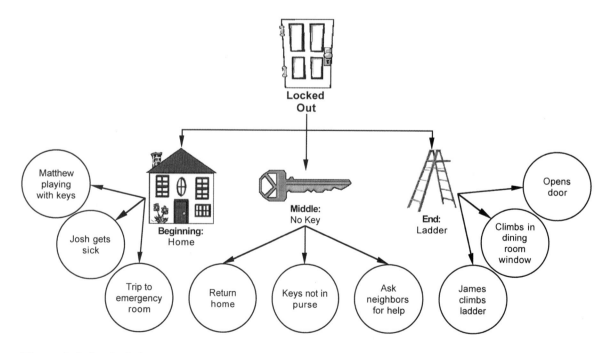

Figure 1-6. Locked Out Revised Story Map

Ella Sarah Gets Dressed

by Margaret Chodos-Irvine
Caldecott Honor Book, 2004

READING

Before Reading

Story Summary
Ella Sarah gets up one morning, looks in her closet, and decides what she will wear for the day. Her family members do not agree with her about what she has chosen. Her mother suggests an outfit, her father suggests another outfit, and her big sister suggests hand-me-down clothing. Ella Sarah ignores them all and puts on the outfit she picked out. When her friends arrive all dressed up for their tea party, it is evident that Ella Sarah picked out just the right outfit. Chodos-Irvine used a process called Collagraph, printing from mixed media, to create the vivid illustrations in this book.

Activating Prior Knowledge
Ella Sarah has very definite ideas on what to wear, but her family does not agree with her. To introduce this book to the students, ask them if they ever have disagreements with their parents over the clothes they wear.

During Reading

Invite the students to join you as you read Ella Sarah's description of the outfit she plans to wear. Project a copy of this repeated refrain and point to the words as you say them. By the end of the book when Ella Sarah is adamant about her choice of outfits, the students will be familiar with the words and their voices will reflect her determination.

After Reading

Ask the students, "Do you think that Ella Sarah made just the right choice of clothes to wear for her special occasion?" Then, invite the students to describe their favorite party outfits.

WRITING

Mini-lesson—Repeated Refrain

- The author uses the repeated refrain describing Ella Sarah's perfect outfit to add emphasis to the story and to show readers that Ella Sarah is one very determined young girl, rather than to state that Ella Sarah is determined to have her way.
- Explain to the students that the author uses the repeated refrain to show them Ella Sarah's determination.

Modeling

- Use a chart such as the one in Figure 1-7, to model for the students how to create their own story using their favorite outfit as the repeated refrain.

Recommended Grade Levels

K–3

Standards for the English Language Arts

1, 3, 4, 5, 6, 12

Information Literacy Standards for Student Learning

3, 5, 9

Objectives

The students will:

- Write a story with a repeated refrain.

Author

The idea for this story came from Margaret Chodos-Irvine's daughter who, at age two and a half, had her very own definite ideas about what she should wear. While it came to her quickly, she took a writing class that helped her develop the story, and even then it was rejected. At the suggestion of her illustration editor, she changed the ending, and the book was finally accepted for publication (Chodos-Irvine, 2003). When she draws her illustrations, she creates a series of proofs before settling on the final image. Some information about the author is on her Web site at http://www.chodos-irvine.com.

Ella Sarah's Family Members	Suggested Clothes	My Family Members	Suggested Clothes
Ella Sarah	pink polka-dot pants, dress with orange-and-green flowers, purple-and-blue striped socks, yellow shoes, red hat		
Mother	blue dress, matching socks, white sandals		
Father	yellow T-shirt, white shorts, tennis shoes		
Big Sister	overalls, old boots		

Figure 1-7. Clothing Choices

- Ask the students to help you complete the first two columns in the chart using the information from the story.
- In the third column, write your name in the second space and write the names of your family members in the other spaces.
- In the fourth column describe your favorite party outfit and then write down things your family members might suggest you wear.
- Use your favorite party outfit to create a repeated refrain.
- Write your repeated refrain on the board and have the students join you as you read.
- For example, you might write something like:

I want to wear my long black dress,
my dangling earrings that sparkle,
my shiny gold bracelet,
and my high heel shoes.

Writing Activity

Younger Students

- Project a copy of the chart or draw the chart on the chalkboard or chart paper to create a repeated refrain to use in a class story. There is a blank chart in the appendix.
- Ask the students to decide who they want to list as the family members. Since not every family consists of a father, a mother, and a sister, the students may want to add grandparents or other relatives.
- Call on different students to suggest items of clothing to put in the fourth column.
- Once the students have completed the chart, begin writing the class story.

Older Students
- Give each student a blank chart. There is a blank chart in the appendix.
- Tell the students to put their name on the first line and to write a description of their favorite party outfit.
- Remind the students to list their family members and then write a description of the clothes they might suggest.
- Using their descriptions of their favorite outfits have the students write their repeated refrains.
- For students who struggle with what to say in their stories, refer them back to the text for ideas.
- If the students have the opportunity to write their stories on the computer, you can show them how to copy and paste the repeated refrain.
- Once the students begin writing their stories, take time to write your story.

Conferencing

- When the students are ready to conference, ask them to read their stories to each other in small groups.
- Have each group select one story to read aloud to the class.
- As the author reads the body of the text, the other members of the group can recite the repeated refrain. If the author does not want to read the story, someone else in the group can read the story for the author.

The Stray Dog

by Marc Simont
Caldecott Honor Book, 2002

READING

Before Reading

Story Summary
During a picnic in the country, a family encounters a stray dog that they name Willy. At the end of the day, they reluctantly leave Willy behind. During that week they all think of Willy, and the next weekend they return to the park hoping he will appear. Suddenly he races by with a dogcatcher in pursuit. The children join the chase and convince the dogcatcher that Willy is theirs. Watercolor illustrations capture the mood and energy of this lively story. This book is also available on audiocassette.

Activating Prior Knowledge
The cover of this book offers tantalizing clues as to the contents of the story. In the background is a man with a net and in the foreground is a wary dog with a ball clenched between its teeth. As you hold the book up for the students to see ask them to predict what is going to happen in this story. The students will be interested to know that this story is one that Marc Simont heard from his friend about how her family adopted a stray dog, as noted on the title page of the book.

❖ ────────────────

Recommended Grade Levels

4–8

Standards for the English Language Arts

1, 2, 3, 5, 6, 11, 12

Information Literacy Standards for Student Learning

3, 9

Objectives

The students will:

- Discover additional story details in the book's illustrations,
- Complete a cause-and-effect chain delineating the story events,
- Create a cause-and-effect chain to organize their stories, and
- Write a story with a cause-and-effect chain.

──────────────── ❖

Author

Marc Simont reports that his father, a magazine illustrator, was his most influential art teacher (Silvey, 2002). Simont was born in France and spent his childhood in France, Spain, and the United States. Frequent moves meant that his schoolwork suffered, but he credits the moves with enhancing his observational skills (Silvey, 2002). Hence, he would rather observe than listen, so in school he was more interested in how his teachers looked than what they said. He won a Caldecott Medal for *A Tree Is Nice* (Udry, 1956) and a Caldecott Honor for *The Happy Day* (Kraus, 1949). He illustrated Marjorie Weinman Sharmat's Nate the Great series.

During Reading

As you read the story, share the pictures with the students and tell them to look for the clues Simont placed in the illustrations to help tell the story.

After Reading

You might begin discussing the story by returning to the illustrations and searching for story details found only in the pictures. Ask the students, "What clues did you find in the illustrations to help you understand the story?" For example, on the two-page spread with the days of the week the illustrations show that the family members are thinking about Willy and not thinking about what they are doing. The dad spills coffee, the daughter trips on the stairs, the son misses a baseball, and the mother burns dinner.

WRITING

Mini-lesson—Cause and Effect Chain

- Tell the students that oftentimes in stories authors use cause-and-effect chains to organize their stories by having one event lead to another event.
- Demonstrate this to the students by having them help you complete a cause-and-effect chain such as the one in Figure 1-8.

Modeling

- Explain to the students that creating a cause-and-effect chain before they begin writing their stories is one way to organize their writing.
- Model this for the students by completing a cause-and-effect chain about an event in your life.
- As you create your cause-and-effect chain, explain it to the students so they will understand how one action leads to another.
- Your cause-and-effect chain might look something like the one in Figure 1-9.

Writing Activity

- Put the students in small groups to talk about experiences in their lives where one event led to another event. Students who are not sure what to write about will be able to get ideas from their classmates.
- Give the students blank templates such as the one in the appendix or have them draw their cause-and-effect chains on blank sheets of paper.

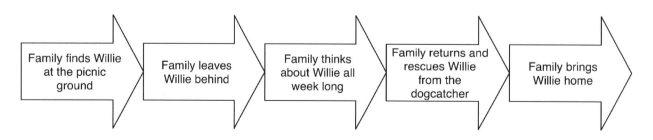

Figure 1-8. Cause-and-Effect Chain for *The Stray Dog*

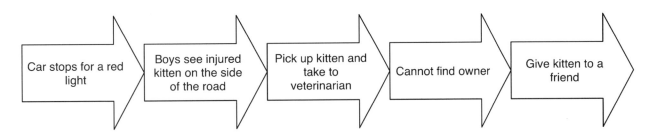

Figure 1-9. Cause-and-Effect Chain for My Story

- Once they complete their cause-and-effect chains, tell them to use the events to write their stories.
- As the students write their stories, begin writing your story.

Conferencing

- Ask the students to read their stories aloud and help them determine if they have left out any details.
- As you listen to their stories jot down any questions you have about them.
- When the students finish reading, ask them the questions you jotted down.
- Suggest that they draw pictures to accompany their stories and perhaps include additional details in their pictures.
- Return to the book to show them how Simont included details in the pictures rather than put all of the details in the text.

When Sophie Gets Angry— Really, Really Angry . . .

by Molly Bang
Caldecott Honor Book, 2000

READING

Before Reading

Story Summary
When it is her sister's turn to play with a favorite toy, Sophie erupts and roars like a volcano. Then, she runs, cries, and climbs her favorite tree. Ensconced in her tree high above the world below, Sophie relaxes, reflects, and regroups. Once she calms down, she climbs down, and returns home to join her family. Bang used gouache for the illustrations, whose colors change to reflect Sophie's moods. For example, when she erupts with anger, bright reds and oranges predominate. Bang also varies the syntactic patterns of the text as Sophie's moods change.

Activating Prior Knowledge
This is the story of how one little girl deals with her anger. As you introduce the story, reassure the students that everyone gets angry and it is important to deal with anger in

❖ ———————————————

Recommended Grade Levels

2–4

Standards for the English Language Arts

1, 2, 3, 5, 12

Information Literacy Standards for Student Learning

3, 9

Objectives

The students will:

- Recognize appropriate ways to respond to anger,
- Complete a character chart, and
- Write a story about a character dealing with anger.

——————————————— ❖

Author

Molly Bang's books often feature folktales she collected while she lived overseas in Japan, India, and Mali. Some of the folktales she illustrated were adapted and translated by her mother Betsy Bang. Molly's book *Picture This: Perception and Composition* (Bang, 1992) describes how the structural elements of pictures come together and cause us to respond to them. The book includes exercises for trying out the techniques. *The Grey Lady and the Strawberry Snatcher* (Bang, 1980) and *Ten, Nine, Eight* (Bang, 1983) were also Caldecott Honor Books. Additional information about Molly Bang and her books can be found at http://www.mollybang.com.

kicks	count to ten
screams	sing
roars	bike ride
runs	play a video game
cries	skate
climbs	hit a pillow

Figure 1-10. Ways to Deal with Anger

acceptable ways. Ask the students what they do when they get angry. When Molly Bang began drawing the illustrations for the book, she used her daughter as the model. Her daughter reminded Molly that she also got angry at times. Therefore, Molly drew the young girl, Sophie, in the story to look like herself as a youngster. The Resources for Librarians and Teachers section at the end of this chapter has lists of books and Web sites that help children deal with their anger.

During Reading

As you read the story aloud, use the color changes in the illustrations as guides to change your tone and voice inflections.

After Reading

Students need to know that getting angry is acceptable, but that their reactions may not be acceptable. Sophie first exhibits unacceptable reactions, but then she regains control and exhibits acceptable ways of dealing with her anger. She uses self-control rather than lashing out or trying to dominate the situation. Return to the book and reread the parts where Sophie reacts to her anger. As you read, ask one of the students to write the ways he or she responds to anger on the board. In the first column in Figure 1-10 are the ways that Sophie reacted to her anger. Notice how her first reactions are inappropriate, but she quickly regains her self-control and channels her anger in more appropriate ways. Now, you are ready for the students to brainstorm other appropriate ways of responding to anger. Their list of ideas might look something like the list in the second column.

WRITING

Mini-lesson—Characterization

- Explain to the students that it is easy to identify with Sophie because her feelings and actions are genuine. Bang develops Sophie's character by revealing her inner thoughts (introspection) and actions. Introspection shows readers how characters react to events in their lives and engages readers in the story (Letchworth, 1996). Readers become engaged in the story because they want to find out how the characters cope with their problems.
- Tell the students that Bang uses strong verbs such as kick, scream, smash, roar, explode, run, and cry to describe Sophie's actions.

- Show the students how Bang repeats the word "run" for emphasis and to let the readers know that Sophie ran for quite awhile.
- Inform the students that before writers begin their stories they have their characters come alive in their imaginations.
- Tell the students that completing a chart such as the one in Figure 1-11 helps them imagine their characters and helps to make their characters more real.

Modeling

- Explain to the students that authors create characters that embody bits of people they know and bits of themselves.
- Caution the students that when they create characters, they do not want to model them too closely after someone they know. However, they can create characters that are composites of different people.
- To model for the students how to imagine a character have them help you complete a chart such as the one in Figure 1-11.

Name
Age
Sex
Hair color
Eye color
Height and weight
Favorite food
Favorite television show
Favorite singer
Favorite song
Number of brothers and sisters
What does the character like to do?
What makes the character angry?
What verbs describe how the character feels when angry?
How does the character deal with anger?

Figure 1-11. Character Chart

Writing Activity

- Distribute a copy of a blank character chart to each student. There is a blank chart in the appendix.
- Have the students work in small groups as they complete their charts. This allows them opportunities to offer each other ideas and support.
- Once the students have described their characters, they can begin writing a story about what makes their characters angry and how their characters deal with anger.
- If the students are unsure of how to begin their stories, you might suggest that they return to the book for ideas.

Conferencing

- Ask the students to read you their favorite part of their story or the part that they think best describes their character's reaction to anger.
- Listen carefully as the students read and try to determine what else you need to know about the character to help you understand the character.
- Ask the students clarifying questions such as, "Why did your character react that way? What other things could your character do when he gets angry?"

A Chair for My Mother

by Vera B. Williams
Caldecott Honor Book, 1983

READING

Before Reading

Story Summary

Rosa, her mother, and her grandmother save their spare change to buy a big, soft, comfortable chair. A fire destroyed all of their belongings and Rosa's mother needs a comfortable place to sit at the end of the day when she comes home exhausted from her job as a waitress. In this matriarchal, multicultural, working-class family, everyone contributes and together they face hardships and celebrate life. Vibrant watercolors framed by simple borders help to tell their story.

Activating Prior Knowledge

"Do you have a favorite chair to sit in at your house?" This might be just the question to get students talking about their favorite chairs and why they like the chairs. If the students are reluctant to share their stories, begin by describing your favorite chair or your favorite chair as a child. Then ask the students, "Have you ever saved your money to buy something you really wanted?" In this story Rosa, her mother, and her grandmother are saving their money to buy a very special chair. Other books featuring Rosa and her family include *Something Special for Me* (Williams, 1983) and *Music, Music for Everyone* (Williams, 1984).

Recommended Grade Levels

4–10

Standards for the English Language Arts

1, 2, 3, 5, 9, 12

Information Literacy Standards for Student Learning

2, 3, 5, 9

Objectives

The students will:

- Examine the organization of a story with a flashback, and
- Write a story with a flashback.

During Reading

As you read the story, ask the students to pay attention to how it develops, because at one point the author uses a flashback to tell the story. A flashback takes the readers back in time to an earlier event. Rather than using chronological order to organize the story, the author begins the story, interrupts it to take us back in time to an earlier event, and returns to the present for the ending. The story begins with the family saving money for a chair, then readers learn that a fire destroyed their belongings, and the story ends with the family enjoying the new chair.

After Reading

These questions will help you get a discussion of the story started:

- How does each of the family members contribute to the purchase of the chair?
- How long do you think it took them to save enough money to buy a chair?
- How did members of the community and Rosa's extended family help after the fire?
- What actions or words show that this is a loving family?
- How do the people in this story help each other?
- How do your family members help each other?
- Why do you think they help each other?
- Did you recognize the flashback in the story?

WRITING

Mini-lesson—Flashback

- Explain to the students that a flashback takes the readers back in time to describe an event from the past that has an immediate impact on the story being told. In this story, the flashback describing the fire tells us why the family is saving for a new chair.
- Have the students help you construct a simple story map showing the main events in the story in chronological order, as depicted in Figure 1-12.
- Ask the students to think about the order in which the events really occurred in the story and create another story map depicting the events of the story, as shown in Figure 1-13.

Modeling

- Share with the students that this story is based on an incident in Williams's life; her mother bought a chair on an installment plan. It was not based on

Author

Vera Williams reports that as a child she had a great deal to say and that she expressed herself in words, pictures, acting, and dancing (Williams, 2002). Her memories and personal experiences provide the details found in her stories and her illustrations. Williams's stories focus on the interdependence of multicultural families, friends, and neighbors as they enjoy life's simple pleasures (Silvey, 2002). Her stories celebrate life including its struggles, hardships, and adventures. She won a Caldecott Honor for *"More More More," Said the Baby: Three Love Stories* (Williams, 1990). Additional information about Williams and her work is at http://www.kidsreads.com/authors/au-williams-vera.asp and http://www.cbcbooks.org/html/vera_williams.html.

Figure 1-12. Chronological Story Map

Figure 1-13. Flashback Story Map

a fire that destroyed her family's belongings. She took one memory from her childhood and used it to create the story. It is not a true story, but it is believable.

- Model this writing activity using an example of a classroom event or something from your own life.
- Create a diagram of your story with a flashback such as the one in Figure 1-14 that depicts how the story unfolds.
- Refer to the story map as you begin writing your story. For example:

> *Pencil in hand, Ben slowly and carefully began printing his note for the tooth fairy. Please leave a dollar, not a quarter, he wrote on the envelope, holding the tiny tooth. The envelope safely stashed under his pillow, he crawled into bed. As he drifted off to sleep, he remembered the visit to the dentist's office earlier in the day. He sat in the big chair as the dentist first gave him a shot and then pulled the stubborn baby tooth that refused to fall out.*

Writing Activity

- Place the students in small groups to talk about events in their lives that they remember or events that had an impact on something else in their lives.
- Once every member of the group has a memory in mind, they draw a diagram of the memory using a blank flashback story map such as the one in the appendix.
- Meet with any students who are having trouble deciding on a topic and discuss classroom mishaps or field trips that might be story ideas.
- As the students begin writing, return to your own writing.

Conferencing

- Have the students show you their story maps.
- Ask them to talk about the events and as they talk, write down the important details they mention on sticky notes.
- Leave the sticky notes with the students so they can check back in their stories to see if they included the details they told you about.

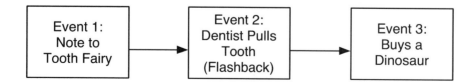

Figure 1-14. Flashback Story Map for the Tooth Pulling

RESOURCES FOR LIBRARIANS AND TEACHERS

Here are the books discussed in this chapter and some other realistic fiction Caldecott Medal and Honor books.

Bang, Molly. 1999. *When Sophie Gets Angry—Really, Really Angry.* New York: Blue Sky.

Chodos-Irvine, Margaret. 2003. *Ella Sarah Gets Dressed.* San Diego, CA: Harcourt.

Isadora, Rachel. 1979. *Ben's Trumpet.* New York: Greenwillow.

Keats, Ezra Jack. 1962. *The Snowy Day.* New York: Viking.

———. 1998, 1969. *Goggles.* New York: Viking.

Kraus, Ruth. 1949. *The Happy Day.* Illustrated by Marc Simont. New York: Harper.

Ness, Evaline. 1966. *Sam, Bangs & Moonshine.* New York: Henry Holt.

Pilkey, Dav. 1996. *The Paperboy.* New York: Orchard.

Raschka, Christopher. 1993. *Yo! Yes?* New York: Orchard.

Rathmann, Peggy. 1995. *Officer Buckle and Gloria.* New York: Putnam.

Shannon, David. 1998. *No! David.* New York: Scholastic.

Shulevitz, Uri. 1998. *Snow.* New York: Farrar Straus Giroux.

Simont, Marc. 2001. *The Stray Dog.* New York: HarperCollins.

Willems, Mo. 2004. *Knuffle Bunny: A Cautionary Tale.* New York: Hyperion.

Williams, Vera B. 1982. *A Chair for My Mother.* New York: Greenwillow.

———. 1990. *"More More More," Said the Baby: Three Love Stories.* New York: Greenwillow.

Yolen, Jane. 1987. *Owl Moon.* Illustrated by John Schoenherr. New York: Philomel.

Web Sites for Dealing with Anger

Dealing with Anger
http://kidshealth.org/kid/feeling/emotion/anger.html
This Web page, written for children, defines anger, describes how you feel when you are angry, explains how to tell if someone else is angry, and gives suggestions on what to do when you are angry. The clear and concise information is easy for children to understand. This Web site has a Spanish version.

Helping Young Children Deal with Anger
http://www.athealth.com/Consumer/issues/childsanger.html
This Web page, written for adults, describes the components of anger, contains information on understanding and managing anger, and includes ideas for helping children express their anger.

Books for Dealing with Anger

Bottner, Barbara. 1992. *Bootsie Barker Bites.* Illustrated by Peggy Rathmann. New York: Putnam.

Sendak, Maurice. 1984. *Where the Wild Things Are.* New York: HarperCollins.

Viorst, Judith. 1972. *Alexander and the Terrible, Horrible, No Good, Very Bad Day.* New York: Atheneum.

RESOURCES FOR STUDENTS

Students who enjoyed reading books by the authors and illustrators in this chapter might enjoy some of their other books.

Bang, Molly. 1980. *The Grey Lady and the Strawberry Snatcher.* New York: Simon & Schuster.

———. 1983. *Ten, Nine, Eight.* New York: Greenwillow.

———. 1985. *The Paper Crane.* New York: Greenwillow.

———. 1991. *Picture This: Perception & Composition.* Boston: Little, Brown.

———. 2004. *My Light.* New York: Blue Sky.

Rathmann, Peggy. 1992. *Ruby the Copycat.* New York: Putnam.

———. 1994. *Goodnight, Gorilla.* New York: Putnam.

———. 1998. *10 Minutes till Bedtime.* New York: Putnam.

———. 2003. *The Day the Babies Crawled Away.* New York: Putnam.

Schoenherr, John. 1991. *Bear.* New York: Philomel.

———. 1995. *Rebel.* New York: Philomel.

Sharmat, Marjorie Weinman. 2002, 1972. Nate the Great. Series illustrated by Marc Simont. New York: Delacorte.

Simont, Marc. 1997. *The Goose That Almost Got Cooked.* New York: Scholastic.

Taylor, Theodore. 2002. *Hello, Arctic!* Illustrated by Margaret Chodos-Irvine. San Diego, CA: Harcourt.

Udry, Janice May. 1956. *A Tree Is Nice.* Illustrated by Marc Simont. New York: HarperCollins.

Willems, Mo. 2003. *Don't Let the Pigeon Drive the Bus.* New York: Hyperion.

———. 2003. *Time to Pee!* New York: Hyperion.

———. 2004. *Pigeon Finds a Hot Dog.* New York: Hyperion.

Williams, Vera B. 1983. *Something Special for Me.* New York: Greenwillow.

———. 1984. *Music, Music for Everyone.* New York: Greenwillow.

———. 1988. *Stringbean's Trip to the Shining Sea.* New York: Greenwillow.

———. 2001. *Amber Was Brave, Essie Was Smart: The Story of Amber and Essie Told Here in Poems and Pictures.* New York: Greenwillow.

Wong, Janet. 2000. *Buzz.* Illustrated by Margaret Chodos-Irvine. San Diego, CA: Harcourt.

———. 2002. *Apple Pie 4th of July.* Illustrated by Margaret Chodos-Irvine. San Diego, CA: Harcourt.

Yolen, Jane. 1967. *The Emperor and the Kite.* Illustrated by Ed Young. New York: Philomel.

———. 2001. *Welcome to the River of Grass.* Illustrated by Laura Regan. New York: Putnam.

———. 2003. *The Flying Witch.* Illustrated by Vladimir Vagin. New York: HarperCollins.

———. 2003. *Hoptoad.* Illustrated by Karen Lee Schmidt. San Diego, CA: Harcourt.

———. 2003. *My Brothers' Flying Machine.* Illustrated by Jim Burke. Boston: Little, Brown.

IDEAS FOR PARENTS AND CAREGIVERS

Enjoying family outings, adventures, and everyday experiences with their parents and caregivers are all sources of inspiration for students as they consider topics for writing realistic fiction. A family journal or scrapbook can be used to record these activities to preserve details that students can use in their writing. Haircuts, picnics, birthday parties, visits from relatives, vacations, trips to the grocery store, dentist visits, the birth of a sibling, and deaths in the family are all topics students can explore in their writing. As children write realistic fiction based on these experiences their parents and caregivers can talk with them to help them organize their thoughts and to help them remember important details. Encourage the children to bring their writing home to read to their parents and caregivers. Parents and caregivers can give students positive support and reinforcement by pointing out what they like best about the writing or asking questions about parts that are unclear. They should refrain from criticizing or correcting the writing, as that will discourage the students from sharing writing with them.

REFERENCES

Bishop, Kay, and Nancy Larimer. 1999. "Literacy through Collaboration." *Teacher Librarian* 27, no. 1 (October): 15–20.

Chodos-Irvine, Margaret. 2003. "Between the Lines: Interview with Theodore Taylor and Margaret Chodos-Irvine." [Online] Available: http://www.harcourtbooks .com/authorinterviews/bookinterview_taylor.asp [cited 24 February 2005].

Gourley, Catherine. 1999. "How Advertisers Persuade." *Writing* 22, no. 1 (September): 6–9.

Inspiration. Version 7.5. Portland, OR: Inspiration Software.

"Jane (Hyatt) Yolen." 2002. *Major Authors and Illustrators for Children and Young Adults,* 2nd ed. Farmington Hills, MI: Gale Group.

Letchworth, Beverly J. 1996. "The Big 'I' in Children's Fiction." *Writer* 109, no. 9 (September): 20–22.

Peck, Jackie, and Judith Hendershot. 1997. "Meet Officer Buckle and Gloria through their Creator's Own Story." *The Reading Teacher* 50, no. 5 (February): 404–408.

Rochelle, Warren. 1991. "A Sense of Responsibility in Realistic Children's Fiction." *Emergency Librarian* 18, no. 5 (May/June): 8–13.

Silvey, Anita, editor. 2002. *The Essential Guide to Children's Books and Their Creators.* Boston: Houghton Mifflin.

Tyson, Cynthia A. 1999. " 'Shut My Mouth Wide Open': Realistic Fiction and Social Action." *Theory into Practice* 38, no. 3 (Summer): 155–159.

Williams, Vera B. 2002. "Voices of the Creators." In *Children's Books and Their Creators,* edited by Anita Silvey. Boston: Houghton Mifflin.

Yolen, Jane. 1999. "The Geography of Hope." *Writer* 114, no. 4 (April): 23.

2 ❖ HISTORICAL FICTION

Historical fiction weaves together realistic stories and stories from history as fictional characters take part in historical events. It allows readers to time travel and to discover how the present and the future are linked inexorably to the past. Historical fiction is not just a dry recitation of the facts, such as might be found in a textbook or an encyclopedia; rather, it is a blend of knowledge and emotions. Richard Peck notes that historical fiction focuses on people and relationships, not on historical events (Rochman, 2004). The facts of history serve as frameworks for the stories. As former school-librarian-turned-author Brenda Rickman Vantrease states, "it (history) is filled with stories" (Williams, 2005, p. 77). Well-told stories have characters that readers care about and the stories explore the social and political issues of the time (Beck, Nelson-Faulkner, and Pierce, 2000). Macleod (1998) cautions that as social climates change, historical revisionism becomes apparent in historical fiction.

Writers of historical fiction may be writing about their own lives, the lives of relatives, about an incident in the life of a historical figure, or about a character who could have lived during the time period. Richard Peck contends that historical novels are memories; they reflect what is felt in the heart (Rochman, 2004). In writing historical fiction, authors are required to immerse themselves in the time period through extensive research, using primary and secondary resources. These resources may include interviews, newspapers, advertisements, diaries, journals, records, and books. Writers conduct research to learn the details of major events and to get a feel for daily life. They write about things in the past that puzzle them. Writers must know the facts but must also remember that as they write, their characters and their readers are there because they are witnessing history before it became history (Martin, 1996).

Historical fiction strengthens the social studies curriculum because it examines history from different perspectives and enables readers to develop empathy for those whose lives were impacted by decisions that were made. Students discover the interdependence of people; they learn that some values and beliefs change over time and some values and beliefs have persisted over time. They also learn that some conflicts of the past are similar to conflicts that confront people and society today.

As they look back into history through stories, students develop an appreciation for their own family histories. Historical fiction enables them to explore the place of children in important events, and in the process gain a sense of their own place in history (Stanek, 1991). It also helps students understand that their daily lives and experiences will one day be written about as the past. Students need to be surrounded by historical fiction and they need a wide variety of information resources in a variety of formats to explore. Librarians not only take the lead in locating and organizing the resources; they also provide help to teachers as they design instruction to meet the diverse needs of their students (Woods, 1997). While collaboration takes time and requires that librarians and teachers each define the roles they can best fulfill, the benefits to students' learning are well worth the time and effort. When librarians and teachers work together, students receive the benefits of the support and resources of both (Schomberg, McCabe, and Fink, 2003).

In picture books, the illustrations and the text combine to help readers visualize the setting (Albright and Vardell, 2003), which in historical fiction is the key to transporting readers back in time (Speer, 1995). For example, the illustrations in *Peppe the Lamplighter* (Bartone, 1993) show the lamps that must be lit every evening, the laundry hanging from windows high above the streets, and the clothing of the time period. The illustrations not only aid in understanding the story, they also evoke questions about the characters and the times in which they lived.

The Man Who Walked Between the Towers

by Mordicai Gerstein
Caldecott Medal Winner, 2004

READING

Before Reading

Story Summary

When Philippe Petit sees balls, he has to juggle and when he sees towers, he has to walk between them on a wire. On a summer day in 1974, Petit walked between the twin towers of the World Trade Center. Gerstein takes readers along as this French aerialist defies gravity and the law to fulfill a dream. When he walked off the wire, he was arrested and sentenced to perform for the children in the city park. Two fold-out pages add to the drama as readers look up and down from dizzying perspectives. On one fold-out page readers soar with the seagulls for a bird's-eye view of Petit's walk, and on the next fold-out page readers, firmly planted on the ground, crane their necks to watch in awe as Petit walks between the towers. The ink and oil illustrations dramatically depict the death-defying events unfolding in this gripping story. This book is available in audiocassette, videocassette, CD, and DVD.

While Gerstein did not see Petit walk between the towers, he did see him perform on the sidewalks of New York (Jacobs, Mitchell, and Livingston, 2004/2005). Petit (2002) tells his own story of his six-year dream in *To Reach the Clouds: My High Wire Walk Between the Twin Towers*. A transcript and a video of an interview with Petit taken from Ric Burns's *The Center of the World* (New York, Episode 8) are available at http://www.pbs.org/wgbh/amex/newyork/sfeature/sf_interviews.html.

Activating Prior Knowledge

Open the book flat to show the entire cover to the students and ask them to determine the point of view or the angle from which they are looking at the picture. Then, ask them to predict what will happen in the story. What would happen if they tried to walk across a wire? Mordicai Gerstein tells the story of Philippe Petit's spellbinding walk between the World Trade Center twin towers.

During Reading

The story is told from Philippe's point of view, but the illustrations allow readers to watch the story unfold from a variety of perspectives. As you read the story, share

❖ ————————————————

Recommended Grade Levels

3–12

Standards for the English Language Arts

2, 3, 5, 6, 8, 9, 11, 12

Information Literacy Standards for Student Learning

2, 4, 6, 8

Objectives

The students will:

• Examine the story and illustrations looking for different points of view, and

• Respond to the story by rewriting a portion of the story from another character's point of view.

———————————————— ❖

❖ ⸺⸺⸺⸺⸺⸺⸺⸺⸺

Author

Mordicai Gerstein lives in Northampton, Massachusetts. When he was a child his mother created a scrapbook museum for him of photographs of famous paintings she cut from *Life* magazine (Gerstein, 2004). He studied the pictures over and over again. He visits art museums and revisits his childhood to find ideas for his writing. He used to think that he had to know the story before he started writing, but now he writes and lets the story tell itself. Gerstein illustrated books for other authors before he started illustrating his own stories. Students may recognize Gerstein as the illustrator of Elizabeth Levy's mystery series Something Queer Is Going On. Gerstein credits Levy with suggesting that he illustrate and write children's books (Jacobs, Mitchell, and Livingston, 2004/2005).

⸺⸺⸺⸺⸺⸺⸺⸺⸺ ❖

the illustrations with the students and talk about the different perspectives they portray.

After Reading

To encourage lively, interactive discussions, Lenihan (2003) suggests posing provocative questions and modeling how to listen and respond appropriately when others speak.

- How do you think Philippe practiced for his walk?
- What plans did he have to make to accomplish this feat?
- What challenges did he have to face?
- How would you describe Philippe?
- Why did the police officers arrest him?
- Why did the judge sentence him to perform for the children in the park? Was this a fair sentence? Why or why not?
- Why was walking the wire between the buildings dangerous to him and to others?
- What do you think his parents thought of his feat?
- What would your parents think if you told them you wanted to walk on a wire between two tall buildings?

WRITING

Mini-lesson—Point of View

- When Petit walked off the wire, the police officers arrested him. What would the story be like if it was told from the point of view of the police officers?
- Ask the children to imagine that they are the police officers.
- Return to the book to look at the police officers and what they are doing, including the page that unfolds with the police officer on his radio.
- Brainstorm with the students about what the police officers are saying, what are they thinking, their actions, their words, their feelings, and their concerns.
- Write their responses on the board so they can refer to them as they write.
- What laws might Petit have broken?
- What did the police tell their friends about the incident?
- How would the story sound if it was told from the point of view of the police?

Modeling

- Invite the students to review the ideas gathered in their brainstorming.
- Select some of their ideas and begin writing your version of the story from the point of view of the police officers, which might look something like this:

    Down the street, I saw a large crowd of people staring toward the sky. They were transfixed. They were blocking the sidewalks. They were standing in the street. Cars halted, drivers got out, and stared upwards. When I looked up, I could not believe what I saw.

Writing Activity

- Place a copy of the book on a table where the students can refer to the pictures for ideas as they write.
- Tell the students that they are going to write their version of how the police officers reacted when they saw Petit high above them crossing the thin, taut wire.
- Remind the students that the book does not give many details about the police officers' version of what happened, so they are free to make up the details.
- Students can also tell the story from the point of view of the seagulls or the people on the street.

Conferencing

- As you conference with the students and you notice students having trouble getting started on their writing, suggest that they use what you have written to begin their writing.
- As the students begin finishing their drafts, allow them to meet in small groups and talk about their writing rather than read it to each other.
- Once they have shared ideas, ask the students to return to their desks and revise their stories using ideas they gained from the conference.

Smoky Night

by Eve Bunting
Illustrated by David Diaz
Caldecott Medal Winner, 1995

READING

Before Reading

Story Summary
Daniel, an African-American boy, gives readers a child's perspective on the riots that erupted in Los Angeles in 1992. When his apartment building catches fire, Daniel and his mother join other tenants as they seek shelter in a nearby church hall. In the confusion, Daniel's cat is lost as is the cat of his Korean neighbor Mrs. Kim. A firefighter finds the two cats howling under the stairs in the apartment building and reunites them with their owners. In this night of chaos and terror, the two cats forged a friendship, as did their owners, who previously did not associate with one another. Bold acrylic paintings surrounded by collages of torn, wrinkled paper and debris from the looted stores illustrate the story. Bunting and Diaz also collaborated on *Going Home* (Bunting, 1996) and *December* (Bunting, 1997).

After three police officers were acquitted of criminal charges in the beating of Rodney King, the Los Angeles riots erupted. This book provides a positive look at disturbing events and serves as a catalyst for talking and reflecting on the issues presented. Kazemek (1995) notes that the book provides no context for the chaotic

❖ ——————————

Recommended Grade Levels

5–12

Standards for the English Language Arts

1, 2, 4, 5, 7, 8, 9, 11, 12

Information Literacy Standards for Student Learning

1, 2, 3, 6, 8, 9

Objectives

The students will:

- Examine the text to determine how the author creates suspense, and
- Write a suspenseful narrative. ❖

——————————

Author

Eve Bunting was born and raised in Northern Ireland. As a child, she attended boarding school and told stories to her classmates. In the 1950s, she moved to California where she enrolled in a writing for publication course. She draws from her personal experiences and news events when she writes. She writes picture books, books for middle school students, and young adult novels. A brief biography and reviews of some of her books are at http://www.childrenslit.com/f_evebunting.htm.

Illustrator

David Diaz was born in Fort Lauderdale, Florida. In the first grade, he decided he was going to be an artist. His wife Cecelia is also an artist and she helps him make decisions about which books to illustrate. In his Caldecott Medal acceptance speech, he acknowledged his high school art teacher, who motivated him to pursue a career as an artist and encouraged him to enter competitions (Diaz, 1995). *Smoky Night* was the first picture book he illustrated, and it is unusual for an illustrator to win the Caldecott for a first book. Diaz's biography and a transcript of an interview can be found on the *Scholastic* Web site by using the Quick Find option at http://www2.scholastic.com/teachers/authorsandbooks/. Additional information about Diaz is available at http://www.nccil.org/diaz.html.

situation it depicts. To provide a context for the story you can learn about the riots by reading television reporter Stan Chambers's personal recollection of the Los Angeles riots and the Rodney King beating at http://www.citivu.com/ktla/sc-ch1.html. Information concerning some of the controversy about this book is in articles by Gerhardt (1995) and Koehnecke (2001).

Activating Prior Knowledge

Eve Bunting's story ideas often come from current events, including this one based on the Los Angeles riots. Sometimes riots occur when people get frustrated and angry about events they cannot control. In this story, when a riot breaks out a little boy and his mother are forced to flee their home. Ask the students about times when they were forced to flee their homes because of events beyond their control.

During Reading

Writers build suspense by letting readers know about things that might happen (Klaven, 1994). In this story, Bunting lets readers know that the boy and his mother are in danger by describing what is happening and letting the reader infer what could possibly happen. As you read, pause periodically and have the students predict what might happen next.

After Reading

This book helps students discuss how events such as the Los Angeles riots affect their lives (Zingher, 1996). If a librarian and teacher are collaborating on this lesson, divide the class into two groups to discuss the book. Students are more likely to contribute to the discussion in smaller groups because they have more opportunities to be heard and may feel more comfortable in a smaller group. Once the students are in their groups, these questions help them think about the book and their personal responses to it.

- How much control do the characters have over what is happening?
- What problems do the characters face over the course of the night?
- What choices do the characters make?
- What stereotypes are evident?
- Did anything in the book surprise you? Why did it surprise you?
- What conditions are necessary to provoke a riot?
- What effect did being part of a crowd have on the looters?
- What was the motive behind the riots?
- How did the riots affect society?
- Why do peaceful demonstrations sometimes turn violent?
- Do you think something like this could happen again? Why or why not?

WRITING

Mini-lesson—Creating Suspense

- Bunting builds suspense by having the young boy describe what he and his mother are doing and letting the readers infer what might happen.
- Project the statements from the book as shown in Figure 2-1. These statements are examples from the book that show students how Bunting builds suspense in her writing.

"Mama and I stand well back from our window."

"I move behind Mama. 'Will they come here?'"

"I am to take off my shoes but leave on my clothes."

Figure 2-1. Creating Suspense

- Point out to the students that, rather than say the boy and his mother are afraid of what might happen, she describes their actions. Describing the characters' actions is one way to build suspense.

Modeling

- Think about a time when something suspenseful happened to you or something suspenseful happened to someone else.
- The narrative below is about a time when a teenage boy and his dog were home alone when a tornado touched down nearby.

> *The pelting rain slackened. The sky turned an eerie shade of green. The wind howled and whipped around the house. The house creaked and shuddered. The wind howled louder. Blanco was shaking. His large, skinny frame pressed hard against my leg. I grabbed his collar and dragged him into the windowless downstairs bathroom in the center of the house. I slammed the door. Together we crouched in the dark on the cold tile floor waiting, waiting.*

Writing Activity

- Put the students into small groups and ask them to talk to each other about a suspenseful or unexpected occurrence that happened to them, such as a thunderstorm, a snowstorm, a dust storm, or a hurricane.
- As they talk, remind them to briefly jot down their feelings, the events, and their reactions to what was happening.
- Then, have the students work together to think of ways to describe rather than tell about their feelings and the events.
- Put a copy of the book in an accessible location so the students can refer to Bunting's text to examine how she created suspense in her writing.

Conferencing

- As you conference with the students ask them open-ended questions about their writing, such as, "What other details can you add to make your readers feel as if they were there with you? How did you feel while it was happening? How did you feel when it was over?"

- After asking a question, wait for the students to respond and listen carefully to their responses. If their answers provide additional details, encourage them to add the details to their narratives.

Mirette on the High Wire

by Emily Arnold McCully
Caldecott Medal Winner, 1993

READING

Before Reading

Story Summary

Bellini, an aerialist, has become fearful of walking across the high wire he once crossed with ease. He takes up residence in the boarding house Mirette's mother operates, and Mirette discovers him walking across a wire he has strung in the courtyard. At first he refuses to teach her to walk across the high wire, but he relents. Mirette helps restore his courage and together they share the high wire. McCully used bright watercolor and gouache illustrations in the French Impressionist style to capture everyday life in nineteenth-century Paris. Other books about these characters are *Starring Mirette and Bellini* (McCully, 1997) and *Mirette and Bellini Cross Niagara Falls* (McCully, 2000). This book is available on videocassette.

Activating Prior Knowledge

Show the students the breathtaking illustration on the cover and ask them to predict what will happen in the book. Making predictions motivates students to listen attentively and develops their imaginations. As students make their predictions help them make connections to their own lives. Tell the students that authors use conversations, thoughts, actions, and descriptions to develop their characters, and that as you read the book, they are to listen for information about the characters Mirette and Bellini.

During Reading

As you read the story pause to point out the characters' conversations, thoughts, actions, and descriptions, and ask the students what they learn about the characters.

After Reading

Martin (1996) contends that characters in historical fiction should have strong personalities and strong beliefs, which when tested create conflict based on the decisions the characters make. Questions such as these help students explore the characters' personalities and beliefs:

- How would you describe Bellini? How old is he? What does he look like? How does he act?
- How would you describe Mirette? How old is she? What does she look like? How does she act?

Sidebar

❖ ─────────

Recommended Grade Levels

4–10

Standards for the English Language Arts

1, 2, 3, 5, 12

Information Literacy Standards for Student Learning

3, 5, 9

Objectives

The students will:

- Examine the story to determine the characters' traits,
- Create character maps of Mirette and Bellini,
- Create a character map of their own character, and
- Use the character map to write a story.

───────── ❖

❖ ─────────

Author

Emily Arnold McCully has been writing and drawing since she was three years old. She acknowledges that Mirette is a highly personal metaphor for the risks that she takes as an illustrator and writer. In her Caldecott acceptance speech, she expressed her gratitude to and respect for librarians and teachers who buy books for students with their own money to assure that their students, no matter what their socioeconomic background, become readers (McCully, 1993). She writes picture books, short stories, fiction, novels, and has written a musical. A biography and reviews for some of her books are available at http://www.childrenslit.com/f_mccully.html.

─────────

- What did you learn about Mirette and Bellini from their conversations?
- What did you learn about Mirette and Bellini from their actions?
- Why was Bellini afraid to walk across the high wire? The author does not tell us, but students can speculate on the reasons.
- Why did Mirette decide she wanted to learn to walk across the high wire?
- Why did Bellini freeze as he began walking across the wire high above the crowd?
- Why did he begin walking once Mirette walked out on the wire?

WRITING

Mini-lesson—Characterization

- Project a copy of a blank character map such as the one shown in Figure 2-2, using either *Inspiration* software or a transparency of the blank character map in the appendix. Each level of the map has its own unique shape to help students differentiate between the types of information that goes in each level.
- Ask the students to return to the story and locate descriptions, actions, thoughts, dialogue, or reactions of others that make Mirette seem real and that provide information about her.

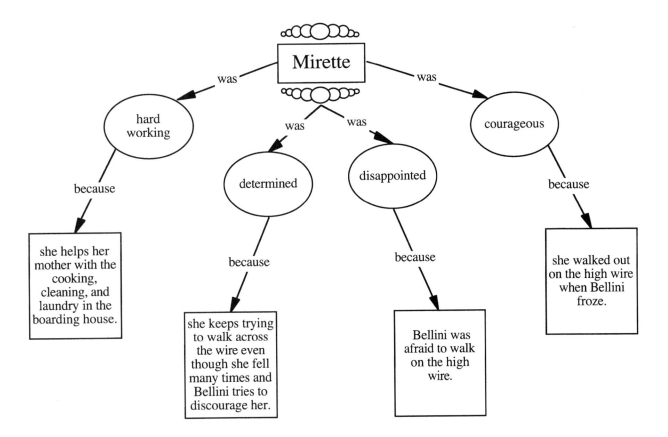

Figure 2-2. Character Map of Mirette

- Record the information in the rectangular boxes in the diagram.
- Then, have the students decide what character trait is indicative of the description and write the trait in the circle.
- Once the character map of Mirette is completed, have the students work in small groups to complete a character map of Bellini.
- Allow the students to share their Bellini character maps.

Modeling

- Once the students have completed the character maps of Mirette and Bellini, model for them how to use a character map to create a character for a story.
- As you decide on a name for your character, talk about names that come to your mind and why you settle on the one that you choose.
- Ask the students for ideas for character traits. Start by describing what the character looks like, the character's age, and how the character acts.
- Once the character traits are written on the character map, ask the students for suggestions for actions that reflect those traits.
- Your completed map might look something like the one in Figure 2-3.
- Begin writing your story which might start something like this:

> *"Why do flies get stuck in spider webs and spiders do not stick?" questioned Frances as she swept the cobwebs from under the kitchen cabinets.*

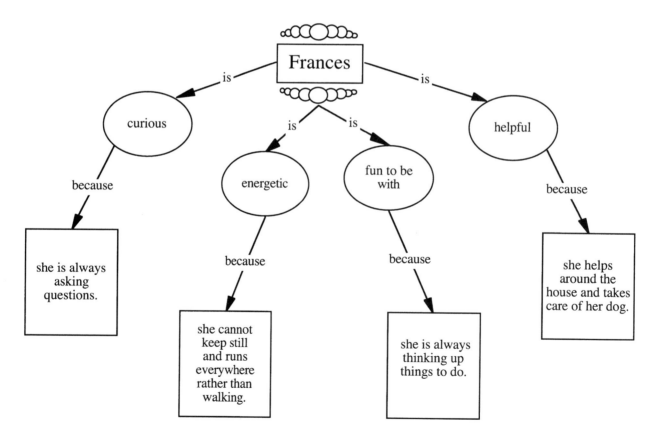

Figure 2-3. Character Map of Frances

The broom was a blur as she jabbed it under the table and crumbs scattered across the floor. She was eager to finish her chores and get outside before the rain came.

Writing Activity

- As older students begin to create their own character maps, allow them to talk with each other and share ideas.
- Once the character maps are completed and the writing begins, ask the students to refrain from talking so that everyone can concentrate on their writing.
- While the students are writing their stories, finish writing your story.

Conferencing

- As you conference with the students ask them to show you how they incorporated the information in their character maps into their stories.
- Encourage them to check off or circle the items in the character maps that they included in their stories.
- Tell the students that it is acceptable to make changes in their character maps as they write.

Coming on Home Soon

by Jacqueline Woodson
Illustrated by E. B. Lewis
Caldecott Honor Book, 2005

READING

Before Reading

Story Summary

During World War II when the men were overseas fighting, women filled their jobs, and in this story a mother leaves her rural homestead for Chicago to take a job working for the railroad and leaves her daughter and her mother behind. A homeless kitten that appears on their doorstep assuages their loneliness. Throughout the story, the refrain "coming on home soon" resounds with hope for the mother's return. This book, as with other books Woodson has written, conveys a sense of optimism. Readers see that while life may not be easy, there is always hope for a better tomorrow. Lewis's earth-toned watercolors have a lifelike quality to them that encourages readers to step into the book and become part of this loving family. Woodson and Lewis also collaborated on *The Other Side* (Woodson, 2001).

Activating Prior Knowledge

This is a story about a child waiting for her mother to return from a job in a distant city. Ask the students if any of them have parents or caregivers who travel on business or are stationed overseas. Encourage the students to talk about how they feel

❖ ───────────────

Recommended Grade Levels

4–12

Standards for the English Language Arts

2, 3, 4, 5, 6, 9, 12

Information Literacy Standards for Student Learning

5, 9

Objectives

The students will:

- Examine the dialogue in a story, and
- Practice writing dialogue.

─────────────── ❖

Author

Jacqueline Woodson was born in Columbus, Ohio. She grew up in South Carolina and New York City, moving back and forth between these two very different locales. Woodson recalls that her sister taught her to write her whole name when she was about three years old and that she loved the power of putting letters on paper and having them mean something (Brown, 2002). By fifth grade, she had become a passionate writer. Her high school English teacher encouraged her to continue writing and to pursue whatever career made her happiest. Her writing ranges from picture books to adult novels. Her Web site is at http://www .jacquelinewoodson.com. On her Web site you can find information about her books including the setting, where she wrote the book, and why she wrote the book. She also has answers to frequently asked questions, a list of awards she has won, and information on how to contact her.

Illustrator

E. B. Lewis was born in Philadelphia and his artistic talent was first noticed when he was in the third grade. Two of his uncles were artists and they inspired him to become an artist (Lewis, 2005). He has a degree in Graphic Design and Illustration and a degree in Art Education. His Web site, located at http://www.eblewis .com, contains a brief biography and an annotated list of books he has illustrated.

when their parents or caregivers are out of town and how they feel upon their return home.

During Reading

Point out to the students how the colors in the illustrations set the mood and tone for the story. Ask the students what they see in the illustrations that remind them of their own lives. For example, those with pets will see themselves in the illustration of the young girl lying on the floor with her kitten. Show the students how Woodson uses italics rather than quotation marks to denote dialogue in the text.

After Reading

- The last illustration in the book shows the mother walking up to the house. Ask the students to describe what they think happened when the mother walked through the front door.
- Questions such as these help the students focus on what might happen next in the story: "What were the child, the grandmother, and the mother feeling?" "What did they do to celebrate the mother's return?"
- Ask the students, "What do you do to celebrate when your parents or caregivers return home after long absences?"

WRITING

Mini-lesson—Dialogue

- Use a document camera to project page three to show the dialogue. If a document camera is not available, make a transparency of the page to project.
- Tell the students that Woodson uses italics to indicate dialogue rather than quotation marks and dialogue tags.
- Have the students read the page with you and look for parts of the text where they think either Ada Ruth or Mama is speaking.
- Ask the students, "Why do you think the author decided not to use quotation marks? How do you know which character is speaking? What clues help you determine which character is speaking?"
- Tell the students that authors use dialogue to develop their characters.
- Ask the students, "What do you learn about Ada Ruth and Mama through their conversation?"
- Point out to the students that when the characters speak they sometimes speak in short phrases rather than complete sentences, which is how we normally talk with our family members and friends.

Modeling

- In order to model the writing of natural-sounding dialogue for the students, recall a conversation you recently had.
- Open a word processing program and project the image on a large screen as you begin writing the conversation, or write the conversation on the board.
- As you write the dialogue replay the conversation in your head, and try to transcribe the conversation. The dialogue should be clear and sparse with

no extraneous words. Think out loud as you write to help the students understand your thought processes and to show them that it is okay to make up the parts of the conversation you do not remember.

- Your conversation might look something like this:

You have to read Ella Enchanted.
Why?
You will love it. You know the story of Cinderella?
Yes.
This is a version of Cinderella. Except in this version the fairy godmother puts a spell on Ella and she cannot say "no." She has to do whatever anyone asks.
So?
One of her stepsisters asks her to go and pick her some flowers. Well, Ella knows she has to do that. So, she goes to pick flowers, but she picks weeds that she knows the stepsister is allergic to.

Writing Activity

- In order to get the students started on the writing assignment, suggest that they think about a recent conversation they had with someone and write it down. Remind them that they can make up the parts of the conversation that they do not remember.
- If there are students who do not have a conversation in mind, ask them to join you in a small group. You can ask two students to volunteer to talk about what they liked about *Coming on Home Soon.* As they talk, ask the other students to listen carefully and take notes about the conversation. Keep the conversation brief.
- Tell the students to return to their desks and write down the conversation. If they do not remember exactly what was said, they can just write down what they remember and make up the rest of it.
- As the students write, remind them to just write the conversation down and not to worry about where to put the punctuation marks as the focus of this exercise is on creating natural-sounding dialogue.

Conferencing

- Ask the students to conference with a partner. Each partner reads the dialogue of one of the characters.
- Once they have read the dialogue aloud, tell them to try to determine which words they can eliminate and which words they need to change to make the dialogue sound natural.

Peppe the Lamplighter

by Elisa Bartone
Illustrated by Ted Lewin
Caldecott Honor Book, 1994

READING

Before Reading

Story Summary

Peppe gets a job lighting the gas streetlights to earn money to help support his sick father and his sisters, but his father does not approve of the work. He continually says negative things about Peppe's job, and so one night Peppe does not light the lamps. His younger sister does not come home that night, because she is scared to walk home in the dark. Peppe's father begs him to light the lamps and at the base of the last lamp Peppe finds his sister, whom he safely guides home. The watercolor illustrations are rich with details of daily life in turn-of-the-century Little Italy, and the interplay of dark and light in the illustrations creates striking contrasts. Bartone and Lewin also collaborated on *American Too* (Bartone, 1996), a companion book to this one.

Activating Prior Knowledge

While the setting, New York City's Little Italy at the turn of the century, may not be familiar to students, the illustrations depict it beautifully. Tell the students that Peppe and his father are immigrants who are struggling to accept the changes in their lives since their arrival in America. Students who have immigrated to America may at this time want to share their experiences with assimilating into a new culture. All of the students, whether or not they are immigrants, can be asked to share disagreements with their parents or caregivers.

During Reading

As you read, pause to point out the development and the resolution of the conflict between Peppe and his father.

After Reading

- Ask the students to describe what Peppe thinks about his job and what his father thinks about Peppe's job. Peppe sees the job as a way of helping to support his family; his father sees the job as not worthwhile and a waste of Peppe's life.
- Encourage the students to discuss both sides of the conflict.
- Have the students work with you to complete a story map diagramming the beginning, middle, and end of the story. Creating a story map is one way to begin a discussion of the plot structure.

WRITING

Mini-lesson—Plot Structure

- Tell the students that the plot gives a focus to the story and shapes the action. The plot structure includes three parts, as shown in Figure 2-4. The first part is the rising action, which creates conflict. The second part is the climax, which involves a turning point in the story. The third part is the falling action or resolution to the conflict.
- Project a blank copy of the plot structure or draw one on the board.
- Give each student a blank plot structure or have them draw one on paper. There is a blank plot structure diagram in the appendix.
- Have the students complete their own plot structures as you complete yours. The completed plot structures will look something like the one in Figure 2-5.

Modeling

- Ask the students about conflicts they have with their siblings or their classmates.
- Have the students help you think about how the event starts by asking a question such as, "What does your brother or sister do to annoy you?"
- As you work on the plot structure diagram ask the children to help you fill in the details.

❖ ———————————

Illustrator

Ted Lewin lives in Brooklyn, New York. His wife Betsy is also a children's book illustrator. Betsy and Ted enjoy traveling and their travels are the subject of many of their books. When he travels, he writes in a journal, makes sketches, and takes photographs to record what he sees and his impressions. In order to pay for his art education he became a wrestler, which he talks about in his biography, *I Was a Teen-Age Professional Wrestler* (Lewin, 1993). Additional information about Lewin and reviews of some of his books are available at http://www .childrenslit.com/f_lewin.htm and http://www.nccil.org/tlewin.html.

——————————— ❖

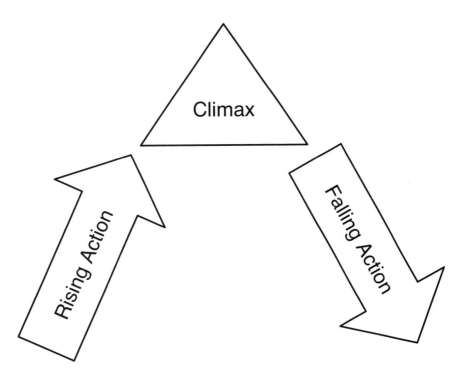

Figure 2-4. Plot Structure

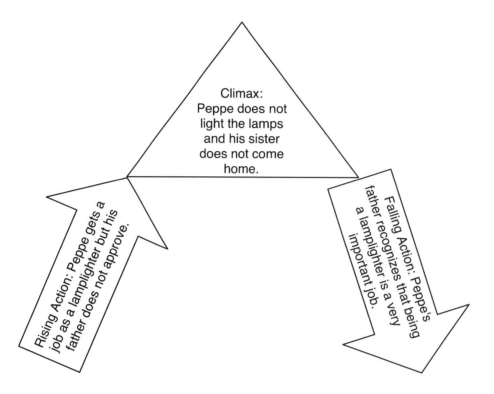

Figure 2-5. Plot Structure for *Peppe the Lamplighter*

Writing Activity

- Place the students in small groups to brainstorm ideas they have about conflicts in their lives.
- Once all of the students have ideas, provide them with copies of the plot structure diagram to complete.
- When the students begin writing ask them to write silently for fifteen to twenty minutes.
- As the students write, remind them that if the conflict was not resolved in the way they felt it should have been, they can change the resolution when they write about it.
- Continue your writing as the students write.

Conferencing

- After the students have been writing for ten to fifteen minutes, begin conferencing with them.
- Ask them to tell you about the conflict they are writing about or ask them to read what they have written.
- Be willing to share your writing with the students and ask them for suggestions for details to add to your writing.

Tar Beach

by Faith Ringgold
Caldecott Honor Book, 1992

READING

Before Reading

Story Summary
Faith Ringgold has fond memories of Tar Beach, the rooftop of the apartment building where she lived as a child during the Depression. While the story is not autobiographical, she does draw upon her childhood experiences of summer evenings eating and sleeping on the rooftop. Cassie flies above the streets of Harlem claiming all that she sees for herself and her family. She claims the George Washington Bridge that opened the day she was born, the building that houses the union that will not allow her father to join because he is African American, and the ice cream factory. Faith Ringgold transformed her story quilt Tar Beach into this picture book. At the end of the book is a photograph of the original story quilt and background information about the story and the author. She created the illustrations using acrylic paint on canvas paper. An animated version of this book, narrated by Natalie Cole, is available on videocassette and DVD. Other books featuring Cassie, the main character in this story, are *Aunt Harriet's Underground Railroad in the Sky* (Ringgold, 1992), *Counting to Tar Beach* (Ringgold, 1999), and *Cassie's Word Quilt* (Ringgold, 2002). Another book to compliment this one is *The People Could Fly* (Hamilton, 2004), which is a folktale about slaves who fly away to escape their sadness and starvation.

Activating Prior Knowledge
In African-American folktales "flying" is a metaphor for escaping from slavery, and in this story, Cassie dreams about flying and escaping the poverty and oppression her parents experience. Ask the students to talk about times when they wanted to escape and dreamed about being somewhere else or dreamed about having the power to change things.

During Reading

Explain to the students that even though this story is set in the past, they will find things in it that are familiar. As you read, pause and help the students make connections between their lives and Cassie's life, because historical fiction allows us to compare our lives to the characters' lives to determine what has changed (Stanek, 1991).

After Reading

One way to discuss the story is to have students complete a Venn diagram showing the connections they made between their lives and Cassie's life. Project a copy of a Venn diagram (see Figure 2-6), and have the students help you complete it. The appendix contains a blank Venn diagram.

❖ ─────────────

Recommended Grade Levels

4–10

Standards for the English Language Arts

1, 2, 3, 4, 5, 6, 9, 11, 12

Information Literacy Standards for Student Learning

2, 3, 5

Objectives

The students will:

- Make connections between their lives and the character's life by completing a Venn diagram,
- Complete a dream chart of the character's dreams,
- Complete a dream chart of their own dreams, and
- Using the chart, they will write about their own dreams.

❖

❖ ─────────────

Author

Faith Ringgold grew up during the Great Depression in Harlem, which is the setting for this book. She was the youngest in the family and was often home sick with asthma. When she was recuperating at home, her mother gave her crayons, paper, and fabric scraps to play with. Her mother, a fashion designer, was an inspiration to her. Faith Ringgold taught art in New York City public schools and notes that she learned a great deal from her students. Ringgold is noted for her story quilts, which combine vibrant painted canvas with pieced fabric and text. Through her quilts, Ringgold examines important social issues (Wolcott, 1998). Additional information about the author is available at http://www.childrenslit .com/f_faithringgold.html and at http://www.faithringgold.com.

❖

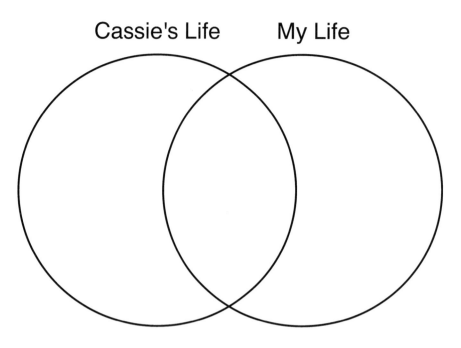

Figure 2-6. Venn Diagram

WRITING

Mini-lesson—Metaphor

- Metaphors are comparisons of two dissimilar things. A good metaphor enables us to see our world from a different perspective (Livingston, 1991).
- Explain to the students that in this book, the metaphor literally and figuratively lets the reader see his or her world from a different perspective. Cassie's "flying" enables her to dream of ways to make changes in her life.
- Tell the students that our dreams enable us to see possibilities in our own lives. Dreams give us the freedom to take charge of our lives and to realize that if we believe in ourselves we can accomplish our dreams. Cassie flies over Harlem and claims buildings and the bridge as her own in order to take control of her life and make changes.
- Put the students into small groups to discuss the story and to complete a chart such as the one in Figure 2-7.

Modeling

- Project a copy of the chart of dreams (see Figure 2-8).
- As you model how to complete the chart, think aloud so that the students realize you are dreaming about things that will benefit others and not just yourself.
- Once you have completed your chart, begin writing so that you can model for the students how you will use the information in the chart to write your story.

Cassie's Dreams   Why She Dreams Them

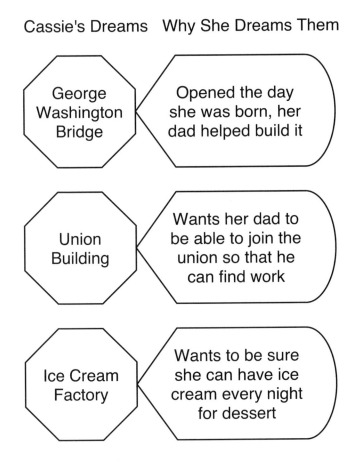

Figure 2-7. Cassie's Dreams

- Your writing might look something like this:

  On hot summer days, I lie in the shade and close my eyes. Before I know it, I am flying over houses in my neighborhood. As I fly over the school, I claim it as my own.

Writing

- Provide the students with a blank dream chart or have them make a list of their dreams on a sheet of paper. There is a blank dream chart in the appendix.
- As they work on their dream charts, remind them to include the reasons why they want to claim things.
- As the students begin writing, continue writing your own story.

Conferencing

- When you conference with the students ask them to read you the one most important thing they dream and to tell you why they dream it.
- During the conference, remember to allow the students to do most of the talking.

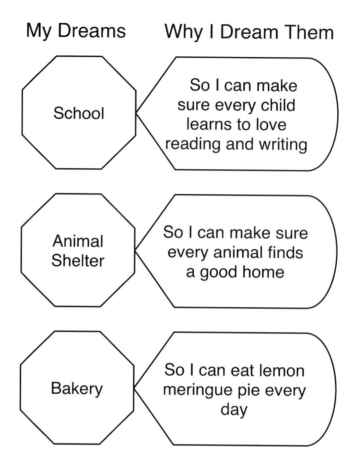

Figure 2-8. My Dreams

- As you conference with the students ask volunteers to read their pieces to the class. The pieces do not have to be complete to share them with the whole class.
- Once the students read their drafts, the other students can ask them questions to help them think about details to include in their stories.

RESOURCES FOR LIBRARIANS AND TEACHERS

Here are the books discussed in this chapter and some other historical fiction Caldecott Medal and Honor books that you might want to consider adding to your curriculum.

Bartone, Elisa. 1993. *Peppe the Lamplighter.* Illustrated by Ted Lewin. New York: Lothrop.
Bunting, Eve. 1994. *Smoky Night.* Illustrated by David Diaz. San Diego, CA: Harcourt Brace.
Gerstein, Mordicai. 2003. *The Man Who Walked Between the Towers.* Brookfield, CT: Roaring Brook.
Hall, Donald. 1979. *Ox-Cart Man.* Illustrated by Barbara Cooney. New York: Viking.
McCully, Emily Arnold. 1992. *Mirette on the High Wire.* New York: Putnam.
Ringgold, Faith. 1991. *Tar Beach.* New York: Crown.

Rylant, Cynthia. 1982. *When I Was Young in the Mountains.* Illustrated by Diane Goode. New York: Dutton.

———. 1985. *The Relatives Came.* Illustrated by Stephen Gammell. New York: Bradbury.

Turkle, Brinton. 1968. *Thy Friend, Obadiah.* New York: Viking.

Woodson, Jacqueline. 2004. *Coming on Home Soon.* Illustrated by E. B. Lewis. New York: Putnam.

RESOURCES FOR STUDENTS

Students who enjoyed reading books by the authors and illustrators in this chapter might enjoy some of their other books.

Bartone, Elisa. 1991. *The Angel Who Forgot.* New York: Simon & Schuster.

———. 1996. *American Too.* Illustrated by Ted Lewin. New York: Lothrop.

Bunting, Eve. 1991. *A Turkey for Thanksgiving.* Illustrated by Diane de Groat. Boston: Houghton Mifflin.

———. 1995. *Spying on Miss Muller.* New York: Clarion.

———. 1996. *The Blue and the Gray.* Illustrated by Ned Bittinger. New York: Scholastic.

———. 1996. *Going Home.* Illustrated by David Diaz. New York: HarperCollins.

———. 1997. *December.* Illustrated by David Diaz. San Diego, CA: Harcourt.

Curtis, Gavin. 1998. *The Bat Boy and His Violin.* Illustrated by E. B. Lewis. New York: Simon & Schuster.

Gerstein, Mordicai. 2002. *What Charlie Heard.* New York: Farrar Straus Giroux.

———. 2003. *Sparrow Jack.* New York: Farrar Straus Giroux.

Grimes, Nikki. 2002. *Talkin' About Bessie: The Story of Aviator Elizabeth Coleman.* Illustrated by E. B. Lewis. New York: Scholastic.

Hamilton, Virginia. 2004. *The People Could Fly: The Picture Book.* Illustrated by Leo and Diane Dillon. New York: Knopf.

High, Linda Oatman. 2003. *The Girl on the High Diving Horse.* Illustrated by Ted Lewin. New York: Philomel.

Johnston, Tony. 2002. *Sunsets of the West.* Illustrated by Ted Lewin. New York: Putnam.

Levy, Elizabeth. 2003. *The Mystery of Too Many Elvises.* Illustrated by Mordicai Gerstein. New York: Aladdin.

Lewin, Ted. 1993. *I Was a Teen-Age Professional Wrestler.* New York: Orchard.

———. 2003. *Lost City: The Discovery of Macchu Picchu.* New York: Philomel.

———. 2003. *Sacred River: The Ganges of India.* Boston: Houghton Mifflin.

McCully, Emily Arnold. 1993. *Grandmas at Bat.* New York: HarperCollins.

———. 1996. *The Ballot Box Battle.* New York: Knopf.

———. 1996. *Bobbin Girl.* New York: Dial.

———. 1997. *The Divide.* New York: Doubleday.

———. 1997. *Starring Mirette and Bellini.* New York: Putnam.

———. 2000. *Mirette and Bellini Cross Niagara Falls.* New York: Putnam.

———. 2001. *Orphan Singer.* New York: Scholastic.

Mollel, Tolowa M. 1999. *My Rows and Piles of Coins.* Illustrated by E. B. Lewis. New York: Clarion.

Ringgold, Faith. 1992. *Aunt Harriet's Underground Railroad in the Sky.* New York: Crown.

———. 1999. *Counting to Tar Beach.* New York: Random.

———. 1999. *If a Bus Could Talk: The Story of Rosa Parks.* New York: Simon & Schuster.

———. 2002. *Cassie's Word Quilt.* New York: Knopf.

Tarpley, Natasha Anastasia. 2002. *Bippity Bop Barbershop.* Illustrated by E. B. Lewis. Boston: Little, Brown.

Woodson, Jacqueline. 2001. *The Other Side.* Illustrated by E. B. Lewis. New York: Putnam.

———. 2001. *Visiting Day.* Illustrated by James Ransome. New York: Scholastic.

———. 2002. *Our Gracie Aunt.* Illustrated by Jon J. Muth. New York: Hyperion.

IDEAS FOR PARENTS AND CAREGIVERS

Historical fiction gives parents, caregivers, and children opportunities to explore their own family heritage through books. Reading and responding to books that reflect their families' past helps children understand their place in history. Parents and caregivers can share their perspectives on historical events that shaped their families' lives. Learning about history from multiple perspectives gives students rich resources to draw upon as they write. Older students can interview family members to learn about their past and the struggles they faced in their lives. They can then write about the interviews and share them with their family members.

REFERENCES

Albright, Lettie K., and Sylvia M. Vardell. 2003. "Focus on History: 1950 to 2000 in Picture Books." *Book Links* 13, no. 1 (September): 21–25.

Beck, Cathy, Shari Nelson-Faulkner, and Kathryn Mitchell Pierce. 2000. "Historical Fiction: Teaching Tool or Literary Experience?" *Language Arts* 77, no. 6 (July): 546–555.

Brown, Jennifer M. 2002. "From Outsider to Insider." *Publishers Weekly* 249, no. 6 (11 February): 156–157.

Diaz, David. 1995. "Caldecott Medal Acceptance." *Horn Book* 71, no. 4 (July/August): 430–433.

"Faith Ringgold." 2002. *Major Authors and Illustrators for Children and Young Adults,* 2nd ed. Farmington Hills, MI: Thomson Gale.

Gerhardt, Lillian N. 1995. "A Prize in Perspective." *School Library Journal* 41, no. 5 (May): 4.

Gerstein, Mordicai. 2004. "Caldecott Medal Acceptance." *Horn Book* 80, no. 4 (July/August): 405–409.

Inspiration. Version 7.5. 2003. Mac/Win. Portland, OR: Inspiration Software.

Jacobs, James, Judith Mitchell, and Nancy Livingston. 2004/2005. "2004 U.S. Children's Literature Award Winners." *The Reading Teacher* 58, no. 4 (December/January): 398–407.

Kazemek, Francis E. 1995. "What Book Awards Tell Us about Ourselves." *Education Week* 14, no. 31 (26 April): 32–33.

Klaven, Andrew. 1994. "The Uses of Suspense." *Writer* 107, no. 5 (May): 13–16.

Koehnecke, Dianne. 2001. "Smoky Night and Crack: Controversial Subjects in Current Children's Stories." *Children's Literature in Education* 32, no. 1 (March): 17–30.

Lenihan, Greg. 2003. "Reading with Adolescents: Constructing Meaning Together." *Journal of Adolescent and Adult Literacy* 47, no. 1 (September): 8–12.

Levine, Gail Carson. 1997. *Ella Enchanted.* New York: HarperCollins.

Lewin, Ted. 1993. *I was a Teen-Age Professional Wrestler.* New York: Orchard.

Lewis, E. B. 2005. "Biography." [Online] Available: http://www.eblewis.com [cited 5 February 2005].

Livingston, Myra Cohn. 1991. *Poem-Making: Ways to Begin Writing Poetry.* New York: HarperCollins.

Macleod, Anne Scott. 1998. "Rewriting History." *Teacher Magazine* 98, no. 9 (April): 34–37.

Martin, William. 1996. "Writing Historical Fiction." *Writer* 96, no. 7 (July): 6–9.

McCully, Emily Arnold. 1993. "Caldecott Medal Acceptance." *Horn Book* 69, no. 4 (July/August): 424–429.

"Mordicai Gerstein." 2002. *Major Authors and Illustrators for Children and Young Adults,* 2nd ed. Farmington Hills, MI: Thomson Gale.

Petit, Philippe. 2002. *To Reach the Clouds: My High Wire Walk Between the Twin Towers.* New York: North Point.

Rochman, Hazel. 2004. "Taking with Richard Peck." *Book Links* 14, no. 1 (September): 44–45.

Schomberg, Janie, Becky McCabe, and Lisa Fink. 2003. "TAG Team: Collaborate to Teach, Assess and Grow." *Teacher Librarian* 31, no. 1 (October): 8–11.

Speer, Morgan. 1995. "Writing Historical Fiction." *Writer* 108, no. 1 (January): 21–23.

Stanek, Lou Willett. 1991. "Whole Language for Whole Kids." *School Library Journal* 37, no. 9 (September): 187–189.

Williams, Wilda. 2005. "Brenda Rickman Vantrease." *Library Journal* 130, no. 4 (March): 77.

Wolcott, Jennifer. 1998. "Faith Ringgold's Patchwork Sojourn." *Christian Science Monitor* 90, no. 246 (16 November): 22.

Woods, Blanche. 1997. "Helping Teachers Sustain the Vision: A Leadership Role." *Emergency Librarian* 25, no. 1 (September/October): 14–18.

Zingher, Gary. 1996. "Gatherings." *School Library Media Activities Monthly* 12, no. 7 (September): 30–33, 36.

3 ❖ TRADITIONAL LITERATURE

Throughout the years and across cultures storytellers have preserved traditional literature, which encompasses fairy tales, folktales, fables, and tall tales. Analogous folk stories appear in different cultures with variations that reflect the culture's moral values (Brickman, 1998). These stories are part of an oral tradition reflecting the culture of the common folk (Krapp, 2004). Sharing these multicultural tales with children equips them with a broad perspective for viewing their world (Mello, 2001). Caldecott books contain a variety of traditional literature, which makes them a rich source of information on diverse cultures from around the world (Chamberlain and Leal, 1999).

Students need a collection of traditional literature to read and respond to before they begin writing their own tales. While most students are familiar with a variety of traditional literature, some are not. Those who do not know the traditional literature will not appreciate the humor parodies of the tales. "Cinderella" is common to many cultures, which makes it an excellent starting point for a study of traditional literature. Aesop's fables are also a good place to start as students are familiar with the morals and the stories are short and are easy for them to comprehend.

Drama, conflict, and action characterize traditional literature. Time passes very quickly, so readers know that the resolution to the characters' dilemmas will be revealed shortly. In traditional literature, it is easy to distinguish between good and evil characters. Additionally, readers know that good will overcome evil and that intelligence will overcome physical strength. Good deeds are rewarded and evil deeds are punished. Traditional literature does not often have strong feminine heroines; the girls and women are portrayed as being passive or as victims (Mello, 2001). However, in this chapter you will find *Lon Po Po* (Young, 1989), which has a strong female character who takes action and overcomes her adversary.

Fairy tales predictably begin with "Once upon a time" and end with the characters living happily ever after. Jacob and Wilhelm Grimm wrote down the German folktales told to them by village storytellers. Charles Perrault collected French fairy tales and published the first book of children's fairy tales in the seventeenth century. Hans Christian Anderson wrote the first fairy tales for children. His first tales were similar to those of the oral tradition but his later ones were original, and some think they were based on his own life experiences.

Fables are short, didactic, allegorical tales that offer practical advice. They usually have animal characters that speak and act like humans, highlighting human foibles. If there are more than two characters in the fable, they are placed in groups. Fables are believed to have originated with Aesop, a sixth-century BC Greek slave. However, fables containing elements and morals similar to those credited to Aesop are found around the world. They are easy to understand, easy to remember, easy to retell, and easy to illustrate. They can be adapted to different times and places so they are easy to retell and to update to suit the audience. Quintilian, a Roman orator; Erasmus, a Dutch humanist; and John Locke, a political philosopher, all advocated using fables with children because they not only entertain; they offer ideas for reflection (Bader, 1991). *Fables* (Lobel, 1980) and *Frederick* by noted fabulist Lionni (1967) are included in this chapter. Avery (1999) found that those traditional fables and Arnold Lobel's fables provided her first graders with a concise structure for writing their own fables.

Tall tales handed down across generations are unverified stories that may contain some elements of truth, but the facts and the exploits are exaggerated. Based on real people, North American tall tales boast about rugged individuals who overcame the hardships of frontier life using strength, skill, and wisdom. Oftentimes the hero or heroine dies or disappears. Students may be familiar with the exploits of Pecos Bill, Paul Bunyan, Johnny Appleseed, Mike Fink, Slufoot Sue, and John Henry.

The humor in picture books can draw older readers into the stories (Halls, 2003) and several of the books presented in this chapter have just the sort of humor that appeals to older readers. Books such as *The Stinky Cheese Man and Other Fairly Stupid Tales* (Scieszka, 1992) and *The Three Pigs* (Wiesner, 2001) provide bizarre twists to classic tales that make them humorous alternatives to the traditional tales. In *Fables* (Lobel, 1980), readers delight in tales with traditional, nontraditional, and romantic morals.

The Three Pigs

by David Wiesner
Caldecott Medal Winner, 2002

READING

Before Reading

Story Summary
From the traditional "Once upon a time" beginning, the text follows the accepted story line as the wolf blows down the pigs' houses and eats them. But wait—if he eats them, why are they running loose? The text and the illustrations suddenly diverge from the traditional version of this tale. The wolf has blown the three pigs right out of the story into the white space beyond the story's frames. Free from the confines of their story the three pigs set off, via a paper airplane that they folded from the pages of the book, to explore other stories. As they venture in and out of the stories, they are transformed from storybook pigs to photorealistic pigs. When they are inside of the traditional story a serif font records the text. When they step outside of the traditional story, the text is sans serif and they speak in word balloons. Along the way, the three pigs encounter the cat and the fiddle and a fairy-tale dragon who join the pigs in their story and help them outwit the wolf. At the end of the story, the pigs are scrambling the letters on the page to write their very own happily-ever-after ending to their surreal adventure. The illustrations were done in watercolor, gouache, colored inks, pencil, and colored pencil. Computer graphic designers worked with Wiesner to crumple pages and set the type to follow the contours of the pages (Giorgis and Johnson, 2002). Other humorous variations of this familiar nursery tale include *The True Story of the Three Little Pigs* (Scieszka, 1989), *Three Little Pigs* (Marshall, 1989), *The Three Little Wolves and the Big Bad Pig* (Trivizas, 1993), and *The Three Little Pigs* (Kellogg, 1997). Sharing different versions of the tale with the students ensures that they have ideas for writing their own retelling of this familiar tale.

❖ ——————————

Recommended Grade Levels

5–12

Standards for the English Language Arts

1, 3, 4, 5, 6, 12

Information Literacy Standards for Student Learning

3, 5

Objectives

The students will:

- Write a retelling that combines two traditional tales.

—————————— ❖

❖ ━━━━━━━━━━━━━━━━━━━

Author

David Wiesner was born in Bridgewater, New Jersey, and was surrounded by creative siblings who shared their artistic talents with him. Wiesner (2002) credits his family members with supporting his artistic efforts. His mother saved everything he drew and his father gave him a large drafting table and researched art schools for him to attend. His first art instruction came from Jon Gnagy's television program, *You Are an Artist.* Both the Renaissance and Surrealist painting movements influence his art as well as science fiction movies. While studying at the Rhode Island School of Design, he met Caldecott Medallist Trina Schart Hyman, who hired him to design a cover for *Cricket* magazine. In his Caldecott acceptance speech, Wiesner (2002) explained that the inspiration for the three pigs' adventures came from a Bugs Bunny cartoon he remembers from his childhood. In the cartoon, Elmer Fudd chases Bugs right through the frames of the film into the white space beyond.

Wiesner works at home where he takes care of his two children while their mother pursues her career (Silvey, 2002). Wiesner also won the Caldecott Medal for *Tuesday* (Wiesner, 1991) and he won Caldecott Honors for *Sector 7* (Wiesner, 1999) and *Free Fall* (Wiesner, 1988). To learn more about David Wiesner and his work, visit his Web pages at http://www.houghtonmifflinbooks.com/authors/wiesner/home.html and http://www.childrenslit.com/f_wiesner.html.

━━━━━━━━━━━━━━━━━━ ❖

Activating Prior Knowledge

Ask the children about what happened in the story of the three little pigs. Then, tell them that this version of the story has some unusual twists and appearances by some unexpected characters.

During Reading

As you read the story, point out how the illustrations and fonts change as the pigs move in and out of the frames.

After Reading

As you discuss the changes in the illustrations, talk about the variations in the pigs themselves. When Wiesner began to paint the pigs, they developed individual personalities, which he represented in part by using three different breeds of pig: Yorkshire, Hampshire, and Duroc. As the pigs' personalities emerged, he had to go back and rewrite parts of the story to match the pigs' personalities (Silvey, 2001). Use these questions as discussion starters for the book:

- What is different about this story when compared to traditional versions of the story?
- What does the wolf think of the changes in this tale?
- Why did the cat and the dragon join the pigs?
- What would have happened to the pigs if they had not returned to their story? Would they have lived happily ever after?
- What would happen if you could step out of your life story?

WRITING

Mini-lesson—Retelling

- Explain to the students that in this retelling of "The Three Little Pigs" there are actually several stories going on in the book at the same time. Wiesner reports that he used familiar stories so as not to disorient the readers when one story is interrupted by another story (Silvey, 2001). By doing this, Wiesner (2002) felt that readers would be able to step outside of the story with the pigs and concentrate on their new adventures.
- Tell the students that they are going to combine two traditional tales and write their own retelling of the tales.
- Remind the students that when they retell stories they are free to make changes and add their own variations to the story. However, a retelling should include enough elements to enable readers to make connections between the traditional tales and the retelling.

Modeling

- Ask the students to help you brainstorm a list of traditional tales. Write the list on the board or an overhead transparency so that the students will be able to refer to the list as they begin writing.
- Select two stories that contain characters that could help each other solve their problems or that have things in common.

- For example, what would happen if there were a race between the ginger-bread boy and the hare, since both characters are noted runners?
- Ask the students to help you think up a list of things that might happen if these two characters raced against each other.

Writing Activity

- Before the students begin writing, ask them to share their ideas with a partner.
- Tell the students that as they talk with their partners they should jot down their ideas to use as guides when they begin writing.
- If some of the students are having difficulty thinking of ideas for their retellings, suggest that they use the ideas generated during the mini-lesson.
- As the students begin writing, return to your retelling.

Conferencing

- When the students are ready to conference ask them to read their retellings to their partners.
- Have them ask their partners to write down any questions that come to mind as they read their drafts aloud (Harper, 1997). The questions must require more than a simple yes or no response.
- Then, the writers choose some of the questions from the list and freewrite responses to them.
- Next, the writer examines the freewriting for ideas to include in the original draft.
- Before having the students attempt this revision strategy on their own the librarian and the teacher can model it for them by asking each other questions about their writing.

Joseph Had a Little Overcoat

by Simms Taback
Caldecott Medal Winner, 2000

READING

Before Reading

Story Summary

When Joseph's overcoat becomes "old and worn," he remakes it into a jacket. When the jacket becomes "old and worn," he remakes it into a vest, then a scarf, a necktie, a handkerchief, and finally a button. When he looses the button, he makes a book about the transformation of the overcoat and ends with "you can always make something out of nothing." The illustrations contain their own story and in them readers discover Yiddish culture and Taback's own family history (Giorgis and Johnson, 2000). In order to create the illustrations he researched his Yiddish heritage by listening to Jewish liturgical music, searching through books, visiting the Jewish museum, and examining

❖ ———————————————

Recommended Grade Levels

2–6

Standards for the English Language Arts

4, 5, 6, 8, 9, 12

Information Literacy Standards for Student Learning

3, 4, 8

Objectives

The students will:

- Write a cumulative tale.

——————————————— ❖

❖ ───────────────
Author

Taback was born in New York City and his mother, a seamstress, encouraged his artistic talent by arranging private art lessons for him. In his Caldecott acceptance speech, he talked about his years as a graphic artist and the misfortunes that accompanied his career as a children's book illustrator (Taback, 2000). For a time he owned a greeting card company and created a line of novelty cards with die cuts (Giorgis and Johnson, 2000). From the years of creating die cut greeting cards came *There Was an Old Lady Who Swallowed a Fly* (Taback, 1997), for which he won a Caldecott Honor. It was the first book he illustrated that incorporated die cuts.

───────────────── ❖

family photographs (Taback, 2000). Taback originally illustrated this story in 1977; however, the illustrations in the two versions are very different. He used watercolor, gouache, pencil, ink, and collage to create the illustrations. Never before has a previously published book by the same illustrator won a Caldecott Medal. This book is available on audiocassette, videocassette, and CD with traditional Klezmer music playing in the background as Taback narrates the story. Taback also sings the song in English and Yiddish.

Activating Prior Knowledge

Relating this cumulative tale to other cumulative tales the students have read is an effective way to introduce this book. They may be familiar with cumulative tales such as *Drummer Hoff* (Emberley, 1987, 1967), *The Napping House* (Wood, 1984), *The Gingerbread Man* (Kimmel, 1993), *There Was an Old Lady Who Swallowed a Fly* (Taback, 1997), and *The Runaway Rice Cake* (Compestine, 2000). The rhyme, rhythm, and repetition in cumulative tales make them fun to read and easy to remember. A cumulative tale has a sequential repetition of actions that move the story along. In this story, the actions involve a tailor remaking a worn overcoat into other items of clothing each smaller than the one before.

During Reading

Strategically placed die cuts help readers predict what the next item of clothing will be (Unsworth and Wheeler, 2002). As you read, point out the die cuts and invite the students to join in as you read the repeated refrain.

After Reading

After you read the book, spend time discussing the illustrations, as the details in the illustrations help readers comprehend the text. The illustrations contain information about pre–World War II Polish Jewish culture. In the illustrations readers discover that Joseph eats flatbread, reads books by Jewish authors, has Jewish sayings on his walls, and according to the address on his envelopes he lives in Poland (Unsworth and Wheeler, 2002). The images of people appearing in the windows when Joseph visits his sister include Taback's daughter and his three grandchildren (Giorgis and Johnson, 2000). Artfully woven into the illustrations is information about Taback's culture and his family and he invites readers to explore and discover his Polish Jewish heritage.

WRITING

Mini-lesson—Cumulative Tale

- To demonstrate how a cumulative tale develops have the students help you create a story map showing the chronological order of the events in the story such as the one in Figure 3-1 created with *Inspiration* software, or create a map with the draw tools in a paint or word processing software program. A story map can also be drawn on chart paper or an overhead transparency.
- As you fill in the story map, point out the repetition in the text to the students. Each time Joseph makes something new it is smaller than the item that preceded it; he immediately does something while wearing his new article of clothing; it gets worn out and he makes something new again.

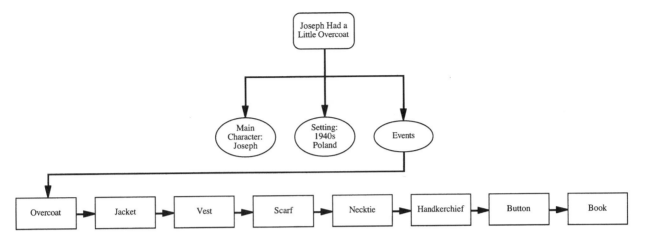

Figure 3-1. *Joseph Had a Little Overcoat* **Story Map**

Modeling

- As you create the story map for your own story talk aloud about what you are thinking as you write.
- You might want to start with a dress rather than a coat. Like a coat, a dress is big enough to transform into successively smaller articles of clothing.
- When you write your story, mimic the repetition of the original story. Each time Joseph made something new, he immediately used it.
- Each time you create a new article of clothing, incorporate one of your daily activities into the story or ask the students for suggestions of things to do wearing your new piece of clothing.

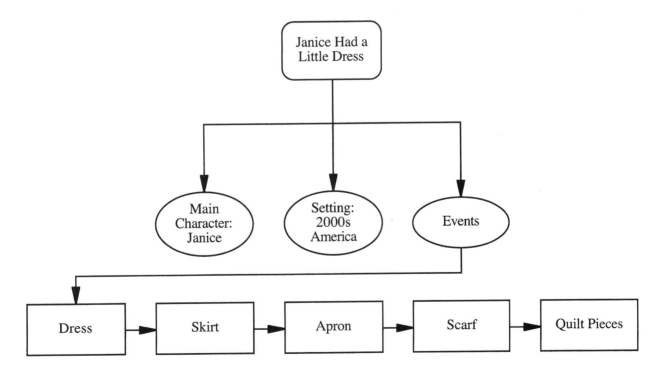

Figure 3-2. Janice Had a Little Dress Story Map

• Your story might look something like this one:

Janice Had a Little Dress

Janice had a little dress. She got tired of wearing it.
So she made a skirt out of it and went to the store.
Janice had a little skirt. She got tired of wearing it.
So she made an apron out of it and baked a cake.
Janice had a little apron. She got tired of wearing it.
So she made a scarf out of it and went for a walk.
Janice had a little scarf. She got tired of wearing it.
So, she cut it into tiny squares and made a quilt to keep her warm.

Writing Activity

• Provide each student with a blank cumulative story map. You can create and save a template of the cumulative story map in *Inspiration* software. If the students do not have access to a computer with *Inspiration* software, there is a blank story map in the appendix.
• As the students create their maps, ask them to share them with a partner to make sure that the events follow in a logical order. For example, if they were altering a piece of clothing the new piece would need to get smaller each time.
• Depending on the writing abilities of the students, encourage them to use the words in the book and make minor changes, or make up their own re-peated refrains.

Conferencing

• As you conference with the students, ask them to tell you their tales using their story maps.
• As they tell their tales, follow along with their written versions of the tales and then help them make revisions.
• If time permits have the students create collage illustrations to accompany their stories.

Recommended Grade Levels

5–10

Standards for the English Language Arts

1, 3, 4, 5, 6, 9, 11, 12

Information Literacy Standards for Student Learning

3, 5

Objectives

The students will:

• Discuss the common characteristics of fairy tales, and
• Write a fairy tale.

Rapunzel

by Paul O. Zelinsky
Caldecott Medal Winner, 1998

READING

Before Reading

Story Summary

The cravings of his pregnant wife send a man over a tall fence into a sorceress's garden to steal her rapunzel. This angers the sorceress who agrees to give the man the rapunzel in exchange for the baby. Afraid that if his wife does not get the rapunzel she will die, the man agrees to the sorceress's demand. As the child grows into a young woman, the sorceress locks her away in a tower to keep her safe. When the sorceress wants to enter the tower, the girl lowers her hair from the window at the top of the tower and the sorceress climbs up. A prince hears the girl singing and tricks her into lowering her hair for him to enter the tower. They marry and when the witch discovers this she banishes the girl to the wilderness and blinds the prince. He wanders through the wilderness eventually finding Rapunzel and their twins. Her tears restore his eyesight and they return to his kingdom where they live happily ever after. This book is available on audiocassette and CD.

Activating Prior Knowledge

Before reading the book, ask the students to brainstorm a list of common characteristics of fairy tales and have them record their responses on the board.

During Reading

As you read the story, ask the students to keep in mind the characteristics of fairy tales that they wrote on the board. Tell them to make note of any other characteristics they discover to add to the list.

After Reading

Questions such as these can be used to start a discussion of the story with the children:

- Why did the sorceress want the baby?
- What would you have done if you were Rapunzel's father?
- Do you think the sorceress took good care of Rapunzel when she was a child?
- Why do you think she locked Rapunzel in the tower?
- Was Rapunzel safe in the tower?
- What do you think it would be like to live in a tower?
- Rapunzel would not have had a television or a computer. What do you think she did all day?
- Why do you think Zelinsky included his family cat in the illustrations?
- Why do you think the cat lived in the tower with Rapunzel?
- This version of the story does not tell us what happened to Rapunzel's parents. Do you think they lived happily ever after?
- What do you think happened to the sorceress?

The author's note at the end of the book contains information Zelinsky uncovered in his research about the evolution of this fairy tale. Linnea Hendrickson (2000), a member of the 1998 Caldecott Award committee, has written a comparison of three picture book versions of *Rapunzel* illustrated by Felix Hoffmann, Trina Schart Hyman, and Paul Zelinsky. This insightful, well-researched article contains a great deal of interesting information that will be helpful if you want to do a critical analysis of the story with older students and an exploration of the origins and variations of the tale.

WRITING

Mini-lesson—Characteristics of Fairy Tales

- Project a copy of a blank chart such as the one in Figure 3-3 and have the students write down the characteristics of fairy tales that they find in *Rapunzel.*

Author

Highlights magazine first published Zelinsky's work in 1957. He was three years old when his family returned from a year in Japan and his fascination with Geishas was reflected in the illustrations he did in preschool, one of which was published in *Highlights* (Lodge, 1998). His fascination with the tractors and steam shovels at the construction site across from his house led him to a new obsession, but he did not totally abandon the Geishas. He simply drew the Geishas as the drivers of the heavy machinery (Brooks, 1998). When he was a child, his parents took him to the Chicago Art Institute and the paintings he saw there influenced his work (Peck and Hendershot, 1999). In his Caldecott acceptance speech, Zelinsky talked about his trips to the Metropolitan Museum to study Italian Renaissance paintings, and purchasing Renaissance art books (Zelinsky, 1998). His wife is an elementary school teachers; they have two children and a Siamese cat who appears in the illustrations in *Rapunzel.* He credits Maurice Sendak with being his illustration teacher (Zelinsky, 1998). Zelinsky won Caldecott Honors for *Hansel and Gretel* (Lesser, 1984), *Rumpelstiltskin* (Zelinsky, 1986), and *Swamp Angel* (Issacs, 1994). Information about Zelinsky and his work is available at http://www.paulozelinsky.com/.

Common Characteristics of Fairy Tales	Rapunzel
Begin "Once upon time," or "A long time ago,"	Begins "Long ago,"
End "They lived happily ever after."	" . . . lived a long life, happy and content."
Rural or forest setting	Tower in wilderness, banished to wilderness
Witches, ogres, giants, sorceresses, fairies	Sorceress
Childless couple	Rapunzel's parents were childless at first
Time passes quickly	Rapunzel is born and grows up quickly
Adventure, action, and drama	Taking the baby, Rapunzel locked in tower, banishing Rapunzel, blinding the prince, Rapunzel and prince reunited
Good overcomes evil	Even though sorceress locks Rapunzel in a tower, banishes her to wilderness, and prince is blinded, the pair overcome adversity
Quest	Prince searches for Rapunzel
Abused and persecuted people	Rapunzel's parents, Rapunzel, prince
Royalty and castles	Prince and his kingdom

Figure 3-3. Fairy-Tale Characteristics found in *Rapunzel*

- Then, ask them to think of other characteristics of fairy tales that were not included in *Rapunzel.* Some other characteristics of fairy tales include the number three, transformations, fortunes or misfortunes of a hero, trials and tests, animal characters, suitor searching for a bride, wise old woman, a lost child, charms, and magic.

Modeling

- Project a copy of a blank chart and have the students offer suggestions as you complete the chart.
- Once you complete the chart, begin writing your fairy tale, which might look something like this:

Belinda

Once upon a time, there was a fair young princess named Belinda. Now, Belinda's favorite companion was her greyhound Lightning, who could run faster than the wind. Every morning Belinda and Lightning took long walks through the forest.

Writing Activity

- Before the students begin writing, have them complete their own fairy-tale characteristics chart to guide them as they write their fairy tales. The appendix contains a blank chart.

Common Characteristics of Fairy Tales	My Fairy Tale - Belinda
Begin "Once upon time,"or "A long time ago,"	"Once upon a time"
End "They lived happily ever after."	"They lived happily ever after."
Rural or forest setting	Forest
Witches, ogres, giants, sorceresses, fairies	Three witches
Quest	Princess searching for lost dog
Royalty and castles	Princess lives in a castle
Number three	Princess meets three witches who give her three charms to use as she searches for her dog
Charms or magic	Three charms help her overcome obstacles as she searches for her dog

Figure 3-4. My Fairy Tale

- Remind the students that they do not need to include all of the characteristics on the chart in their fairy tales.
- As the students complete their charts, some of them may prefer to work with a partner or in small groups so they can talk and share ideas.
- Once the charts are completed the students should write quietly so as not to disturb the other writers in the room.

Conferencing

- As you conference with the students, ask them to tell you their fairy tales rather than read them to you.
- Write down any questions you have about the tale on sticky notes.
- When you finish the conference, leave the sticky notes with the students for them to use to add details to their writing.
- In addition to conferencing with the teacher and the librarian, the students can conference with one another.
- Using their own fairy tales, the librarian and the teacher can model how to conference for the students.

❖ ———————————————

Recommended Grade Levels

4–8

Standards for the English Language Arts

1, 3, 4, 6, 9, 11, 12

Information Literacy Standards for Student Learning

5, 9

Objectives

The students will:

- Look for dialogue tags in the story, and
- Write dialogue to accompany a story illustration.

❖

❖ ———————————————

Author

Ed Young was born and raised in China, and moved to America to go to college. His original plan was to study architecture, but he ended up studying art. His endeavors were influenced by his artistic mother and encouraged by his father (Gauch, 1990). As a child he remembers that he had an active imagination and played alone for hours without props, just using his imagination to be a lone hero (Young, 1990). He won Caldecott Honors for *Seven Blind Mice* (Young, 1992) and *The Emperor and the Kite* (Yolen, 1967). There is a biography, a booklist, and an interview transcript available at http://www2.scholastic.com/teachers/authorsandbooks. Additional information about Ed Young is available at http://www.nccil.org/young.html.

❖

Lon Po Po: A Red-Riding Hood Story from China

by Ed Young
Caldecott Medal Winner, 1990

READING

Before Reading

Story Summary

When their mother goes to visit their grandmother (Po Po) on her birthday, three sisters remain home alone. A cunning wolf (lon) comes calling in the dark of night and he tricks the younger sisters into letting him in the house. When the oldest sister realizes that this is a wolf and not her grandmother, the clever girl lures the wolf outside with the promise of magic gingko nuts. The three girls escape to safety in the highest branches of the gingko tree. Since the wolf cannot climb the tree and the nuts do not taste as sweet unless you pick them yourself, the girls agree to pull the wolf up the tree in a basket. In their attempts to hoist the wolf high into the tree, they repeatedly drop the basket and the repeated falls eventually kill the wolf. The watercolor and pastel illustrations are contained within panels and they present the story from different characters' perspectives. Readers share horrifying glimpses of the wolf in the dark; they travel up the tree with the girls; and they join the wolf as he plummets to the ground.

Activating Prior Knowledge

This ancient Chinese tale translated and retold by Ed Young is a variation of "Little Red Riding Hood." Help students make connections between the two tales by retelling the story of Little Red Riding Hood before reading this story. If the students are familiar with Little Red Riding Hood as you tell the story, pause periodically and let them tell what happens next.

During Reading

As you read the story, share the illustrations as they capture the suspense and terror of the large, shadowy wolf. This story includes dialogue so if you have multiple copies of the book you can assign students to read the dialogue of the different characters. Rather than having one student read a character's lines, you could have a small group of students read the character's lines in unison.

After Reading

A discussion of this story might focus on the lessons that students learn from these brave, clever girls who cooperate to defeat the wolf. Most traditional literature portrays girls and women as passive or as victims; however, this story has a strong, clever female character who takes control of the situation and overcomes an adversary. Working alone, the girls would not have been able to defeat the wolf, but by cooperating they were able to drag him high enough in the air to drop him to his death. This book also provides an opportunity to talk with the students about safety tips to follow when they are left at home alone.

WRITE

Mini-lesson—Dialogue

- Tell the students that dialogue tags such as said, answered, shouted, asked, called out, begged, and sang denote when a character in the story is speaking.
- Use a document camera to project the pages of the book and have the students search for the dialogue tags.
- If several copies of the book are available, have the students work in small groups to find the dialogue tags.
- As the students find the tags, record them on chart paper for the children to refer to as they write.
- Project a copy of the eighth page in the book to use to analyze the dialogue. The eighth page has the shadow of the wolf at the top and the three frightened girls at the bottom.
- Ask the students to read the dialogue aloud and then briefly analyze the dialogue, which will help them make their own dialogues more effective (Wolf and Wolf, 2002).
- The librarian and the teacher can guide the students as they discover the rules of punctuating dialogue by looking for punctuation patterns in the dialogue.
- As the students discover the rules, write them on the board. The rules might be stated as shown below in Figure 3-5.

Modeling

- Project a copy of the girls in bed with the wolf and use that illustration to model writing dialogue.
- Remind the students that when the girls are in bed with the wolf they ask questions about his hairy tail and his claws.
- The librarian and the teacher can talk aloud as they ask the wolf other questions.
- Record the conversation using word processing software on a computer connected to a projection device or written down on an overhead transparency.
- Once the dialogue is recorded ask the students to help punctuate the conversation, referring to the chart of rules for punctuating dialogue created earlier.

- When speakers change, start a new paragraph.
- Place quotation marks around the speaker's words.
- Capitalize the speaker's first word.
- When the dialogue comes before the speaker tag, the dialogue ends with a comma, a question mark, or an exclamation point.
- Commas, question marks, and exclamation points go inside the quotation marks.
- When the speaker tag is at the end of the sentence, it is followed by a period.

Figure 3-5. Rules for Punctuating Dialogue

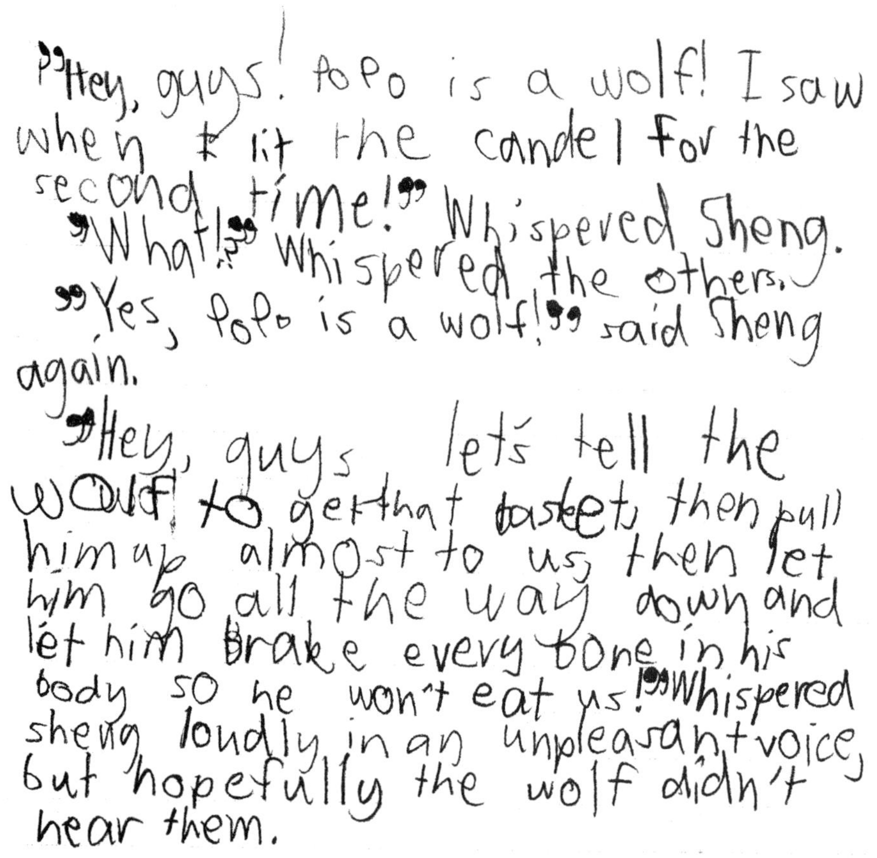

> "Hey, guys! PoPo is a wolf! I saw when I lit the candel for the second time!" Whispered Sheng.
> "What?" Whispered the others.
> "Yes, PoPo is a wolf!" said Sheng again.
> "Hey, guys lets tell the wolf to get that basket, then pull him up almost to us, then let him go all the way down and let him brake every bone in his body so he won't eat us!" Whispered Sheng loudly in an unpleasant voice, but hopefully the wolf didn't hear them.

Figure 3-6. *Lon Po Po* **Dialogue**

Writing Activity

- Use a document camera to project the illustration of the three girls high in the tree with the wolf staring up at them or have the students turn to that illustration in their books. The illustration used for this activity needs to show the characters interacting with each other (George, 1998).
- Tell the students to imagine that the girls are deciding what to do about the wolf and to write down what they think the girls are saying to each other.
- Remind them to begin a new paragraph each time the speaker changes.
- Once the students have the dialogue written they can work in groups or with partners to punctuate the dialogue.
- First graders wrote the dialogue below. Two boys working as partners wrote the dialogue in Figure 3-6.

A first grade girl wrote the dialogue in Figure 3-7.

Conferencing

- As you conference with the students remind them to refer to the rules for punctuating dialogue as they begin to edit their work.
- The students enjoy sharing their dialogues, so give them opportunities to perform their dialogues for their classmates.

"That isn't are popo". shang whisperd.

"It's a wolf. Tao and Paotze where suprised." "I have a plane. whisperd shang

"what is it? asked Paotze and Tao.

"We get the wolf to bring us a rope and a bucket." shang told her sisters

"And we pull him up drop him." pull him higher drop." pull him up almost to the top and drop him". "Great idea"! said Tao.

Figure 3-7. *Lon Po Po* **Dialogue**

Fables

by Arnold Lobel
Caldecott Medal Winner, 1981

READING

Before Reading

Story Summary

A bear draped in a sheet with a frying pan for a hat and paper bags for shoes graces the cover of this book and immediately tells readers that some hilarious animal antics await them. The animals in these fables portray human foibles and there are lessons to be learned from their actions. A flying pig, a smitten ostrich, a camel in a tutu, and a wolf disguised as an apple tree are just some of the animals with cautionary tales to tell. The maxims they offer include warnings such as, friends do not always give good advice, some people will believe anything, and a child's conduct is a reflection of his parents. The animals' expressions in the detailed watercolor illustrations give tantalizing clues as to what to expect in the fables.

❖ ————————————————

Recommended Grade Levels

4–8

Standards for the English Language Arts

1, 2, 3, 4, 5, 6, 8, 11, 12

Information Literacy Standards for Student Learning

1, 2, 3, 8

Objectives

The students will:

• Read a variety of fables,

• Determine the characteristics of fables, and

• Complete a story map and write a fable.

———————————————— ❖

"the place where the rainbow ends"

"never once did I tell you that I was telling the truth"

"too happy to be hungry"

"dance just for myself"

"a thumbtack in this chair"

"his shirt front was covered with crumbs"

Figure 3-8. Book Bits for *Fables*

Author

Arnold Lobel was born in Los Angeles, California, and grew up in Schenectady, New York. He is remembered for creating the steadfast friends Frog and Toad, through whom readers learn about friendship, bravery, nature, and the comfort of home (Lobel, 2000). Memorable characters, humor, and universal truths are hallmarks of his timeless books. Arnold Lobel won Caldecott Honors for *Hildilid's Night* (Ryan, 1971) and for *Frog and Toad are Friends* (Lobel, 1970). He won a Newbery Honor for *Frog and Toad Together* (Lobel, 1972). His wife Anita won a Caldecott Honor for *On Market Street* (Lobel, 1981), for which he wrote the text.

Activating Prior Knowledge

To help students make connections between a book and their prior experiences, Yopp and Yopp (2001) suggest using book bits, short quotes from the text, to introduce the book. Each child will need his or her own book bit (See Figure 3-8) written on a slip of paper. First, they read their book bit and briefly reflect on its meaning. Second, they walk around the room reading their book bits aloud to each other without discussing them. They reflect on what they have heard, discuss their reflections in small groups, and make predictions about the text. They can also write about their reflections.

During Reading

As you read the fables give the students opportunities to make comments when they recognize the fable that matches their book bit.

After Reading

At the end of each fable, take time to discuss the moral with the students. To ensure that the students comprehend the fable, ask them how they think it relates to their own lives. Depending on the ages and backgrounds of the students, you may need to spend time explaining the morals and helping them understand how the morals offer practical advice that can be applied to their own lives. After you read the first few fables to the students and tell them the morals, let the students tell you what lessons they have learned from the fables rather than revealing the moral written at the end of the fable.

WRITING

Mini-lesson—Characteristics of Fables

- After the students have read and discussed a variety of fables, ask them to brainstorm a list of characteristics of fables.

Short

Action revolves around one crucial act

Can happen any time or place

Animal characters who act like humans

Sometimes they have humans and inanimate objects

Usually two characters

Contain a lesson to be learned, usually stated at the end of the fable

Offer practical advice

Easy to understand

Clear, simple language

Figure 3-9. Characteristics of Fables

- Write the characteristics on the board or an overhead transparency.
- The chart in Figure 3-9 contains common characteristics of fables.

Modeling

- Project a story map such as the one in Figure 3-10, showing the elements of a fable, to use to organize your thoughts.
- Ask the students to help you decide on a moral for your fable, or maybe there's a bit of practical advice their parents have given them such as, "look both ways before you cross the street," "do not talk to strangers," "do not judge a book by its cover," or "honesty is the best policy."
- Use a fable story map such as the one in Figure 3-10 to organize your story.
- Your fable might look something like this:

The Rabbit and the Giraffe

Rabbit and his friends were playing football on the playground at recess. Rabbit threw a long, high pass that landed in the branches of a tall tree. Rabbit and his friends stared up into the tree and realized they were not going to be able to get their football down. Giraffe stopped playing baseball with his friends and plucked the football from the tree. He returned the football to Rabbit.

When Giraffe's baseball rolled deep into a rabbit hole on the playground, Rabbit raced over, wiggled down the hole, and returned Giraffe's baseball to him. Moral: One good turn deserves another.

Art students at the University of Massachusetts–Amherst have been retelling fables and illustrating them on the computer since 1974 and their work is located at http://www.umass.edu/aesop/contents.html. Some of the fables have traditional as well as contemporary retellings. As the graphic tools available on the Internet have

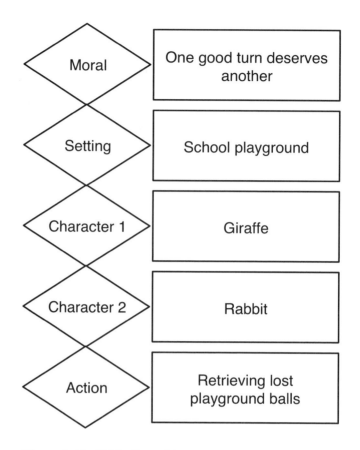

Figure 3-10. Fable Story Map

become more sophisticated, so have the retellings, with some of them including an-imation and sound. This site offers many excellent examples to use as models for students if you are interested in having them create contemporary versions of the fa-bles. You will need to preview the fables and select one or two to share with the stu-dents. Not all of the retellings are suitable for elementary and middle school students.

Writing Activity

- Give each student a blank story map like the one in Figure 3-10. There is a blank story map in the appendix.
- Tell the students that they can create their own fable or write a retelling of their favorite fable.
- Students who immediately know what they are going to write about can share their ideas with other students to help them get started on their fables.
- Provide the students with fable collections to refer to as they write.
- Some students might prefer to begin by illustrating their fables. Once they have the illustrations drawn, they can use the illustrations as inspiration for their writing.
- Using the fables on the University of Massachusetts–Amherst Web site as models, the students can also write and illustrate their fables on the com-puter.

Conferencing

- In Nanette Avery's (1999) class, the students conference by listening to each others' fables and offering advice for revising. For the final drafts of their fables, her students selected writing paper that matched their fables and some students included illustrations.
- As the students finish writing their fables, pair them up to peer conference.
- Tell the students to listen carefully as their partners read so they can offer helpful suggestions for improving the fables.

John Henry

by Julius Lester
Illustrated by Jerry Pinkney
Caldecott Honor Book, 1995

READING

Before Reading

Story Summary
John Henry is an African-American folk hero whose most famous exploit matched him with a steam drill tunneling through a mountain. John Henry beat the steam drill, but the exertion killed him. This version of the story includes anthropomorphism, hyperbole, simile, and contemporary details. The rich, descriptive writing begs to be shared more than once, relished, and explored. Evocative colored-pencil and watercolor illustrations portray this larger-than-life legend. The idea for this book first came from the illustrator, Jerry Pinkney (Lester, 1996). Lester was not sure he could tell a children's story where the hero dies, but he recognized the possibilities of the story after talking to Pinkney and thinking about Martin Luther King, Jr. Lester contends that rather than role models, children need heroes and heroines to inspire them. This book is available on audiocassette, videocassette, and CD. Lester and Pinkney have also collaborated on other books, including *Black Cowboy, Wild Horses* (Lester, 1998), *The Tales of Uncle Remus: The Adventures of Brer Rabbit* (Lester, 1999), *Uncle Remus Complete Tales* (Lester, 1999), and *Sam and the Tigers: A Retelling of Little Black Sambo* (Lester, 2000).

Background information about John Henry: The Steel Driving Man is on the Web at http://www.ibiblio.org/john_henry/index.html. This Web site has two different versions of the story, song lyrics, sound bites of the songs, and links to other Web resources.

Activating Prior Knowledge
Using an anticipation guide to introduce this story motivates children to read to find answers to the questions raised by the guide. An anticipation guide contains statements or questions from the story that the students agree or disagree with before reading (Readence, Bean, and Baldwin, 1998). Including thought-provoking or controversial statements or questions in the guide can pique the students' interest in the story. Figure 3-11 is an example of an anticipation guide used to introduce *John Henry.*

❖ ———————————

Recommended Grade Levels

4–10

Standards for the English Language Arts

3, 4, 5, 6, 8, 11, 12

Information Literacy Standards for Student Learning

3, 5, 8

Objectives

The students will:

- Determine the characteristics of tall tales,
- Complete a tall tale prewriting chart, and
- Write a tall tale.   ❖

———————————

❖ ———————————

Author

Julius Lester is a professional musician, a university professor, and an author. A major influence in Lester's life was the stories his father, a Methodist minister, and his colleagues told (Lodge, 2001). Born in 1939 in the segregated South and active in the civil rights struggles in the 1960s, Lester's life experiences shape his stories. His writing speaks to children of possibilities. *To Be a Slave* (Lester, 1968) is a Newbury Honor book. You can find out more about Julius Lester and his children's books at http://www.childrenslit .com/f_lester.html.

——————————— ❖

Agree	Disagree	
_____	_____	John Henry was faster than the wind.
_____	_____	Machines are better at many jobs than humans.
_____	_____	A mean person might cry if he had a nice thought.
_____	_____	"What matters is how you do your living."
_____	_____	"He grew and grew until his head busted through the roof."

Figure 3-11. *John Henry* **Anticipation Guide**

During Reading

Explain to the students that one of the characteristics of tall tales is exaggeration or hyperbole. Ask the students to listen for examples of exaggeration that describe John Henry's feats as you read the book. This is a finely crafted story that is an excellent example of text written for reading aloud. It incorporates descriptive text that paints pictures in the readers' minds.

After Reading

When you finish reading the story, ask the students which of John Henry's feats were exaggerated. This discussion might include talking about how the story is more interesting and fun to tell with the exaggerations. Invite the students to make up some exaggerations about things they do.

Reading the author's note at the beginning of the story provides another focus for a discussion of this story. In the note, Lester makes a connection between John Henry and Martin Luther King, Jr. Students knowledgeable about Martin Luther King, Jr.'s work may be interested in exploring this connection. The discussion could also focus on Lester's (1996) comments that children need heroes and heroines to inspire them to go beyond the boundaries of what they think is possible. These heroes and heroines show children the potential their lives hold. Nikola-Lisa (1998) compares this book to *John Henry: An American Legend* (Keats, 1965) and to *The Legend of John Henry* (Small, 1994), should the students be interested in comparing versions of the tale.

WRITING

Mini-lesson—Characteristics of Tall Tales

- Explain to the students that a tall tale has a hero or heroine who accomplishes superhuman deeds using strength, skill, and wisdom. Superhuman deeds one accomplishes as a child often foreshadow the deeds to come as an adult.
- Tell the students that common characteristics of tall tales include: a specific job for the main character; a powerful object and/or companion; real people and places; nature, people, or progress that impede the main character's work; and that the main character dies or disappears.
- Have the students work with you to create a chart such as the one in Figure 3-12 to depict some of the characteristics of tall tales found in *John Henry*.

❖ ───────────

Illustrator

Jerry Pinkney was born in Philadelphia and was one of six children. He remembers that he began drawing when he was about four years old and his artistic talent was encouraged in school (Pinkney, 2005). This was important because his dyslexia made reading and spelling difficult. Having his artistic talent recognized by his teachers bolstered his self-esteem and motivated him to work hard. A great deal of research goes into his illustrations. He has collections of clothes that he uses to dress people who pose as his characters. He takes photographs of the character models and works from the photographs. He also has a reference collection of books on nature and animals that he uses to research animals that he illustrates. Jerry Pinkney won Caldecott Honors for *Mirandy and Brother Wind* (McKissack, 1988), *The Talking Eggs: A Folktale from the American South* (San Souci, 1989), *The Ugly Duckling* (Andersen, 1999), and *Noah's Ark* (Pinkney, 2002). Pinkney's son Brian has won two Caldecott Honor awards. Additional information about Pinkney and his work is at http://www.childrenslit .com/f_pinkney.html.

❖

Name	John Henry
Description	African American, very hard worker, fast runner, tall, big, strong
Superhuman Deeds as a Child (Hyperbole)	Grew up in one day; next day added onto the house, fixed the porch, built an indoor swimming pool
Superhuman Deeds as an Adult (Hyperbole)	Running faster than a horse, breaking boulder that dynamite could not budge, faster than a steam drill
Specific Job	Road builder
Powerful Objects	Two sledge hammers
Companion	Rainbow around his shoulders
Real Places	Big Bend Tunnel; Chesapeake & Ohio Railroad; Summer County, West Virginia
Nature, People, or Progress impede them	Steam drill was replacing skilled road builders
Dies or Disappears	Dies after he tunnels faster than the steam drill

Figure 3-12. Characteristics of Tall Tales

- Tell the students that sometimes in tall tales, the main characters' jobs become obsolete as technological advances bring new ways of doing things.
- Ask the students what technological advance is making John Henry's job obsolete. In this story, the steam drill is replacing the road builders.
- Explain to the students that tall tales often include figurative language including simile, onomatopoeia, and anthropomorphism. A simile compares two unlike things using "like" or "as." Onomatopoeia refers to words whose sounds suggest their meanings. Anthropomorphism is giving human characteristics to animals, plants, or objects.
- Ask the students to return to the text and locate examples of some of the figurative language included in *John Henry*.
- Figure 3-13 includes some of the figurative language in the tall tale.

Modeling

- Project a blank tall tale prewriting chart and ask the students for suggestions as you complete the chart.
- Your chart might look something like the one in Figure 3-14.
- Use the completed chart to write your tall tale. Your tall tale might begin like this one:

Sally Jane

Have you ever heard about Sally Jane? As a child, she could read a fat book with no pictures in a minute and she could spell faster than a lightning bolt.

Simile	"a mountain as big as hurt feelings" "muscles as hard as wisdom" "voice like bat wings on tombstones"
Onomatopoeia	"BANG" "KERBOOM BLAMMITY-BLAMMITY" "RINGGGG!"
Anthropomorphism	sun getting scared; sun brushing and flossing; sun crying

Figure 3-13. Figurative Language in *John Henry*

Writing Activity

- Give each student a blank tall tale prewriting chart. There is one in the appendix.
- Put the students into small groups so they can share and discuss their ideas.
- As the group members complete their charts, they can read their charts to each other.
- The group members can provide feedback on whether or not the information in the chart is clear and that the main characteristics of a tall tale are included in the chart before the students begin writing their tall tales.

Name	Sally Ann
Description	Smart, kind, caring, enthusiastic, helpful
Superhuman Deeds as a Child (Hyperbole)	Reads a 300-page book in a minute, spells faster than a bolt of lightning
Superhuman Deeds as an Adult (Hyperbole)	Finds books and articles on any topic in thirty seconds
Specific Job	Librarian
Powerful Object	Computer
Companion	Mouse
Real Places	School library
Nature, People, or Progress ImpedeThem	Computer search engines
Dies or Disappears	Disappears into the computer

Figure 3-14. Tall Tale Prewriting Chart

- As the students begin writing remind them to write quietly so that everyone can think and concentrate on their writing.

Conferencing

- As the students complete their drafts, ask them to read them aloud to a partner or their group members.
- The group members can offer suggestions for ideas they want clarified.
- As the students are conferencing circulate around the room and help students who are still working on their writing.

The Stinky Cheese Man and Other Fairly Stupid Tales

by Jon Scieszka
Illustrated by Lane Smith
Caldecott Honor Book, 1993

READING

Before Reading

Story Summary

The Stinky Cheese Man, unlike his gingerbread counterpart, is avoided by everyone and hence chased by no one. Scieszka was so tired of reading "The Gingerbread Boy" to his daughter that he rewrote the classic tale for himself. The other brief fractured tales included in this book are "Chicken Licken," "The Princess and the Bowling Ball," "The Really Ugly Duckling," "The Other Frog Prince," "Little Red Running Shorts," "Jack's Bean Problem," "Cinderumpelstiltskin," and "The Tortoise and the Hair." Jack, famous for beanstalk climbing, narrates this hilarious collection of tales. The squawking Little Red Hen, who frequently interrupts his narration with her complaints about the dog, the cat, and the mouse, meets an untimely yet perhaps just end. Smith's illustrations were done in oil paints applied in layers with an acrylic varnish sprayed between the layers. Scieszka and Smith collaborated on the Time Warp Trio series and several picture books including *Math Curse* (Scieszka, 1995), *The True Story of the Three Little Pigs* (Scieszka, 1997), *Squids Will Be Squids: Fresh Morals, Beastly Fables* (Scieszka, 1998), and *Science Verse* (Scieszka, 2004).

Activating Prior Knowledge

Before reading this book to the children, display it in a prominent place and invite them to explore the book on their own. Then, when you introduce the book to the students you can begin by reviewing book conventions, such as the table of contents being at the front of the book. Students who have previewed the book will be delighted to tell you how this book breaks the rules, including a table of contents that is not at the front of the book, a story that begins on an end page, and a title page labeled "Title Page." Not only does the book poke fun at book conventions; it also

❖ ─────────────────

Recommended Grade Levels

1–6

Standards for the English Language Arts

1, 3, 6, 8, 11, 12

Information Literacy Standards for Student Learning

3, 5, 8

Objectives

The students will:

- Compare a fairy tale parody to the original tale,
- Complete a fairy tale parody chart, and
- Write a parody.

───────────────── ❖

❖ ━━━━━━━━━━━━━━
Author

Jon Scieszka was born in Flint, Michigan. His father was an elementary school principal and his mother was a nurse. He has held various jobs including elementary school teacher, apartment painter, lifeguard, and magazine writer. He credits his years in the elementary school classroom with helping him to understand children's sense of humor and the importance of not talking down to them (Petrolle, 1997). Dr. Seuss's stories gave Scieszka the confidence to write humorous children's stories (Brodie, 2004). Scieszka's picture books contain sophisticated humor that appeals to older children and to young adults. Distressed by the number of boys who are reluctant readers, he started the "Guys Read" campaign to encourage boys to read. The Web site http://www.guysread.com has information on this campaign.

━━━━━━━━━━━━━━ ❖

pokes fun at fairy tales (Marcus, 2001). You can mention that these tales are parodies, humorous imitations of classic tales including fairy tales, nursery tales, and fables.

During Reading

As you read the stories to the students, tell them to think about a story they know that reminds them of the one you are reading.

After Reading

After you read each fairy tale ask the students which fairy tale it parodies. Then, ask a student to retell the familiar version of the fairy tale. Questions such as these can help focus the students' discussion:

- What is different about the version in the book and the classic version of the tale?
- What changes did Scieszka make in the story?
- What makes this version funny?
- Which version do you like better?

WRITING

Mini-lesson—Parody

- To help the students understand how a parody relates to the original tale, work with them to complete a chart such as the one in Figure 3-15. In "The Princess and the Bowling Ball," the prince realizes the absurdity of feeling a pea buried under 100 mattresses and so when he finds the girl he wants to marry he puts a bowling ball under the mattresses.
- Explain to the students that to create parodies of the fairy tales they need to look for things to poke fun at in the tales.

Title	The Princess and the Pea	The Princess and the Bowling Ball
Characters	King, Queen, Prince, Princess	King, Queen, Prince, Princess
Setting	Once upon a time . . .	Once upon a time . . .
Beginning	Princess sleeping on one hundred mattresses	Princess sleeping on one hundred mattresses
Middle	Parents put a pea under the mattresses	Prince puts a bowling ball under the mattresses of girl of his dreams
End	Prince and princess live happily ever after	Prince and princess live happily ever after

Figure 3-15. Fairy Tale Comparison

- Remind them that writing an effective parody requires that the author have a through understanding of the subject under scrutiny (Gehring, 2005). Hence, when they select a tale to parody, it needs to be one they know well.

Modeling

- To model this activity project a blank fairy tale parody chart.
- Decide on a tale you will parody, such as Hansel and Gretel.
- Ask the students to help you retell the tale by completing the second column of the comparison chart.
- Then, in the third column record the changes you will make in the classic tale such as in Figure 3-16.

Writing Activity

- Remind the students that there are many variations of the classic fairy tales and there can be many variations of the parodies of them.
- Tell the students they can use one of the tales Scieszka parodied and create their own parody of the tale.
- The students can also combine two fairy tales as Scieszka did in "Cinderumpelstiltskin" or they can parody a fable as Scieszka did in "The Tortoise and the Hair."
- Once the students have selected the tale or tales they will parody, give them a blank fairy tale comparison chart. There is a blank fairy tale comparison chart in the appendix or the students can create their own charts.
- Explain to the students that in the second column of the chart, they record their notes on the original tale.
- In the third column they write their ideas for the parody.
- Once they have the chart completed, they begin writing their tale.

❖ ───────────

Illustrator

Lane Smith was born in Tulsa, Oklahoma. In order to earn extra money when he was in college, he worked as a janitor at Disneyland. He works as a freelance artist in addition to illustrating children's books. He admits that sometimes he gets carried away with the layering technique he uses in his illustrations and ruins them (Smith, 2000). Once he has the layers just right, he adds the details to the illustrations. He admires the work of other illustrators including Maurice Sendak, Edward Lear, and Tomi Ungerer. Smith's wife, Molly Leach, designed the layout of the book and her layout makes the jokes work. Britton (2002) refers to her "fresh and irreverent" design as a watershed event in children's book publishing.

───────────── ❖

Title	Hansel and Gretel	Hansel, Gretel, and the Gingerbread House
Characters	Woodcutter, stepmother, Hansel, Gretel, witch	Woodcutter, stepmother, Hansel, Gretel, witch
Setting	Once upon a time in a forest,	Once upon a time in a forest,
Beginning	Not enough food so Hansel and Gretel are left in the forest	Not enough food so Hansel and Gretel are left in the forest
Middle	Hansel and Gretel nibble at the gingerbread house, mistreated by the witch, whom they shove in the oven and escape with her riches.	Hansel and Gretel nibble at the gingerbread house, mistreated by the witch, whom they shove in the oven
End	They return home to find the stepmother dead and live happily ever after	They finish eating the gingerbread house, grow obese, and use the witch's money to pay their medical bills

Figure 3-16. Fairy Tale Parody

Title	Cinderella	Denerella
Characters	Cinderella, evil step sisters, evil step mother, and Prince,	Denerella, evil step sisters, Kenerella step mother. Prin;
Setting	Once upon a time, village, Kingdom	One day, Castle.
Beginning	doing chores	cleans the Castle.
Middle	Birds make a dress for Cinderella and evil sisters rip it up	Animels makes Denerella a Dress.
End	She Gets merred.	She does not get merred

Figure 3-17. *Cinderella* and *Denerella* **Comparison**

Conferencing

- As you conference with the students, bring along your chart and tale in order to share it with them and get their feedback.
- Bringing your writing to the conference provides you an opportunity to conference with the students as one writer to another.

Denerella

One day there was a buttful princess named Denerella. She lives in a castle. She had to clean the castle ever day. She had evil step sisters and a evil step mother. One day she got a invetaen to a ball. She showed her step sisters and step mother. Denerella said "I got invelaen to a ball." The evil step sisters said "no your not we are going to that ball." Denerella Said "but it's tonight." The evil step sissters went to work on there dress. When the evil step sisters got to the ball Denerella seek out the window and she started runing to the ball. When she got there she daced with the price. she did not get merred but she lived happly ever after.

Figure 3-18. *Denerella*

❖ ——————————————
Recommended Grade Levels

4–8

Standards for the English Language Arts

3, 7, 8, 11, 12

Information Literacy Standards for Student Learning

1, 2, 3, 8

Objectives

The students will:

• Determine the theme of a story,
• Create a story map based on a theme of their choice, and
• Write a story using their story map.
—————————————— ❖

❖ ——————————————
Author

Leo Lionni was born in Amsterdam, Holland. He moved to the United States in 1939 and later divided his time between the United States and Italy. His first children's book, *Little Blue and Little Yellow* (Lionni, 1959), came from a story he made up for his restless grandchildren on a train trip. Lionni was an author, a painter, a sculptor, a photographer, and a filmmaker (Smith, 1991). Through the stories of the animals in his picture books, he crafted metaphors that revealed his soul and the complexities of the world (Heller, 2000). In *The Girl with the Brown Crayon,* Paley (1997) writes about the year her kindergarten class spent immersed in Leo Lionni's books. Paley (2000), in a conversation with Leo Lionni, asked him the question she and her kindergarten class often pondered: Which of the characters in his books was most like himself? It was the character Swimmy. Lionni also won Caldecott Honors for *Inch by Inch* (Lionni, 1960), *Swimmy* (Lionni, 1963), and *Alexander and the Wind-Up Mouse* (Lionni, 1969).
—————————————— ❖

Frederick

by Leo Lionni
Caldecott Honor Book, 1968

READING

Before Reading

Story Summary
Frederick is the story of Lionni's most famous mouse. As the other field mice spend the summer gathering food for the long winter ahead, Frederick sits on a rock gathering sunshine, colors, and words. When the food is gone and the cold, gray winter lingers, Fredrick shares the sunshine, the colors, and the words he gathered. Collage illustrations capture the quiet elegance of this fable that confirms why the arts are important to society. This book is available on videocassette and CD.

Activating Prior Knowledge
Show the students the pictures of the field mice gathering food for the winter and ask them to describe what they see. Questions such as these can get the students thinking about the story before reading it:

• Why is one mouse sitting off to the side and not helping gather food?
• What is that mouse doing?
• Why are the field mice gathering food?
• What chores do you do around your house?
• How do you help at home?

During Reading

As you read, pause long enough on each page for the students to examine the details in the illustrations.

After Reading

As with other Lionni books, this is one to read aloud and then ponder the lessons in the book. These questions can help start a discussion of the theme of the book:

• Would it have been better for Frederick to help gather food?
• Why was it important for Frederick to gather the sunshine, the colors, and the words?
• Why did Frederick let the other field mice do all of the work?
• Frederick resisted doing what the other field mice wanted him to do. Why did he refuse to conform?
• What would have happened if Frederick had stopped gathering sunshine, colors, and words?
• Have you ever not conformed to what everyone else was doing?
• When might it be important to do what everyone else is doing and when might it be important not to conform?
• Why do you think Lionni wrote this fable?
• What did Lionni want you to learn from this fable?

Another discussion could focus on the similarities and differences between this story and Aesop's fable "The Ant and the Grasshopper." In this fable, the grasshopper sings all summer rather than gathering food for the winter, and when winter comes the ant does not share food with the grasshopper since he did not help gather the food. Print versions of this fable are available in *Aesop's Fables* (Pinkney, 2000), *Aesop's Fables* (Ash and Higton, 1990), and *Aesop and Company: With Scenes from His Legendary Life* (Bader, 1991), and it is available online at http://www.bartleby.com/17/1/36.html. After you read "The Ant and the Grasshopper," discuss with the students why the field mice were willing to share their food with Frederick but the ant was not willing to share food with the grasshopper.

WRITING

Mini-lesson—Theme

- Explain to the students that the theme of a story is a lesson or lessons readers learn from a story that can sometimes be stated in one sentence (Roy, 2003).
- Tell the students that authors develop the theme through the characters' actions and the outcome of the story. Readers' prior experiences and perspectives influence what they understand from stories and their understanding of the themes of stories.
- Explain to the students that in *Frederick,* they learn about the importance of the arts in our lives, about conformity, and about saving for the future. In "The Ant and the Grasshopper" readers learn about saving for the future.

Modeling

- Project a blank story map such as the one in Figure 3-19.
- Explain to the students that you are going to start with the theme of your story and then write down the other information in the story map.
- Ask the students to help you brainstorm a list of possible themes.
- Write the list on the board for the students to refer to as they begin deciding on themes for their stories.
- Once you decide on the theme of your story write it on the story map and have the students help you complete the rest of the story map.

Writing Activity

- Suggest that the students select one of the themes from the list on the board to use in their stories.
- Once the students decide on a theme, have them complete a story map as a prewriting activity.
- Provide the students with copies of the blank story map in the appendix or they can draw a story map on a blank sheet of paper.
- Remind the students that our best writing comes from our personal experiences, so they should think about events in their own lives that they can incorporate into their writing.
- Remind the students that fables usually have animal characters with human failings. Using animal characters helps to disguise the actions of real humans that might cause them embarrassment.

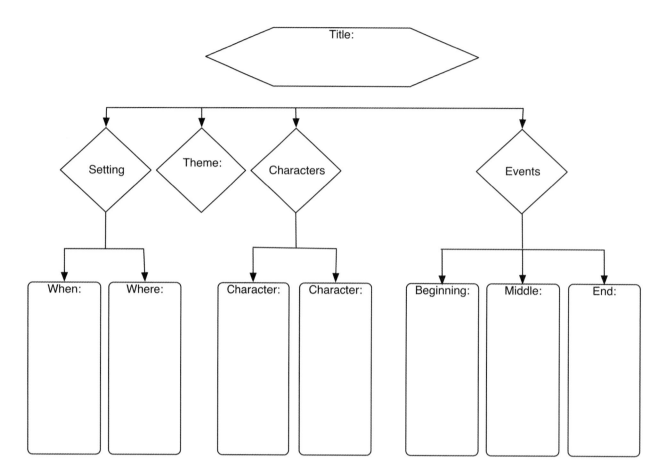

Figure 3-19. Story Map with Theme

- If students are finding it difficult to decide on their own story, allow them to write a retelling of "The Ant and the Grasshopper."

Conferencing

- As you conference with the students, help them determine if their story reflects the theme they have chosen.
- Once they have written their stories, provide the students with time to share them with their classmates by reading them aloud or involving other students in a dramatization of the stories.

RESOURCES FOR LIBRARIANS AND TEACHERS

Here are the books discussed in this chapter and some other traditional tales in Caldecott Medal and Honor books that you might want to consider adding to your curriculum.

Aardema, Verna. 1975. *Why Mosquitoes Buzz in People's Ears.* Illustrated by Leo and Diane Dillon. New York: Dial.

Andersen, Hans Christian. 1999. *The Ugly Duckling.* Illustrated by Jerry Pinkney. New York: William Morrow.

Cendrars, Blaise. 1982. *Shadow*. Translated and illustrated by Marcia Brown. New York: Simon & Schuster.

de Paola, Tomie. 1975. *Strega Nona*. New York: Prentice-Hall.

Emberley, Barbara. 1987, 1967. *Drummer Hoff*. Illustrated by Ed Emberley. New York: Simon & Schuster.

Goble, Paul. 1978. *The Girl Who Loved Wild Horses*. New York: Atheneum.

Hodges, Margaret. 1984. *Saint George and the Dragon*. Illustrated by Trina Schart Hyman. Boston: Little, Brown.

Hogrogian, Nonny. 1971. *One Fine Day*. New York: Macmillan.

Hyman, Trina Schart. 1983. *Little Red Riding Hood*. New York: Holiday House.

Issacs, Anne. 1994. *Swamp Angel*. Illustrated by Paul O. Zelinsky. New York: Dutton.

Jarrell, Randall. 1970. *Snow-White and the Seven Dwarfs*. Illustrated by Nancy Ekholm Burkert. New York: Farrar Straus Giroux.

Jeffers, Susan. 1973. *Three Jovial Huntsmen*. New York: Simon & Schuster.

Kimmel, Eric. 1989. *Hershel and the Hanukah Goblins*. Illustrated by Trina Schart Hyman. New York: Holiday House.

Leodhas, Sorche Nic. 1965. *Always Room for One More*. Illustrated by Nonny Hogrogian. New York: Holt, Rinehart and Winston.

Lesser, Rika. 1984. *Hansel and Gretel*. Illustrated by Paul O. Zelinsky. New York: Dodd.

Lester, Julius. 1994. *John Henry*. Illustrated by Jerry Pinkney. New York: Dial.

Lionni, Leo. 1960. *Inch by Inch*. New York: Obolensky.

———. 1963. *Swimmy*. New York: Pantheon.

———. 1967. *Frederick*. New York: Pantheon.

———. 1969. *Alexander and the Wind-Up Mouse*. New York: Pantheon.

Lobel, Arnold. 1970. *Frog and Toad Are Friends*. New York: Harper.

———. 1980. *Fables*. New York: Harper.

———. 1981. *On Market Street*. Illustrated by Anita Lobel. New York: Greenwillow.

Marshall, James. 1988. *Goldilocks and the Three Bears*. New York: Dial.

McDermott, Beverly Brodsky. 1974. *The Golem: A Jewish Legend*. New York: HarperCollins.

McDermott, Gerald. 1972. *Anansi the Spider: A Tale from the Ashanti*. New York: Holt.

———. 1974. *Arrow to the Sun*. New York: Viking.

———. 1993. *Raven: A Trickster Tale from the Pacific Northwest*. New York: Harcourt.

McKissack, Patricia C. 1988. *Mirandy and Brother Wind*. Illustrated by Jerry Pinkney. New York: Knopf.

Mosel, Arlene. 1972. *The Funny Little Woman*. Illustrated by Blair Lent. New York: Dutton.

Perrault, Charles. 1952. *Puss in Boots*. Translated and illustrated by Marcia Brown. New York: Farrar Straus Giroux.

———. 1954. *Cinderella, or The Little Glass Slipper*. Translated and illustrated by Marcia Brown. New York: Atheneum.

———. (Trans. by Malcolm Arthur.) 1990. *Puss in Boots*. Illustrated by Fred Marcellino. New York: Farrar Straus Giroux.

Plume, Ilse. 1980. *The Bremen-Town Musicians*. New York: Doubleday.

Ransome, Arthur. 1968. *The Fool of the World and the Flying Ship*. Illustrated by Uri Shulevitz. New York: Farrar Straus Giroux.

San Souci, Robert D. 1989. *The Talking Eggs: A Folktale from the American South*. Illustrated by Jerry Pinkney. New York: Dial.

———. 1995. *The Faithful Friend*. Illustrated by Brian Pinkney. New York: Simon & Schuster.

Scieszka, Jon. 1992. *The Stinky Cheese Man and Other Fairly Stupid Tales.* Illustrated by Lane Smith. New York: Viking.

Shulevitz, Uri. 1979. *The Treasure.* New York: Farrar Straus Giroux.

Snyder, Dianne. 1988. *The Boy of the Three-Year Nap.* Illustrated by Allen Say. Boston: Houghton Mifflin.

Steptoe, John. 1984. *The Story of Jumping Mouse: A Native American Legend.* New York: Lothrop.

———. 1987. *Mufaro's Beautiful Daughters: An African Tale.* New York: Lothrop.

Stevens, Janet. 1995. *Tops & Bottoms.* New York: Harcourt Brace.

Taback, Simms. 1997. *There Was an Old Lady Who Swallowed a Fly.* New York: Viking.

———. 1999. *Joseph Had a Little Overcoat.* New York: Viking.

Wiesner, David. 2001. *The Three Pigs.* Boston: Houghton Mifflin.

Wood, Audrey. 1985. *King Bidgood's in the Bathtub.* Illustrated by Don Wood. New York: Harcourt.

Yolen, Jane. 1967. *The Emperor and the Kite.* Illustrated by Ed Young. Chicago: World.

Young, Ed. 1989. *Lon Po Po: A Red-Riding Hood Story from China.* New York: Philomel.

———. 1992. *Seven Blind Mice.* New York: Philomel.

Zelinsky, Paul O. 1986. *Rumpelstiltskin.* New York: Dutton.

———. 1997. *Rapunzel.* New York: Dutton.

Zemach, Harve. 1973. *Duffy and the Devil.* Illustrated by Margot Zemach. New York: Farrar Straus Giroux.

Zemach, Margot. 1977. *It Could Always Be Worse.* New York: Farrar Straus Giroux.

Fable Collections

Ash, Russell, and Bernard Higton. 1990. *Aesop's Fables.* San Francisco: Chronicle.

Bader, Barbara. 1991. *Aesop and Company: With Scenes from His Legendary Life.* Boston: Houghton Mifflin.

Pinkney, Jerry. 2000. *Aesop's Fables.* San Francisco: Chronicle Books.

Resource Books

Compestine, Ying Chang. 2000. *The Runaway Rice Cake.* Illustrated by Tungwai Chau. New York: Simon & Schuster.

Hoffmann, Felix. 1961. *Rapunzel.* New York: Harcourt.

Keats, Ezra Jack. 1965. *John Henry: An American Legend.* New York: Pantheon.

Kellogg, Steven. 1997. *The Three Little Pigs.* New York: Morrow.

Kimmel, Eric A. 1993. *The Gingerbread Man.* New York: Holiday House.

Marshall, James. 1989. *Three Little Pigs.* New York: Penguin Putnam.

Rogasky, Barbara. 1982. *Rapunzel.* Illustrated by Trina Schart Hyman. New York: Holiday House.

Roy, Jennifer Rozines. 2003. *You Can Write a Story or Narrative.* Berkeley Heights, NJ: Enslow Publishers.

Small, Terry. 1994. *The Legend of John Henry.* New York: Doubleday.

Trivizas, Eugene. 1993. *The Three Little Wolves and the Big Bad Pig.* Illustrated by Helen Oxenbury. New York: Simon & Schuster.

Wood, Audrey. 1984. *The Napping House.* Illustrated by Don Wood. San Diego: Harcourt.

Web Sites

These are some Web sites where you will find fairy tales, folktales, fables, and legends. A word of caution about the tales on these sites: they are not appropriate for all age groups and it is highly recommended that you preview the tales before directing the students to the Web sites.

Hans Christian Andersen Fairy Tales and Stories
http://hca.gilead.org.il/#intro
This page has a list of Hans Christian Anderson's fairy tales and there are hyperlinks to many of the tales. There are also links to other pages about Hans Christian Anderson.

Tales of Wonder: Folk and Fairy Tales from Around the World
http://www.darsie.net/talesofwonder/
This page has links to fairy tales from around the world grouped by country.

National Geographic Grimm's Fairy Tales
http://www.nationalgeographic.com/grimm/index2.html
There are twelve tales on this site based on a 1914 translation. Four of the tales have an audio component.

SurLaLune Fairy Tale Pages
http://www.surlalunefairytales.com/
Annotated fairy tales, collections of illustrations, a discussion board, and links to other resources are on this site.

Grimm Fairy Tales
http://www.grimmfairytales.com/en/main
Animated Grimm fairy tales and text versions of the tales along with games and activities are on this site.

Myths, Folktales & Fairy Tales
http://teacher.scholastic.com/writewit/mff/index.htm
On this site, students can learn about and write myths, folktales, and fairy tales with noted children's authors. They can explore writing myths with Jane Yolen, writing folktales with Alma Flor Ada and Rafe Martin, and writing fractured fairy tales and fables with Jon Scieszka.

Aesop's Fables: Online Collection
http://www.aesopfables.com/
This site houses over 655 fables and 127 of Hans Christian Anderson's fairy tales. Some of the fables and fairy tales are narrated.

Harvard Classics, Vol. 17, Part 1 Fables
http://www.bartleby.com/17/1/
Eighty-two of Aesop's fables as retold by Joseph Jacobs are on this Web site. You may want to print these out for the children as the advertisements in the margins may not be suitable for children and you will want to preview the fables before sharing them with the students.

Aesop's Fables: Traditional and Modern
http://www.umass.edu/Aesop/contents.html

Since 1994, art students taking Introduction to Computing in the Fine Arts at the University of Massachusetts–Amherst have been illustrating traditional and some modern retellings of Aesop's fables. The original fables and the modern retellings provide students with wonderful examples of how to create their own versions of the fables. Over the years, the illustrations have evolved from still images to animated graphics.

RESOURCES FOR STUDENTS

Students who enjoyed reading books by the authors and illustrators in this chapter might enjoy some of their other books.

Coerr, Eleanor. 1993. *Sadako.* Illustrated by Ed Young. New York: Putnam.

Collodi, Carlo. 1996. *Pinocchio.* Illustrated by Ed Young. New York: Philomel.

Lester, Julius. 1968. *To Be a Slave.* New York: Dial.

———. 1998. *Black Cowboy, Wild Horses.* Illustrated by Jerry Pinkney. New York: Penguin Putnam.

———. 1999. *The Tales of Uncle Remus: The Adventures of Brer Rabbit.* Illustrated by Jerry Pinkney. New York: Penguin Putnam.

———. 1999. *Uncle Remus Complete Tales.* Illustrated by Jerry Pinkney. New York: Penguin Putnam.

———. 2000. *Sam and the Tigers: A Retelling of Little Black Sambo.* Illustrated by Jerry Pinkney. New York: Penguin Putnam.

Lionni, Leo. 1959. *Little Blue and Little Yellow.* New York: Obolensky.

———. 1970. *Fish Is Fish.* New York: Pantheon.

———. 1991. *Matthew's Dream.* New York: Knopf.

———. 1992. *A Busy Year.* New York: Knopf.

Lobel, Arnold. 1972. *Frog and Toad Together.* New York: Harper.

———. 1979. *Days with Frog and Toad.* New York: Harper.

Louie, Ai-Ling. 1982. *Yeh-Shen: A Cinderella Story from China.* Illustrated by Ed Young. New York: Philomel.

Pinkney, Jerry. 2002. *Noah's Ark.* New York: North-South.

Pollock, Penny. 1996. *The Turkey Girl: A Zuni Cinderella Story.* Illustrated by Ed Young. Boston: Little, Brown.

Ryan, Cheli Durán. 1971. *Hildilid's Night.* Illustrated by Arnold Lobel. New York: Macmillan.

San Souci, Robert D. 1997. *The Hired Hand: An African-American Folktale.* Illustrated by Jerry Pinkney. New York: Dial.

Schroeder, Alan. 1996. *Minty: A Story of Young Harriet Tubman.* Illustrated by Jerry Pinkney. New York: Dial.

Scieszka, Jon. 1995. *Math Curse.* Illustrated by Lane Smith. New York: Viking.

———. 1997. *The True Story of the Three Little Pigs.* Illustrated by Lane Smith. New York: Viking.

———. 1998. *Squids Will Be Squids: Fresh Morals, Beastly Fables.* Illustrated by Lane Smith. New York: Viking.

———. 1998. *Summer Reading Is Killing Me!* Illustrated by Lane Smith. New York: Viking.

———. 2004. *Science Verse.* Illustrated by Lane Smith. New York: Viking.

Taback, Simms. 2002. *This Is the House that Jack Built.* New York: Putnam.

Van Leeuwen, Jean. 1993. *More Tales of Oliver Pig.* Illustrated by Arnold Lobel. New York: Puffin.

———. 1993, 1979. *Tales of Oliver Pig.* Illustrated by Arnold Lobel. New York:
  Puffin.
Wiesner, David. 1988. *Free Fall.* New York: Lothrop.
———. 1991. *Tuesday.* New York: Clarion.
———. 1999. *Sector 7.* New York: Clarion.
Young, Ed. 2004. *The Sons of the Dragon King: A Chinese Legend.* New York:
  Atheneum.
Ziefert, Harriet. 1996. *Two Little Witches: A Halloween Counting Story.* Illustrated by
  Simms Taback. Cambridge, MA: Candlewick.

IDEAS FOR PARENTS AND CAREGIVERS

Parents and relatives introduce children to family folktales as they recount family stories handed down through the generations (Coody, 1997). These impromptu storytelling sessions transmit family memories and help develop children's understanding
of oral stories and story structure. Anita Lobel (2000) notes that some of the most
pleasant moments she remembers spending with her children were the times she read
them bedtime stories. Favorite stories were read in unison accompanied by giggles
when they recognized familiar events. While reading, they would stop to discuss an illustration or look back in the text for clarification. Whether they are telling stories or
reading stories, parents and caregivers transmit to children an understanding of story
structure that helps them comprehend stories and provides them with an organization
to follow as they write their own stories.

REFERENCES

"Arnold (Stark) Lobel." 1999. *St. James Guide to Children's Writers,* 5th ed.
  Farmington Hills, MI: St. James.
———. 2002. *Major Authors and Illustrators for Children and Young Adults,* 2nd ed.
  Farmington Hills, MI: Gale Group.
Avery, Nanette L. 1999. "From Aesop to Lobel: Fabulous Fables." *Teaching PreK–8*
  30, no. 3 (November/December): 62–63.
Bader, Barbara. 1991. *Aesop and Company: With Scenes from His Legendary Life.*
  Boston: Houghton Mifflin.
Brickman, Bette. 1998. "A Moral to the Story: Folk Tales in the ESL Writing Class."
  Teaching English in the Two-Year College 25, no. 1 (February): 67–68.
Britton, Jason. 2002. "A Watershed Event." *Publishers Weekly* 249, no. 43 (28
  October): 29.
Brodie, Carolyn S. 2004. "Making Kids Laugh: John Scieszka." *School Library
  Media Activities Monthly* 21, no. 1 (September): 45–47.
Brooks, Donna. 1998. "Paul O. Zelinsky: Geishas on Tractors." *Horn Book* 74, no. 4
  (July/August): 442–449.
Chamberlain, Julia, and Dorothy Leal. 1999. "Caldecott Medal Books and
  Readability Levels: Not Just 'Picture' Books." *Reading Teacher* 52, no. 8
  (May): 898–902.
Coody, Betty. 1997. *Using Literature with Young Children,* 5th ed. Madison, WI:
  Brown & Benchmark.
"Ed (Tse-chun) Young." 2002. *Major Authors and Illustrators for Children and Young
  Adults,* 2nd. ed., 8 vols. Farmington Hills, MI: Gale Group.

Gauch, Patricia Lee. 1990. "Ed Young." *Horn Book* 66, no. 4 (July/August): 430–435.

Gehring, Wes D. 2005. "Trying to Parody the Classics." *USA Today Magazine* 133, no. 2716 (January): 51.

George, Jack. 1998. "Writing Dialogue (With a Little Help from Norman Rockwell)." *Teaching PreK–8* 29, no. 3 (November/December): 56–57.

Giorgis, Cyndi, and Nancy J. Johnson. 2000. "2000 Caldecott Medal Winner: A Conversation with Simms Taback." *Reading Teacher* 54, no. 4 (December): 418–422.

———. 2002. "Interview with the 2002 Caldecott Medal Winner, David Wiesner." *Reading Teacher* 56, no. 4 (December): 400–404.

Halls, Kelly Milner. 2003. "When Picture Books Grow Up." *Book Links* 12, no. 5 (April/May): 51–54.

Harper, Laura. 1997. "The Writer's Toolbox: Five Tools for Active Revision Instruction." *Language Arts* 74, no. 3 (March): 193–200.

Heller, Steve. 2000. "Tribute: Leo Lionni, 1910–1999." *Print* 54, no. 3 (May/June): 36–38.

Hendrickson, Linnea. 2000. "The View from Rapunzel's Tower." *Children's Literature in Education* 31, no. 4 (December): 209–223.

Inspiration. Version 7.5. Portland, OR: Inspiration Software.

"Jon Scieszka." 2002. *Major Authors and Illustrators for Children and Young Adults,* 2nd ed. Farmington Hills, MI: Gale Group.

Krapp, JoAnn Vergona. 2004. "So Many Books: Genres of Children's Fiction." *School Library Media Activities Monthly* 21, no. 2 (October): 44–45.

Lester, Julius. 1996. "John Henry." *Horn Book* 72, no. 1 (January/February): 28–31.

Lionni, Leo. 1967. *Frederick.* New York: Pantheon.

Lobel, Anita. 2000. "Future Classics." *Horn Book* 76, no. 6 (November/December): 684–685.

Lobel, Arnold. 1980. *Fables.* New York: Harper.

Lodge, Sally. 1998. "Paul Zelinsky's Surprising Debut." *Publishers Weekly* 245, no. 13 (30 March): 27.

———. 2001. "Working at His Creative Peak." *Publishers Weekly* 248, no. 7 (12 February): 180.

Marcus, Leonard S. 2001. "A Collaborative Effort." *Publishers Weekly* 248, no. 29 (16 July): 84–87.

Mello, Robin. 2001. "Cinderella Meets Ulysses." *Language Arts* 78, no. 6 (July): 548–555.

Nikola-Lisa, W. 1998. "John Henry: Then and Now." *African American Review* 32, no. 1 (Spring): 51–56.

Paley, Vivian Gussin. 1997. *The Girl with the Brown Crayon.* Cambridge, MA: Harvard.

———. 2000. "The Mouse that Roared." *School Library Journal* 46, no. 1 (January): 46–49.

Peck, Jackie, and Judy Hendershot. 1999. "Release from 'Grimm' Captivity: Paul O. Zelinsky Talks about the Making of *Rapunzel,* the 1998 Caldecott Medal Winner." *Reading Teacher* 52, no. 6 (March): 570–575.

Petrolle, Jean. 1997. "*Stinky Cheese Man* Author Keeps Them Laughing at Convention." *Language Arts* 74, no. 36 (March): 226.

Pinkney, Jerry. 2005. "Jerry Pinkney." [Online] Available: http://www.harperchildrens.com/catalog/author_xml.asp?authorid=12598 [cited 04 April 2005].

Readence, John E., Thomas W. Bean, and R. Scott Baldwin. 1998. *Content Area Reading: An Integrated Approach,* 6th ed. Dubuque, IA: Kendall/Hunt.

Roy, Jennifer Rozines. 2003. *You Can Write a Story or Narrative.* Berkeley Heights, NJ: Enslow Publishers.

Silvey, Anita. 2001. "Pigs in Space." *School Library Journal* 47, no. 11 (November): 48–50.

———. 2002. "David Wiesner." *Horn Book* 78, no. 4 (July/August): 401–405.

Smith, Amanda. 1991. "The Lively Art of Leo Lionni." *Publishers Weekly* 238, no. 16 (5 April): 118–119.

Smith, Lane. 2000. "About Lane Smith." [Online] Available: http://www .penguinputnam.com/nf/Author/AuthorPage/0,,0_1000029880,00.html [cited 28 March 2004].

Taback, Simms. 2000. "Caldecott Medal Acceptance." *Horn Book* 76, no. 4 (July/August): 402–408.

Unsworth, Len, and Janet Wheeler. 2002. "Re-valuing the Role of Images in Reviewing Picture Books." *Reading* 36, no. 2 (July): 68–74.

Wiesner, David. 2002. "Caldecott Medal Acceptance." *Horn Book* 78, no. 4 (July/August): 393–399.

Wolf, Shebly Anne, and Kenneth Paul Wolf. 2002. "Teaching True and to the Test in Writing." *Language Arts* 79, no. 3 (January): 229–240.

Yopp, Ruth Helen, and Hallie Kay Yopp. 2001. *Literature-Based Reading Activities,* 3rd ed. Needham Heights, MA: Allyn & Bacon.

Young, Ed. 1990. "Caldecott Medal Acceptance." *Horn Book* 66, no. 4 (July/August): 425–429.

Zelinsky, Paul O. 1998. "Caldecott Medal Acceptance." *Horn Book* 74, no. 4 (July/August): 433–441.

4 ❖ MEMOIRS, AUTOBIOGRAPHIES, AND BIOGRAPHIES

Memoirs, autobiographies, and biographies consist of life stories about the events, people, and moments that shape lives. These are personal stories that force readers to pause and make connections between their lives and the lives of the people in the stories. These stories create bonds between the past and the present, between generations, and between cultures. Readers find common threads that help them see that the similarities between people outweigh the differences. These life stories help readers develop empathy for others, see things from others' points of view, and become emotionally involved in the lives of others. Writing their own life stories causes students to pause and to reflect on their lives. Writing others' life stories requires students to research and to reflect on others' lives and to make connections between their lives and the lives of their subjects. Reflecting and writing helps students make sense of their world.

While writing an autobiography or a biography may be a daunting task for students, writing a memoir of a special time in their lives is a more manageable task. Writing about their memories shows students how powerful it is to write about what they know best. Memoirs encourage students to use authentic voice as they write. Writing about personal experiences helps students make connections to one another as they discuss similar experiences. Memoirs present personal glimpses into students' lives as they write about people, events, and places in their lives. Writing and sharing their memories establishes connections between students in the classroom and helps them develop understanding and empathy for one another; a safe, nonjudgmental climate in the classroom assures that they feel comfortable sharing their memories. The memories may be about a particular time in their lives, as in *When I Was Young in the Mountains* (Rylant, 1982), or the description of one day in their lives, as in *Working Cotton* (Williams, 1992). Students can also write their autobiographies chronicling the significant events in their lives, as in *Bill Peet: An Autobiography* (Peet, 1989).

Before writing biographies, students need to have biographies read aloud to them and discussed. They need multiple opportunities to interact with a selection of biographies in order to develop a feeling of expertise before they begin writing. Judy Freeman (2000) worked collaboratively with teachers using a variety of activities in her library including book talks and read alouds to introduce elementary students to the biographies in the library. Madeleine Hoss (2000) worked with an elementary teacher to conduct a biography party during which Louisa May Alcott, portrayed by a parent volunteer, visited with the students. Library media specialists can help teachers select biographies for the classroom and can provide students with print and electronic resources to locate information on the subjects of their biographies.

Students need the freedom to find someone they admire for the subject of their biography (Ramsland, 1990). James Cross Giblin (2002) selects a subject for a biography because something in that person's life makes him curious and makes him want to learn more about the forces that affected the person's actions. As he writes, he works to show rather than tell and to evoke an emotional response in his readers. Giblin includes information on the person's strengths and weaknesses in his biographies. After conducting intensive research on his subject, he writes in a lively style and includes revealing anecdotes about the person. Giblin notes that Jean Fritz and Russell Freedman combine solid research, insight, and storytelling in the biographies they write.

As part of their science curriculum, fourth-grade students wrote biographies of scientists (McCarty and Betterton, 1999). To introduce the unit the teacher placed information on a diverse collection of scientists on a bulletin board. To guide their research the students grouped their information into broad categories including vital statistics, life experiences, character traits, locations visited or lived, successes, conflicts, and impact on society (McCarty and Betterton, 1999). They recorded their notes in booklets and met in groups to discuss their research. These discussions gave the students opportunities to reflect on their notes and to decide on the important points to include in their biographies.

Picture-book biographies combine outstanding illustrations and a narrative writing style to tell the story of people's lives. *Snowflake Bentley* (Martin, 1998) combines narrative with facts and quotes set in sidebars. *The Glorious Flight: Across the Channel with Louis Blériot* (Provensen and Provensen, 1983) focuses on just one aspect of Blériot's life, as reflected in the title of the book. These books and the other books in this chapter provide students with a variety of models to examine as they write biographies. You can share information on other biographies that students can use as models for their writing. Some of the biographies may be read aloud and others put on display for the students to read and explore on their own. The books provide them with ideas and help them understand what is expected when they write (Barrs, 2000; Graham, 2001; Thomason and York, 2000).

Snowflake Bentley

by Jacqueline Briggs Martin
Illustrated by Mary Azarian
Caldecott Medal Winner, 1999

READING

Before Reading

Story Summary
Wilson A. "Snowflake" Bentley was passionate about snowflakes. He was ridiculed for his obsession with snowflakes and considered to be an eccentric by his neighbors. When he was sixteen his parents spent their life savings to buy him a camera with a microscope so that he could photograph snowflakes. Bentley's life is an inspiration for children and the word imagery used to tell his story paints vivid pictures in readers' minds (Cooper, 1998). The sidebars in this picture-book biography contain additional information about Bentley's work and the science of snowflakes (Giorgis and Johnson, 1999/2000). His photographs proved that no two snowflakes are alike and a book of his photographs is still used and studied today. This biography includes credits for sources, a photograph of Bentley, a quote from him about the importance of his work, and three of his photographs of snowflakes. Students interested in learning more about Wilson A. Bentley can visit the Web site at http://www.snowflakebentley.com. Mary

❖ ————————————

Recommended Grade Levels

5–10

Standards for the English Language Arts

1, 3, 4, 5, 6, 7, 8, 11, 12

Information Literacy Standards for Student Learning

1, 4, 6, 8

Objectives

The students will:

- Consult print and electronic resources to locate information on the subject of their choice,

- Complete a biography chart, and

- Write a brief biography.

———————————— ❖

Author

Jacqueline Briggs Martin states that writing books is not easy, but that she would not want to be doing anything else. Ideas for her books come from her childhood experiences, articles she has read, her love of rivers, her family history, things she loves to do, and sometimes from questions that pique her interest. To write this book she read articles Bentley wrote, looked at some of his snowflake photographs, read about his life, and visited his home (Martin, 2001). Martin's Web page is at http://www .jacquelinebriggsmartin.com/.

Illustrator

To gather ideas for her woodcuts for this book, Mary Azarian visited Bentley's hometown where there is a small museum dedicated to his work. In the museum, she found his camera and some of his photographs of snowflakes. This research ensured that the illustrations in the book were accurate (Giorgis and Johnson, 1999/2000). In her acceptance speech for the Caldecott award, Azarian noted that her initial excitement about a project is followed by dismay and she develops sudden urges to reorganize and clean rather than begin working (Azarian, 1999). Additional information about Azarian is available at http://www.maryazarian.com/ and http://www.nccil.org/azarian.html.

Azarian illustrated the book using woodcuts tinted with watercolors. This book is available on audiocassette, videocassette, CD, and DVD.

Activating Prior Knowledge

In the author and illustrator sections below you will find information about the research they did on Bentley's life and work before they began writing and illustrating. Sharing this information with the students helps them understand the different ways authors and illustrators gather information before they begin working. Read aloud Bentley's comment that he "loved snow more than anything else in the world." Invite the students to think about things that they love more than anything else. What things are they passionate about? Things they are passionate about provide them with topics to explore in their writing.

During Reading

During the first reading of the book, read aloud the narrative portion of the biography. Then, read aloud the scientific information in the sidebars or allow the students to read this part of the biography on their own.

After Reading

Use questions such as the ones below to initiate a discussion of this biography.

- What was the most interesting thing you learned about Snowflake Bentley?
- What was the most interesting thing you learned about snowflakes?
- What else would you like to know about Snowflake Bentley?
- How did his family support his endeavors?
- Why is it important to follow your passion?
- What things are you passionate about?
- Can you think of another famous person who is passionate about something?

WRITING

Mini-lesson—Research

- Brainstorm with the students to create a list of people that they are interested in learning more about.
- If there is a local celebrity in your area, consider having the students write that person's biography. They can visit relevant sights and conduct interviews to gather information to include in the biography.
- Select one of the people on the list for your personal research.
- Provide the students with copies of the biography chart in Figure 4-1, which is available in the appendix.
- Explain to the students that as they research their subjects they will record the information on the chart.
- If *TimeLiner* software is available, the students can use it to record and organize their research.

Modeling

- Put together a collection of print and electronic resources to be used to find information about biography subjects.

Birth: When and Where	
Places lived or visited	
Major Life Events	
Successes	
Obstacles	
Character Traits	
Why I selected this person	

Figure 4-1. Biography Chart

- Select the resources you will use to gather information about your subject.
- Project a copy of the biography chart.
- Skim through your resources to find details to record in the chart.
- When you find a piece of information, think aloud as you determine how to rephrase the information instead of writing it down exactly as it appears in the resource.
- Record the information on the biography chart.

Writing Activity

- Ask the students to talk to each other in small groups to decide who will be the subjects of their biographies.

- Once the students have selected their subjects, have them begin using the available resources to find information to fill in their charts.
- Circulate around the room as the students work to help them rephrase the text rather than copy it word for word onto their charts.
- Once they complete the chart have the students begin writing their biographies.

Conferencing

- As you conference with the students ask them to tell you why they selected their subjects.
- Also have them tell you the most interesting things they learned about their subjects and remind them to include them in the biography charts and in the biographies.

Song and Dance Man

by Karen Ackerman
Illustrated by Stephen Gammell
Caldecott Medal Winner, 1989

❖ ──────────────

Recommended Grade Levels

3–6

Standards for the English Language Arts

3, 4, 5, 6, 12

Information Literacy Standards for Student Learning

2, 3, 5

Objectives

The students will:

- Distinguish between the beginning, middle, and end of the story,
- Examine the text to locate sensory words, and
- Record their personal memories incorporating sensory words in their writing.

────────────── ❖

READING

Before Reading

Story Summary

Readers step back in time as Grandfather dons his hat, laces up his tap shoes, and grabs his cane. The attic becomes a vaudeville stage as Grandfather performs his act that includes songs, dances, jokes, and magic tricks. His adoring grandchildren laugh, clap, and cheer his performance. Grandfather demonstrates that you are only as old as you feel and that you can step back in your memories to favorite times and places. Stephen Gammell's colored-pencil illustrations vibrate with splashes of color and Grandfather's animated shadow. This book is also available on videocassette.

Activating Prior Knowledge

This is the story of a very special afternoon spent with a very special grandfather. Ask the students about how they spend time with their grandparents or older relatives.

During Reading

Before you read the book aloud, ask the students to listen for the author's descriptions about what the children smelled, heard, saw, and felt as Grandfather performed.

After Reading

The book has a well-defined beginning, middle, and end. Mention to the students that they can organize their ideas for their memories using that structure. To help them understand the structure of the story you can group your discussion questions around the beginning, middle, and end of the story.

Beginning

- Why are the children visiting their grandparents?
- What did you think was going to happen when the children followed Grandfather up to the attic?

Middle

- How can you tell from the illustrations that the children enjoyed the performance?
- How do you know that Grandfather enjoys performing?
- Do you think this is the first time Grandfather performed for the children? Why or why not?
- Why do you think Grandfather performed for the children?

End

- How do you think the children felt when Grandfather finished performing?
- How do you think Grandfather felt when he finished performing?

WRITING

Mini-lesson—Sensory Words

- Tell the students that by describing what the children smelled, heard, saw, and felt the author draws readers into the story and makes them feel as though they were there in the attic as Grandfather performed.
- Return to the text to reread passages such as the ones in Figure 4-2.
- As you read the passages, ask the students which of the five senses the author evokes by her words.

Modeling

- Talk with the students about a memory you have about a relative.
- Think aloud about the memory and write down your thoughts. As you write, try to include sensory words.

❖

Author

Karen Ackerman always remembers having stories to write or tell and she was encouraged in her journalistic efforts by her mother, who supplied her with paper to keep her from writing on the walls (Ackerman, 2003). Her own childhood memories were the basis for this book. Ackerman advises young authors to keep writing and not to get discouraged. She writes at home surrounded by her twelve cats who sprawl on her desk, her shoulders, and her neck. For additional information about Karen Ackerman, visit her Web pages at http://community-2.webtv.net/ KAbooks/KarenAckermanBooks/.

❖

". . . the smell of cedar chips and old things saved fills the attic."

". . . his tap shoes make soft, slippery sounds . . ."

". . . all we can see is a song and dance man . . ."

". . . it feels like the whole attic is shaking . . ."

Figure 4-2. Sensory Words

Food	marked down turnip greens—limp, some leaves still bright green, smell of overripe bananas marked down pale meat with bright orange stickers marked down dented cans—not too dented careful purchases—sale items, generic brands
Grandma	black and grey hair pulled into a tight bun always neat and tidy navy blue Keds carries a large, menacing black umbrella no-nonsense style, at times gruff

Figure 4-3. Grocery Shopping with Grandma

❖ ─────────────

Illustrator

Stephen Gammell was born in Des Moines, Iowa. His father was a magazine art editor who encouraged his son's artistic endeavors by supplying him with magazines, pencils, and stacks of paper of different colors and thicknesses (Silvey, 2002). Gammell would cut the illustrations out of the magazines and create scrapbooks. He works in his study every day, whether he is working on a book or not. In addition to illustrating books for other authors, Gammell writes and illustrates his own books. He finds writing books to be very hard work. When Gammell sent in biographical information for the back cover of this book, he included the fact that he likes chocolate chip cookies and milk (Schwartz, 1989). Gammell won Caldecott Honors for *Where the Buffaloes Begin* (Baker, 1981) and *The Relatives Came* (Rylant, 1985).

- Describe what you smelled, the sounds you heard, what you felt, and what you saw.
- Figure 4-3 is a list of remembrances I have of shopping trips to the Piggly Wiggly with my grandmother.

Writing Activity

- Before the students begin writing, provide them with some time to discuss their memories with partners or in small groups.
- Suggest to the students that they write down some notes about the memories before they begin writing and to include sensory words to help describe the memories.
- When the students write, begin writing your memory for ten to fifteen minutes before you begin conferencing with the students.

Conferencing

- As you conference with the students ask them to read a portion of the memory that they think is the best or a portion they need help with.
- Offer positive comment to the students about their writing.
- If there is a part where you think they can add sensory words, ask them about what they were smelling, hearing, tasting, seeing, or feeling.
- Write their responses on sticky notes to leave with them at the end of the conference so they can add the sensory words to their writing.

The Glorious Flight: Across the Channel with Louis Blériot

by Alice Provensen and Martin Provensen
Caldecott Medal Winner, 1984

READING

Before Reading

Story Summary

While out with his family for a ride in their new car one sunny day, the sight and sound of an airship soaring over the city of Cambrai, France, attracted Louis Blériot's attention. Blériot, who made a fortune from his invention of an automobile searchlight, invested that fortune in developing a high-performance airplane. His experiments began with the Blériot I and culminated in 1909 with the Blériot XI, which carried him over the English Channel in thirty-seven minutes. He was the first person to fly solo across the English Channel. Six years earlier, the Wright brothers had made their first flight, and eighteen years later Charles Lindbergh flew across the Atlantic Ocean. The focus of the book is on the series of airships Blériot invented, which encourages readers to focus on the inventor's passion for his work and the wonder of his airships (Marantz, 1983). Alice and Martin Provensen's fascination with aviation provided inspiration for this book and the idea for the book came from their research on the history of aviation. The Provensen's extensive research and fascination with flying are evident in the accurate, intriguing illustrations of the flying machines. Detailed acrylic, pen, and ink illustrations capture Blériot's struggles and triumphs in turn-of-the-century France. This book is available on audiocassette.

Activating Prior Knowledge

Read the title of the book to the students and show them the cover. Ask them to predict what will happen in the book.

During Reading

As you read the book ask the students to listen carefully to determine why the Provensens selected Blériot as the subject for a biography.

After Reading

Use these questions to start a discussion of the book:

- Why did the Provensens find Blériot's life interesting?
- What did you learn from reading this biography?
- What questions come to mind about Blériot's flying adventures?
- Would you have flown with Blériot?
- How would flying in 1909 be different from flying today? How would it be the same?

❖ —————————
Recommended Grade Levels

4–8

Standards for the English Language Arts

1, 3, 7, 8, 9, 12

Information Literacy Standards for Student Learning

1, 2, 3, 6, 8

Objectives

The students will:

- Use print and electronic resources to select a biography subject.
————————— ❖

❖ —————————
Authors

Alice and Martin Provensen work so closely together that they cannot tell nor can their readers tell that two people did the work. They both had parents who supported their artistic endeavors, both were born in Chicago, both enjoyed reading, and both enjoyed attending daredevil flying exhibitions (Marcus, 2001). Alice and Martin Provensen received a 1982 Caldecott Honor for illustrating *A Visit to William Blake's Inn: Poems for Innocent and Experienced Travelers* (Willard, 1981). Additional information on Alice Provensen can be found on this Web site: http://www.kidspoint.org /columns2.asp?column_id=807 &column_type=author.
————————— ❖

WRITING

Mini-lesson—Choosing a Biography Subject

- Explain to the students that when deciding on a subject for this biography the Provensens began with their fascination with aviation.
- Then, they searched for someone in the field of aviation whose exploits interested them.
- Tell the students that author James Cross Giblin (2002) notes that he looks for subjects whose life stories make him curious to learn more about the person and he includes revealing anecdotes about the person when he writes a biography.
- Ask the students to make a list of things that interest them and then ask them to think of famous people who have similar interests. For example, students who are interested in sports may be interested in learning more about their favorite sports figures.
- Provide the students with access to A&E Television Network's Web site at http://www.biography.com, which contains a searchable database of biographies. Students can type in an occupation and retrieve a list of famous people in that field. They can then skim the brief biographies to find someone they are interested in researching for their biography.

Modeling

- One way to model how you selected someone for your biography would be to project the http://www.biography.com Web site on a large screen and demonstrate how to use the Web site.
- For example, type in "inventor" and from the list of inventors that appear, click on the hyperlink for Thomas Edison.
- Another way would be to explore your own personal interests and then seek out biography collections in the reference section of the library. As you browse through the collections select someone that interests you.
- Demonstrate to the students how you went about making your selection and explain your reasons for selecting that particular person.
- Describe what it was about that person that made you curious and convinced you that you wanted to learn more about the person.

Writing Activity

- Some students may immediately decide on a person they will research, so ask them to tell their classmates who they selected and why they are curious to learn more about the person. This sharing session may give other students ideas about whom they will research.
- If some students are interested in the same person allow them to research the same person as they will probably focus on different things in their reports and students will be more motivated to research people they are genuinely interested in learning more about.
- For the students who have not decided on a biography subject suggest that they brainstorm a list of their interests.
- Working from their lists, the students can access http://www.biography .com to look for biography subjects.

- Introduce students to biography collections to use in their search for people they are interested in researching. There are a few reference books listed in the resource section at the end of this chapter that contain brief biographies of famous people.
- At the end of the class period, have the students meet in small groups to discuss the person they will write about and why they selected the person.

Conferencing

- As you conference with the students, ask them if they discovered any revealing or interesting anecdotes about the person to include in the biography.
- Ask the students what was the most surprising thing they learned about the subject.
- Your questions will help the students focus on interesting aspects of the person's life.

Duke Ellington: The Piano Prince and His Orchestra

by Andrea Davis Pinkney
Illustrated by Brian Pinkney
Caldecott Honor Book, 1999

READING

Before Reading

Story Summary

As a child Duke Ellington wanted to play baseball rather than practice the piano, so he quit his piano lessons. Years later, when he heard ragtime music, he began playing the piano again but this time he played his own special ragtime rhythm. He played at parties and in pool halls. His orchestra eventually played at Harlem's swankiest nightspot, the Cotton Club, and New York's Carnegie Hall. The text contains idioms that paint vivid pictures in the reader's mind that rival the vivid pictures in the book, such as "cuttin' the rug." The rhythmic prose blends with the energetic lines of the scratchboard, gouache, and oil illustrations, making Duke Ellington's music come alive on the pages of this book (Giorgis and Johnson, 1999). Students may be interested in learning that when the Pinkneys write biographies they do a great deal of research at the library; they may also make a weekend excursion to a relevant location, and interview people who knew the person they are researching (Winarski, 1997). The book concludes with additional information about Ellington and a list of sources. This book is also available on audiocassette, videocassette, and CD. The Duke Ellington Web site at http://www.dukeellington.com includes a biography, quotes, photographs, and awards.

❖ ————————————

Recommended Grade Levels

4–12

Standards for the English Language Arts

2, 4, 6, 7, 8, 9, 12

Information Literacy Standards for Student Learning

1, 2, 3, 4, 5, 8

Objectives

The students will:

- Critically examine the illustrations to develop an appreciation of how the illustrator incorporated the sounds of the instruments into the illustrations,
- Develop an understanding of idioms, and
- Research and write about a musician or artist of their choice.

————————————— ❖

❖ ——————————————

Author

Andrea Davis Pinkney was born in Washington, DC. When she was young, Pinkney enjoyed reading and writing stories. After graduating from college with a degree in journalism, she began editing magazines and writing articles (Winarski, 1997). From there she became involved in writing and editing books. She writes both fiction and nonfiction books for toddlers to young-adult readers. Additional information about Andrea Davis Pinkney is available at http://voices.cla.umn.edu/vg/Bios/entries/pinkney_andrea_davis.html.

—————————————— ❖

❖ ——————————————

Illustrator

Brian Pinkney was born in Boston, Massachusetts. As a child, he had his own painting studio modeled after his father's (Jerry Pinkney) studio except that Brian's was smaller and located in a walk-in closet. Pinkney enjoys collaborating with his wife (Winarski, 1997). He likes illustrating stories about African Americans because it gives him an opportunity to learn more about his culture and heritage. The inspiration for his books comes from his own childhood experiences. Pinkney garnered his first Caldecott Honor for *The Faithful Friend* (San Souci, 1995). More information about Brian Pinkney is available at http://www.eduplace.com/kids/hmr/mtai/bpinkney.html.

—————————————— ❖

Activating Prior Knowledge

Listening to selections from a CD of Duke Ellington's music, such as *The Very Best of Duke Ellington* (Ellington, 2000), introduces students to this famous musician.

During Reading

While reading this biography share the illustrations with the students and show them how Pinkney wove the sounds of the instruments into the illustrations.

After Reading

Mention to the students that this biography focuses on Ellington's music and not the personal details of his life. Some of these questions can be used to start a discussion of the book:

- Why did Duke Ellington give up playing the piano as a child? Why did he begin again?
- Why do you think the biography includes only a few personal details about Ellington's life?
- What examples of figurative language did you notice in the story?
- How did the illustrations enhance the story?
- What did the illustrator do to make the pictures look like they are moving?
- What revealing anecdotes about Duke Ellington did the author include in this biography?
- Ask the students if they play a musical instrument?
- How often do they practice the instrument?
- Why did they select the instrument they play?

WRITING

Mini-lesson—Idioms

- Explain to the students that an idiom is a phrase whose meaning cannot be determined by examining the literal meaning of the words. Understanding and learning to use idioms is a skill that develops over time.
- Tell the students that examining idioms, learning to discern the meaning of idioms from their linguistic context when possible, and using idioms in their writing are strategies that help them understand idioms (Nippold, Moran, and Schwarz, 2001).
- Caution the students that while idioms add energy and spice to writing, they need to be used in moderation (Rafenstein, 1999).
- Project a copy of Figure 4-4, which includes some of the idioms in the book.
- Read the idioms with the students and help them determine the literal and figurative meanings of the idioms.
- Have the students work with you to create a wall chart of idioms for them to refer to as they write.
- Provide the students with blank paper to illustrate both the literal and figurative meanings of the idioms.
- Hang the illustrations on the wall for the students to refer to as they write.

> "fingers rode the piano keys"
> "press on the pearlies"
> "made tracks for New York City"
> "each cat took the floor"
> "cuttin' the rug"
> "ivory eighty-eights"

Figure 4-4. Idioms

Marvin Terban's books contain an extensive collection of idioms: *In a Pickle and Other Funny Idioms* (Terban, 1983), *Mad as a Wet Hen! And Other Funny Idioms* (Terban, 1987), *Punching the Clock: Funny Action Idioms* (Terban, 1990), and *Scholastic Dictionary of Idioms* (Terban, 1998). Fred Gwynne also has a collection of books filled with idioms and amusing illustrations: *The King Who Rained* (Gwynne, 1970), *A Chocolate Moose for Dinner* (Gwynne, 1976), *A Sixteen Hand Horse* (Gwynne, 1980), and *A Little Pigeon Toad* (Gwynne, 1988).

Modeling

- Select a musician as the subject of your biography and gather some research on the individual before the writing lesson.
- Select a revealing anecdote about the person.
- Introduce the musician to the students by having them listen to a musical selection.
- Begin writing the biography on the chalkboard or on an overhead transparency.
- For example, in Ray Charles's autobiography on his Web site, at http://www.raycharles.com/, there is an interesting anecdote from his childhood.
- Your biography might begin something like this:

Ray Charles
   When Wylie Pitman sat down at his piano to practice, three-year-old Ray Charles climbed on the bench beside him and began banging on the keys. Ray remembers fondly that rather than send him on his way Wylie would give him piano lessons.

- Once you have this much written ask the students to help you find a place that an idiom might fit.
- For example, another way of saying "banging on the keys" would be "tickling the ivories."
- Another way of saying "send him on his way" would be "sending him packing."
- Select only one of the idioms to incorporate into the autobiography and remind the students not to put in too many idioms.

Writing Activity

- Prior to beginning the activity, put up a bulletin board and encourage students to write the names of their favorite musicians and artists on the bulletin board.
- Introduce the students to encyclopedias such as *The Billboard Encyclopedia of Music* (DuNoyer, 2003), *The Encyclopedia of Popular Music* (Lakin, 1998), and the *Encyclopedia of Artists* (Vaughn, 2000) to provide them with resources for selecting a musician or an artist to research and write about.
- As they gather information encourage the students to focus on a particular incident or a revealing anecdote to begin their biography and to use as a focus for their research.

Conferencing

- Once the students have completed a draft of their writing, have them work with a partner or in small groups to go back through their writing and determine if they can add any idioms.

❖ ────────────────────

Recommended Grade Levels

1–6

Standards for the English Language Arts

1, 2, 3, 9, 11, 12

Information Literacy Standards for Student Learning

1, 2, 3

Objectives

The students will:

- Infer the main character's feelings,
- Complete a feelings chart, and
- Describe their feelings in writing.

──────────────────── ❖

Working Cotton

by Sherley Anne Williams
Illustrated by Carole Byard
Caldecott Honor Book, 1993

READING

Before Reading

Story Summary

Readers spend the day in the cotton fields with young migrant worker Shelan and her family, who arrive in the fields in the dark and leave the fields in the dark. Leading a harsh life does not mean the family does not have time to stop and relish the world around them. When a late cotton bloom catches her father's eye, he pauses to appreciate this gift of nature and remarks that it will bring the family good luck. More than just a day in the life of a migrant worker, this story describes a way of life told in the child's dialect. The text is based on verses from *The Peacock Poems* (Williams, 1975). The dramatic, acrylic mural-like paintings were created on Stonehenge white paper.

Activating Prior Knowledge

For students who are not familiar with the lives of migrant workers, you might introduce this story by telling them that many of the fruits and vegetables they eat are picked by workers who travel around the country picking fruits and vegetables to earn a living. The students may have read other books about migrant workers such as *Going Home* (Bunting, 1996), *Tomas and the Library Lady* (Mora, 1997), and *Harvesting Hope: The Story of Cesar Chavez* (Krull, 2003). If they have read these books, help the students make connections between the texts.

During Reading

Before reading tell the students that during the course of the story the main character, Shelan, expresses the feelings of pride, hope, weariness, impatience, and acceptance (Hurst, 2004); however, these words are not used in the story. Ask them to listen carefully and see if they can determine which feelings she is experiencing at different times in the story.

After Reading

Ask the students to describe Shelan's day. Encourage them to include their thoughts about how she was feeling at different times during the day.

Working Cotton can also be used to provide students with an opportunity to explore social issues from a critical perspective. As students examine complex social issues, they need a variety of print, electronic, fiction, and nonfiction resources as well as opportunities to delve deeply into the topic over time (Busching and Slesinger, 2002). When librarians and teachers collaborate to find these resources, they can work from their areas of expertise to provide students with an optimal environment for exploration. Some other Caldecott Medal and Honor books that are discussed in this book and can be used to explore social issues include *Tar Beach* (Ringgold, 1991), *Peppe the Lamplighter* (Bartone, 1993), *Smoky Night* (Bunting, 1994), and *Coming on Home Soon* (Woodson, 2004).

WRITING

Mini-lesson—Characterization

- Explain to the students that one way authors develop characters is to describe their feelings, desires, and experiences.
- Point out to the students that as Williams describes Shelan's day, they learn about her feelings, desires, and experiences. Williams does not tell them what Shelan is feeling; instead she describes what Shelan is feeling. For example, rather than tell readers that Shelan is "tired," the author writes "Sometime I still be sleep."
- Invite the students to return to the text and find other descriptions of Shelan's feelings. Figure 4-5 contains examples of some of Shelan's feelings.
- Ask the students about feelings, desires, and experiences they might have during the course of a day and write their responses on the board.

Author

Sherley Anne Williams was born in Bakersfield, California. She writes about her life experiences, including working in cotton fields and fruit fields alongside her parents. By the time she was sixteen, she was an orphan and she was working in cotton fields to support herself. She read books by African-American authors who wrote about their lives. These books and a caring science teacher influenced her to become a writer.

Illustrator

Carole Byard was born in Atlantic City, New Jersey. She is a sculptor and painter whose work examines humanity from the perspective of an African American and whose work reflects her life experiences (Porter, 1999). Through her work, she conveys the struggles of African Americans and women. Her sculptures usually include earth in combination with other materials including cotton, wood, canvas, mud, and branches (Murphy, 1994).

Pride	"Daddy pick so smooth and fast."
Hope	"Sometime, it's a little piece of meat in your bowl."
Tired	"Sometime I still be sleep."
Cold	". . . both sides can't get warm at once."
Acceptance	"Not big enough to have my own sack . . ."

Figure 4-5. Shelan's Feelings

Event	Feeling	Description
Waking up	Sleepy	When my alarm clock buzzes, I bury my head under my pillow and try to ignore it.
Eating breakfast	Engergized	My thoughts are racing a mile a minute as I begin thinking about all the things I have to do today.

Figure 4-6. My Feelings

- Then, have the students select one or two of the responses and suggest ways to describe the feelings without using the feeling in the description.

Modeling

- Begin by writing a brief chronology of the normal events of your day.
- For example, waking up, eating breakfast, getting dressed, driving to school, working with students, driving home, fixing dinner, grading papers, and going to bed.
- Next to each event in the list write down how you might be feeling at that time.
- Then, think of ways to describe how you are feeling rather than telling how you feel, as in Figure 4-6.

Writing Activity

Younger Students

- Give each child a blank sheet of paper.
- Ask them to draw a picture of something they do every day.
- As they finish their pictures have them write a one-sentence description about how they feel.

Older Students

- Ask the students to make a list of things they do every day either on a blank sheet of paper or a copy of the feelings chart that is in the appendix.
- Next to each item on their list, ask them to write down how they felt yesterday or today when they were doing each thing.
- Then, have them write down a description of their feelings.

Conferencing

Younger Students

- Have the students read their sentences to you and help them write the words correctly.
- If the students have not included their feelings in the sentence, help them write another sentence that includes their feelings.

Older Students

- When the students have finished writing their descriptions, have them read the descriptions to a partner.
- After they read each description aloud, have their partner tell them what feeling was described.
- If they decide that the description does not match the feeling, the students can work together to rewrite the descriptions.
- Have the students store their descriptions in their writing folder or notebook so that they can refer back to them when they are developing characters for their stories.

Bill Peet: An Autobiography

by Bill Peet
Caldecott Honor Book, 1990

READING

Before Reading

Story Summary
Peet entrances readers with the details of his life using descriptive text and profuse pencil illustrations that add drama and interest to the story. Readers relate to his life experiences, including wishing for muscles in order to make the football team, a summer in the country on his grandparents' farm, and his love of the circus. His father was a traveling salesman who was usually on the road, and when he was home he and his wife quarreled. When Peet graduated from art school he took a job filling in the colors on greeting cards and then worked for the Disney Company for twenty-seven years. While working for Disney, he began writing and illustrating children's books and one year, on his birthday, he quit Disney. Then, he began working full-time writing and illustrating children's books.

Activating Prior Knowledge
While students may be familiar with biographies written about famous people's lives, they may not be familiar with autobiographies that people have written about their own lives. Explain to the students that author Bill Peet has written his life stories to share with the readers of his books. A resource section at the end of this chapter includes a list of autobiographies written by children's book authors and illustrators for students to use as models when they write their life stories.

During Reading

This long book will take several readings to finish. In between readings have it available for students to peruse on their own so they can examine the detailed illustrations depicting Peet's life. As you read the book, keep a list of key events in Peet's life written on chart paper and hung on the wall. After you finish reading a section of the book, invite students to add to the list of events they remember from the autobiography. As

❖ ———————————————

Recommended Grade Levels

4–10

Standards for the English Language Arts

2, 4, 5, 8, 12

Information Literacy Standards for Student Learning

3, 5

Objectives

The students will:

- Use *Timeliner* software or an autobiography chart to record key events in their lives, and
- Write their autobiographies.

——————————————— ❖

Early Years	
Preschool Years	
Elementary Years	
Middle School Years	

Figure 4-7. Autobiography Chart

the reading of the book progresses, have the students begin making lists of key events in their lives using *TimeLiner* software, or they can record their thoughts on a chart like the one in Figure 4-7. A copy of Figure 4-7 is in the appendix. Encourage the students to discuss their lists or charts with their family members who can help them fill in details of their lives that they may have been too young to remember.

After Reading

These questions can help spark discussions about Peet's life:

- What event do you think had the most profound effect on his life?
- Why do you think he worked for Disney for such a long time?
- What finally made him decide to leave Disney? Why do you think he left on his birthday?

- Why do you think the attic was Peet's favorite place to draw?
- Do you have a favorite place to draw or write or just to sit and think?
- What was the most interesting thing you learned about Peet's life from reading his autobiography?
- Did anything in the autobiography surprise you?
- What historical events did you learn about in his autobiography?
- What was life like when Peet was a boy?
- What did you learn about Peet's life that reminded you of your own life?
- Was there a part of his life that you would like to know more about?

WRITING

Mini-lesson—Important Details

- Ask the students what they think was the most remarkable or memorable thing about Peet's life. Encourage them to refer back to the class list of key events that they created.
- Help the students recognize that Peet did not include every event in his life; rather, he focused on the details that had a lasting impact, such as winning a prize at the Indiana State Fair Art Exhibition for his portrait of his cousin Eli and meeting his future wife.
- Remind the students that as they write their autobiographies they need to consider which events to include as well as which ones to omit. For example, rather than including information about every birthday, they would include information about a birthday when they received a special present or had a memorable party.

Modeling

- You can use an autobiography chart such as the one in Figure 4-7 to record some of the events in your life, or simply focus on a particular aspect of your life.
- For example, I decided to begin my autobiography with all of the different places I lived as a child.

    Moving is what I remember about my childhood. By the time I was in third grade, I had lived in California, Louisiana (twice), Iowa, North Carolina (twice), and Hawaii. I had experienced life in northern, southern, eastern, and western United States and my three siblings and I were each born in a different region. Third grade was particularly memorable because my dad retired from the Marine Corps and I went to three different schools that year.

- As you write talk about your thought processes to help the students understand how you make changes, and simply write down what comes to mind knowing that you can make revisions later.

Writing Activity

- Ask the students to take out the lists or charts about their lives and allow them to work with a partner to decide which details and events they will include and which ones they will leave out.

❖

Author

As a boy, Bill Peet drew in his books and on tablets of paper. His favorite place to draw was the attic and it was such a special place that he included it in the cover illustration of his autobiography (Kerzner, 2002). In his autobiography, Peet tells of his disappointments, his struggles, and his poverty. Readers come to realize that his talent and his persistence enabled him to become the success he was. His parents' troubles and the devastating effect of his grandmother's death with its accompanying change in the family circumstances resonate with some readers. Look for additional information about Bill Peet at http://www.houghtonmifflinbooks.com/catalog/authordetail.cfm?authorID=2175.

❖

- As the students begin working, if they are unsure about what to write suggest that they reread portions of Peet's autobiography or other autobiographies in the library to gather ideas.
- As the students work, encourage them to examine which events Peet included and to look closely at his descriptions of the events.
- Encourage the students to create illustrations for their autobiographies or to bring pictures from home to include.
- Suggest that the students talk to their parents and caregivers about events to include and to provide them with additional details about the events.
- Figure 4-8 contains the first page of an autobiography written by a middle school student.

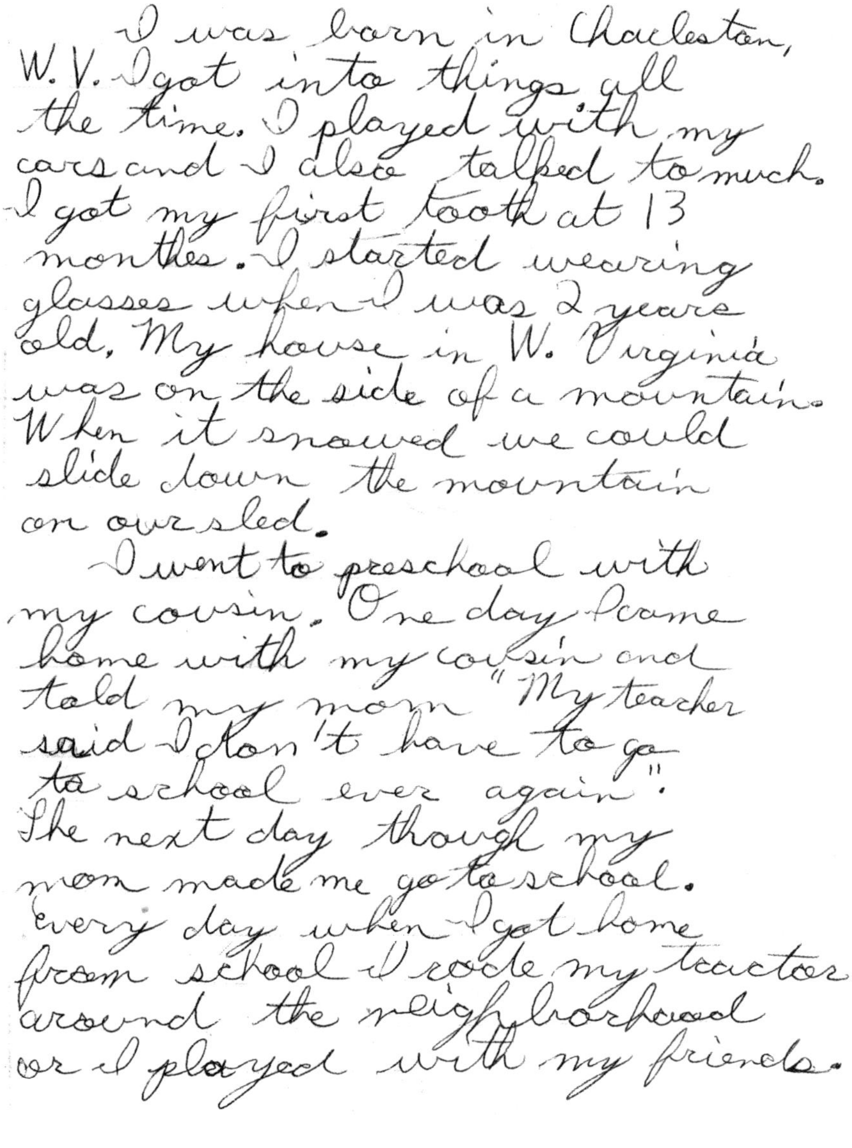

I was born in Charleston, W.V. I got into things all the time. I played with my cars and I also talked to much. I got my first tooth at 13 months. I started wearing glasses when I was 2 years old. My house in W. Virginia was on the side of a mountain. When it snowed we could slide down the mountain on our sled.

I went to preschool with my cousin. One day I came home with my cousin and told my mom "My teacher said I don't have to go to school ever again". The next day though my mom made me go to school. Every day when I got home from school I rode my teacter around the neighborhood or I played with my friends.

Figure 4-8. Autobiography

Conferencing

- Sometimes talking about ideas helps writers determine what to write next, so as you conference with the students ask them about where they are in their writing and what you can do to help them.
- Ask them to read you their favorite part of their writing or a part they think needs some work.
- As they read, write down any questions that come to you about their writing.
- When they finish reading, share your questions with them and help them determine if there are additional details they can include in their writing.

When I Was Young in the Mountains

by Cynthia Rylant
Illustrated by Diane Goode
Caldecott Honor Book, 1983

READING

Before Reading

Story Summary

The young girl in this story relishes the happy memories of life in rural West Virginia during the Great Depression. She lived with her grandparents in a home filled with love and respect for what life has to offer. The repeated refrain of "When I was young in the mountains . . ." reinforces the setting of the book and the repetition gently lulls readers into listening to the quiet melody of the words. Readers glimpse a simple life and the pleasures to be found in a cousin's baptism in the swimming hole, drawing water from a well, and a grandfather who arrives home each evening, covered with coal dust, with a kiss for a very special little girl. Watercolor illustrations set just the right tone for this loving recollection of a time gone by. In Tennessee, second graders each contribute to a class book called *When I Was Young in Nashville* (Schneider, 2002). This article contains other writing ideas and books for children to use as models for writing about special times and places in their lives.

Activating Prior Knowledge

Cynthia Rylant dedicated this book to her grandparents, with whom she lived in rural West Virginia during the Great Depression while her mother attended nursing school. Tell the students that Rylant is sharing her life with them through her recollections. Rylant writes about what matters most to her—family, friends, and pets. In this book she describes her life with her grandparents. Writing about things that are important to them gives authors powerful topics. Introduce this book by asking the students about the things that matter most to them. Write their responses on chart paper and hang the responses on the wall for them to refer back to when they are looking for topics for their writing.

❖ ─────────────

Recommended Grade Levels

2–6

Standards for the English Language Arts

1, 2, 4, 5, 9, 12

Information Literacy Standards for Student Learning

3, 5, 9

Objectives

The students will:

- Develop an understanding of how the author uses a repeated refrain to reinforce the setting, and
- Write about a personal memory using a repeated refrain to reinforce the setting.

───────────── ❖

❖ ────────────────────
Author

Cynthia Rylant was borne in Hopewell, Virginia. She sifts through her life experiences and weaves stories from them (Ward, 1993). Sometimes the words come in a rush and other times it may be weeks or months before the words come. She keeps her life quiet and simple so that when the creative urge moves her she can immediately begin writing or painting (Frederick, 1997). Rylant's own words say it best: "You have to respect whatever it is you have to do to write, and for me, this is how I have to live" (Frederick, 1997, p. 178). She has written the Lighthouse Family series, the Mr. Putter and Tabby series, and the Henry and Mudge series. This Web site has additional information about Rylant: http://www.eduplace.com/kids/hmr/mtai/rylant.html.

──────────────────── ❖

❖ ────────────────────
Illustrator

Diane Goode also writes and illustrates her own children's books. Her Italian father and her French mother took Diane and her brother to Europe every summer. They visited cathedrals and museums, which helped her develop an appreciation for art and life. Her son Peter provides critiques of her work. She sketches her illustrations lightly in pencil and then she adds watercolors. Sometimes she uses color pencils with the watercolors.

──────────────────── ❖

During Reading

Tell the students that the author repeats the title of the book throughout the text to emphasize the setting of the book. Invite them to join in each time you read the repeated refrain, "When I was young in the mountains."

After Reading

These questions can be used to start a discussion of the book:

- What words did Rylant use to describe the setting?
- Does she use the refrain on every page? Why or why not?
- How did the refrain help the author establish the setting for the book?
- What other books do you remember having read that have a repeated refrain?
- How might you use a repeated refrain when writing a memoir to help establish the setting?
- What events in your life are similar to the ones in the book?

WRITING

Mini-lesson—Setting

- Remind the students that the setting of the story includes the place and time.
- Write the repeated refrain on the board, "When I was young in the mountains."
- Point out to the students how Rylant includes both the place and time in the refrain.
- Explain to the students that in this story, Rylant uses the setting to create the mood and the background for her story.
- Refer back to the illustrations in the story to show the students how the illustrations help them understand the setting for the story.

Modeling

- Talk to the students about a favorite place that holds warm memories for you. It could be your grandparents' house, a favorite place to picnic, a place you lived as a child, or a favorite place you like to vacation.
- Brainstorm a list of words and phrases you can use in your writing to describe the place and the time. (See Figure 4-9.)
- As you write, model for the students how to use words and phrases from your list to describe the setting and your experiences.
- Your writing might look something like this.

When I was young in Hawaii, I played on hot sandy beaches as huge, blue-green waves crashed on the shore. I stayed a safe distance from the menacing waves as I built castles in the sand.

Writing Activity

- Invite the students to talk in small groups or with a partner about favorite places.

huge, blue-green waves
strong, salty waves crashing on the shore
hot, sandy beaches
cold, salty water lapping at your toes
red, gold campfires on the beach at night
loud thumps as coconuts fell from tall, swaying trees
hats woven from slim, green fronds
masses of rainbow-colored flowers

Figure 4-9. When I Was Young in Hawaii

- Working together, they can help each other think about the details that will need to be included and sort through their ideas for the one place that they remember most vividly or one they want to explore more fully through writing.
- They may choose to focus on an ordinary event in their life that they can closely examine, explore, and savor, such as their dog's joyous greeting when they arrive home from school.
- Once they decide on the memory they will write about, ask them to brainstorm a list of words to use to describe that place or event.
- Then have the students decide on a repeated refrain that reflects the setting of their recollection.
- As they write, remind the students to use words from their lists in their writing as they describe their favorite places and remind them to describe the memory rather than tell about the memory.

Conferencing

- As the students read their work to you during conferences, listen carefully.
- When they finish, briefly summarize for them what you learned about the setting for their recollection.

RESOURCES FOR LIBRARIANS AND TEACHERS

In this section of the chapter are additional autobiographies and biographies that provide models for students' writing. There are also reference books and other resource books that you will find helpful as you explore memoirs, biographies, and autobiographies with the students.

Caldecott Memoirs, Biographies, and an Autobiography

Ackerman, Karen. 1988. *Song and Dance Man*. Illustrated by Stephen Gammell. New York: Knopf.
Kerley, Barbara. 2001. *The Dinosaurs of Waterhouse Hawkins*. New York: Scholastic.
Lawson, Robert. 1940. *They Were Strong and Good*. New York: Viking.

Martin, Jacqueline Briggs. 1998. *Snowflake Bentley.* Illustrated by Mary Azarian. Boston: Houghton Mifflin.

Peet, Bill. 1989. *Bill Peet: An Autobiography.* Boston: Houghton Mifflin.

Pinkney, Andrea Davis. 1998. *Duke Ellington: The Piano Prince and His Orchestra.* Illustrated by Brian Pinkney. New York: Hyperion.

Provensen, Alice, and Martin Provensen. 1983. *The Glorious Flight: Across the Channel with Louis Blériot.* New York: Penguin.

Rappaport, Doreen. 2001. *Martin's Big Words: The Life of Dr. Martin Luther King, Jr.* Illustrated by Brian Collier. New York: Hyperion.

Ringgold, Faith. 1991. *Tar Beach.* New York: Crown.

Rylant, Cynthia. 1982. *When I Was Young in the Mountains.* Illustrated by Diane Goode. New York: Dutton.

Say, Allen. 1993. *Grandfather's Journey.* Boston: Houghton Mifflin.

Sís, Peter. 1996. *Starry Messenger.* New York: Farrar Straus Giroux.

Williams, Sherley Anne. 1992. *Working Cotton.* Illustrated by Carole Byard. New York: Harcourt Brace.

Autobiographies Written by Children's Book Authors

Berenstain, Stan, and Jan Berenstain. 2002. *Down a Sunny Dirt Road: An Autobiography.* New York: Random.

Carle, Eric. 1997. *Flora and Tiger: 19 Very Short Stores from My Life.* New York: Philomel.

Cleary, Beverly. 1988. *A Girl from Yamhill: A Memoir.* New York: Morrow.

———. 1995. *My Own Two Feet: A Memoir.* New York: Morrow.

Cole, Joanna, with Wendy Saul. 1996. *On the Bus with Joanna Cole: A Creative Autobiography.* Portsmouth, NH: Heinemann.

Crews, Donald. 1991. *Bigmama's.* New York: HarperCollins.

de Paola, Tomie. 1999. *26 Fairmont Avenue.* New York: Putnam.

———. 2000. *Here We All Are.* New York: Putnam.

———. 2002. *On My Way: A 26 Fairmont Avenue Book.* New York: Putnam.

———. 2002. *What a Year.* New York: Putnam.

———. 2003. *Things Will Never Be the Same.* New York: Putnam.

Fritz, Jean. 1982. *Homesick: My Own Story.* New York: Putnam.

Joyce, William. 1997. *The World of William Joyce Scrapbook.* New York: HarperCollins.

Lewin, Ted. 1993. *I Was a Teen-Age Professional Wrestler.* New York: Orchard.

Lowry, Lois. 1998. *Looking Back: A Book of Memories.* Boston: Houghton Mifflin.

McPhail, David. 1996. *In Flight with David McPhail.* Portsmouth, NH: Heinemann.

Naylor, Phyllis Reynolds. 2001, 1987. *How I Came to Be a Writer.* New York: Simon & Schuster.

Nixon, Joan Lowery. 2002. *The Making of a Writer.* New York: Delacorte.

Paulsen, Gary. 1998. *My Life in Dog Years.* New York: Delacorte.

Rylant, Cynthia. 1989. *But I'll Be Back Again: An Album.* New York: Scholastic.

Stevenson, James. 1986. *When I Was Nine.* New York: Greenwillow.

Biography Reference Books

Alter, Judy. 2001. *Extraordinary Explorers and Adventurers.* New York: Children's.

Ciovacco, Justine. 2003. *The Encyclopedia of Explorers and Adventurers.* New York: Franklin Watts.

Culligan, Judy, editor. 1999. *Scientists and Inventors.* New York: Macmillan Library Reference.

Daintith, John, and Derek Gjertsen, editors. 1997. *The Grolier Library of Science Biographies.* Danbury, CT: Grolier Educational.

Saari, Peggy, and Daniel B. Baker. *Explorers and Discoverers: From Alexander the Great to Sally Ride.* 1995. New York: UXL.

Saari, Peggy, and Stephen Allison, editors. 1996. *Scientists: The Lives and Works of One Hundred Fifty Scientists.* New York: Gale.

Sullivan, Otha Richard. 2002. *African American Women Scientists and Inventors.* New York: Wiley.

Webster, Raymond B. 1999. *African American Firsts in Science and Technology.* Detroit: Gale.

World Book Biographical Encyclopedia of Scientists. 2002. Chicago: World Book.

Yount, Lisa. 1998. *Asian-American Scientists.* New York: Facts on File.

———. 1999. *A to Z of Women in Science and Math.* New York: Facts on File.

Zierdt-Warshaw, Linda, Alan Winkler, and Leonard Bernstein. 2000. *American Women in Technology: An Encyclopedia.* Santa Barbara, CA: ABC–CLIO.

Books about Idioms

Gwynne, Fred. 1970. *The King Who Rained.* New York: Simon & Schuster.

———. 1976. *A Chocolate Moose for Dinner.* New York: Simon & Schuster.

———. 1980. *A Sixteen Hand Horse.* New York: Simon & Schuster.

———. 1998. *A Little Pigeon Toad.* New York: Simon & Schuster.

Terban, Marvin. 1983. *In a Pickle and Other Funny Idioms.* Boston: Houghton Mifflin.

———. 1987. *Mad as a Wet Hen! And Other Funny Idioms.* Boston: Houghton Mifflin.

———. 1990. *Punching the Clock: Funny Action Idioms.* New York: Clarion Books.

———. 1998. *Scholastic Dictionary of Idioms.* New York: Scholastic.

Books about Migrant Workers

Bunting, Eve. 1996. *Going Home.* New York: HarperCollins.

Krull, Kathleen. 2003. *Harvesting Hope: The Story of Cesar Chavez.* New York: Harcourt.

Mora, Pat. 1997. *Tomas and the Library Lady.* New York: Knopf.

Books about Social Issues

Bartone, Elisa. 1993. *Peppe the Lamplighter.* New York: Lothrop.

Bunting, Eve. 1994. *Smoky Night.* San Diego, CA: Harcourt Brace.

Ringgold, Faith. 1991. *Tar Beach.* New York: Random.

Woodson, Jacqueline. 2004. *Coming on Home Soon.* New York: Putnam.

Biography Web Sites

Biographical Dictionary
http://www.s9.com/biography
This Web site contains information on over 28,000 men and women. The information can be searched in a variety of ways, including by birth years, professions, and literary works.

Biography.com
http://www.biography.com
This Web site sponsored by A&E Television networks houses a database of over 25,000 biographies.

RESOURCES FOR STUDENTS

Students who enjoyed reading books by the authors and illustrators in this chapter might enjoy some of their other books.

Ackerman, Karen. 1994. *By the Dawn's Early Light.* New York: Atheneum.

———. 1995. *The Night Crossing.* Illustrated by Elizabeth Sayles. New York: Random.

———. 1998, 1990. *Araminta's Paint Box.* Illustrated by Betsy Lewin. New York: Simon & Schuster.

Azarian, Mary. 2000. *A Gardener's Alphabet.* Boston: Houghton Mifflin.

Baker, Olaf. 1981. *Where the Buffaloes Begin.* Illustrated by Stephen Gammell. New York: Warne.

Brown, Margaret Wise. 2004. *Christmas in the Barn.* Illustrated by Diane Goode. New York: HarperCollins.

Dunlap, Julie, and Marybeth Lorbiecki. 2002. *Louisa May & Mr. Thoreau's Flute.* Illustrated by Mary Azarian. New York: Dial.

Gammell, Stephen. 2000. *Once upon MacDonald's Farm.* New York: Simon & Schuster.

———. 2001. *How about Going for a Ride?* San Diego, CA: Harcourt.

Goode, Diane. 2001. *Tiger Trouble!* New York: Blue Sky Press.

———. 2002. *Monkey Mo Goes to Sea.* New York: Blue Sky Press.

———. 2003. *Thanksgiving Is Here!* New York: HarperCollins.

Greenfield, Eloise. 1983, 1980. *Grandma's Joy.* Illustrated by Carole Byard. New York: Philomel.

Peet, Bill. 1965. *Chester the Worldly Pig.* Boston: Houghton Mifflin.

———. 1970. *The Whingdingdilly.* Boston: Houghton Mifflin.

———. 1990. *Cock-a-Doodle Dudley.* Boston: Houghton Mifflin.

Pinkney, Andrea. 1994. *Dear Benjamin Banneker.* Illustrated by Brian Pinkney. New York: Harcourt.

———. 1996. *Bill Pickett: Rodeo-Ridin' Cowboy.* Illustrated by Brian Pinkney. New York: Harcourt.

———. 2000. *Let It Shine!: Stories of Black Women Freedom Fighters.* New York: Harcourt.

———. 2002. *Ella Fitzgerald: The Tale of a Vocal Virtuosa.* Illustrated by Brian Pinkney. New York: Jump at the Sun.

Provensen, Alice. 1990. *The Buck Stops Here: The Presidents of the United States.* New York: Harper & Row.

———. 2003. *A Day in the Life of Murphy.* New York: Simon & Schuster.

Provensen, Alice, and Martin Provensen. 2001, 1978. *The Year at Maple Hill Farm.* New York: Simon & Schuster.

Rylant, Cynthia. 1985. *The Relatives Came.* Illustrated by Stephen Gammell. New York: Simon & Schuster.

———. 1995. *Dog Heaven.* New York: Blue Sky.

———. 1997. *Cat Heaven.* New York: Blue Sky.

———. 2002. *Christmas in the Country.* Illustrated by Diane Goode. New York: Blue Sky.

San Souci, Robert D. 1995. *The Faithful Friend*. Illustrated by Brian Pinkney. New York: Simon & Schuster.

Stewart, Sarah. 1995. *The Library*. Illustrated by David Small. New York: Farrar Straus Giroux.

———. 2000. *The Gardener*. Illustrated by David Small. New York: Farrar Straus Giroux.

———. 2001. *The Journey*. Illustrated by David Small. New York: Farrar Straus Giroux.

Willard, Nancy. 1981. *A Visit to William Blake's Inn: Poems for Innocent and Experienced Travelers*. Illustrated by Martin and Alice Provensen. New York: Harcourt.

IDEAS FOR PARENTS AND CAREGIVERS

As your students write, their memoirs and autobiographies enlist their parents' and caregivers' assistance by suggesting that they construct a memory timeline with their children. The timeline might include places they have lived, special events in their lives, and favorite celebrations. Parents and guardians might also help the children gather a collection of their favorite things. These items can help the children decide on memories to include in their writing. Parents, guardians, and other relatives can share stories with the children about what they were like when they were younger. These shared memories can be included in the children's autobiographies. Some parents and guardians may be willing to write about the events with the students or come to the classroom to share the stories with your students. In *The Girl with the Brown Crayon*, Paley (1997) recounts how family members came to her first-grade classroom and told stories about their lives.

REFERENCES

Ackerman, Karen. 2003. "Ohio Authors and Illustrators for Young People." [Online] Available: http://green.upper-arlington.k12.oh.us/ohioauthors/ackerman,karen .htm [cited 17 February 2004].

———. 2004. "Karen Ackerman Books for Kids HomePage." [Online] Available: http://community-2.webtv.net/KAbooks/KarenAckermanBooks/ [cited 17 February 2004].

"Andrea Davis Pinkney." 2003. *Contemporary Authors Online*. Farmington Hills, MI: Thomson Gale.

Azarian, Mary. 1999. "Caldecott Medal Acceptance." *Horn Book* 75, no. 4 (July/August): 423–429.

Barrs, Myra. 2000. "The Reader in the Writer." *Reading* 34, no. 2 (July): 54–60.

Busching, Beverly, and Betty Ann Slesinger. 2002. *"It's Our World Too": Socially Responsive Learners in Middle School Language Arts*. Urbana, IL: The National Council of Teachers of English.

Cooper, Ilene. 1998. "Review of *Snowflake Bentley*." *Booklist* 95, no. 3 (1 October): 323.

"Diane Goode." 2000. *Contemporary Authors Online*. Farmington Hills, MI: Thomson Gale.

DuNoyer, Paul, editor. 2003. *The Billboard Encyclopedia of Music*. New York: Billboard.

Ellington, Duke. 2000. *The Very Best of Duke Ellington*. RCA. Compact disk.

Fountas, Irene C., and Gay Su Pinnell. 1996. *Guided Reading: Good First Teaching for All Children.* Portsmouth, NH: Heinemann.

Frederick, Heather Vogel. 1997. "Cynthia Rylant: A Quiet and Reflective Craft." *Publishers Weekly* 244, no. 29 (21 July): 178–179.

Freeman, Judy. 2000. "Investigating Biographies." *Library Talk* 13, no. 4 (September/October): 14–16.

Giblin, James Cross. 2002. "Biography for the 21st Century: An Author Examines His Craft and the Needs of Today's Readers." *School Library Journal* 48, no. 1 (January): 44–45.

Giorgis, Cyndi, and Nancy J. Johnson. 1999. "Children's Books: Visual Literacy." *The Reading Teacher* 53, no. 2 (October): 146–153.

———. 1999/2000. "Caldecott and Newbery Medal Winners for 1999." *The Reading Teacher* 53, no. 4 (December/January): 338–343.

Graham, Lynda. 2001. "From Tyrannosaurus to Pokemon: Autonomy in the Teaching of Writing." *Reading* 37, no. 1 (April): 18–26.

Hoss, Madeleine M. 2000. "Biography Party." *Library Talk* 13, no. 5 (November/December): 18.

Hurst, Carol Otis. 2004. "Review of Working Cotton." [Online] Available: http://www.carolhurst.com/titles/workingcotton.html [cited 13 February 2004].

"Jacqueline Briggs Martin." 2001. *Contemporary Authors Online.* Farmington Hills, MI: Thomson Gale.

Kerzner, Valerie. 2002. "Places that Inspired Writers." *Appleseeds* 4, no. 7 (March): 8–10.

Knoth, Maeve Visser. 1993. "Working Cotton." *Horn Book* 69, no. 1 (January/February): 81–82.

Lakin, Colin, editor. 1998. *The Encyclopedia of Popular Music.* New York: Muze.

Marantz, Kenneth. 1983. "Review of *The Glorious Flight: Across the Channel with Louis Blériot.*" *School Library Journal* 30, no. 12 (December): 68.

Marcus, Leonard S. 2001. "A Collaborative Effort." *Publishers Weekly* 248, no. 29 (16 July): 84–87.

McCarty, Diane, and Maribelle Betterton. 1999. "Scientifically Speaking . . . Connecting the Past." *Teaching PreK–8* 29, no. 5 (February): 48–50.

Murphy, Anthony C. 1994. "Portfolio: Various Media—Always with a Message." *American Visions* 9, no. 4 (August/September): 20–29.

Nippold, Marilyn A., Catherine Moran, and Lisa E. Schwarz. 2001. "Idiom Understanding in Preadolescents: Synergy in Action." *American Journal of Speech-Language Pathology* 10, no. 2 (May): 169–179.

Paley, Vivian Gussin. 1997. *The Girl with the Brown Crayon.* Cambridge, MA: Harvard.

Porter, Evette. 1999. "Art for Our Sake." *Essence* 21, no. 1 (May): 78–81.

Rafenstein, Mark. 1999. "Idioms: Don't Take Them Literally!" *Writing* 22, no. 1 (September): 16–19.

Ramsland, Katherine. 1990. "Writing Biographies: The Problems and the Process." *Writer* 103, no. 10 (October): 13–17.

Schneider, Dean. 2002. "When I Was Young in Nashville: Writing about the Times of Our Lives." *Book Links* 11, no. 5 (April/May): 9–14.

Schwartz, Anne. 1989. "Stephen Gammell." *Horn Book* 65, no. 4 (July/August): 456–459.

"Sherley Anne Williams." 2000. *Contemporary Authors Online.* Farmington Hills, MI: Thomson Gale.

Silvey, Anita, editor. 2002. *Children's Books and Their Creators.* Boston: Houghton Mifflin.

"Stephen Gammell." 2002. *Contemporary Authors Online.* Farmington Hills, MI: Thomson Gale.

Thomason, Tommy, and Carol York. 2000. *Write on Target: Preparing Young Writers to Succeed on State Writing Achievement Tests.* Norwood, MA: Christopher-Gordon.

TimeLiner. Version 5. Watertown, MA: Tom Snyder Productions.

Vaughn, William, editor. 2000. *Encyclopedia of Artists.* New York: Oxford University Press.

Ward, Diane. 1993. "Cynthia Rylant." *Horn Book* 69, no. 4 (July/August): 420–423.

Williams, Sherley Anne. 1975. *The Peacock Poems.* Middletown, CT: Wesleyan University Press.

Winarski, Diana L. 1997. "The Rhythm of Writing and Art." *Teaching PreK–8* 28, no. 2 (October): 38–40.

5 ❖ POETRY

Surround children with the sounds, rhythms, and language of poetry when they enter the library, in their classrooms, as they wait in lines, and as they walk down the hallways. Immerse students in poetry because they learn poetry the same way they learn language: by hearing it and using it (Higashi, 1998). Bauer (1995) suggests modeling our own excitement and enthusiasm for poetry. Poet Mel Glenn advocates reading poetry aloud with passion in order to grab students' attention (Lesesne, 1998a). Frequent, pleasurable encounters with poetry demonstrate to students that poetry is fun and enjoyable. Frequent poetry encounters help students understand how poetry shows us the extraordinary in the ordinary (Potts, 2004). The more poetry that children hear the more poetry they will understand (Schliesman, 2004).

Students of all ages and ability levels can succeed at reading and writing poetry. The nonsense in Mother Goose rhymes encapsulates children's worlds where everything is alive and so matches their experience of the world (Willard, 2001). *The Rooster Crows* (Petersham and Petersham, 1945), a Caldecott Medal winner, contains familiar nursery rhymes, songs, jingles, and finger plays that are perfect for introducing poetry to young writers. Begin by reading aloud poetry written or selected for children in order for them to understand and appreciate the meaning (Schliesman, 2004). Read aloud poetry written by children from *Salting the Ocean: 100 Poems by Young Poets* (Nye, 2000). Miguez (2005) suggests having a poetry file of favorite poems, developing a poetry unit with teachers, and staging impromptu poetry breaks as ways to surround children with poetry.

Spark students' interest in poetry by creating a poetry corner in the library. Display books of poetry and feature pictures of faculty and staff members next to copies of their favorite poems. In addition to poetry books, include pictures, photographs, and interesting objects for inspiration; and pencils, pens, makers, and paper for writing. When classes come to the library or you work with students in their classrooms, start each lesson by sharing a poem to quickly and easily engage students in poetry. The library media specialist and the teacher might each share one of their favorite poems by reading them aloud with expression and feeling (Timblin, 1998). Project a copy of a poem related to the lesson topic, state the title of the poem and the author's name. Former Poet Laureate Billy Collins (2004) suggests that you read the poem slowly in a relaxed voice and pause only when there are punctuation marks. Encourage the students to join you as you read the poem a second time.

Brightman (1998) works with teachers to engage the students in a weekly poetry writing activity that begins in the library and continues in their classrooms. Before they can write poetry students need to be exposed to lots of poetry, so they have models in their heads of what poetry sounds like, feels like, and looks like. Modeling their own poems after ones they have read helps young poets discover their own voice (Certo, 2004). Livingston (1991) reminds students that we learn by imitating others and that when we feel confident we experiment and develop our own writing style. Routman (2000; 2001) suggests this model for the poetry-writing process: ten to fifteen minutes of the teacher or librarian reading aloud poems written by students; ten to twenty minutes where the instructor models how to write a poem and talks about the process; five to ten minutes of brainstorming ideas with the students; twenty to twenty-five minutes of sustained writing; and ten to fifteen minutes of sharing what the students have written. Routman (2001) enjoins us not to be afraid to write a poem on the spot in front of students, as they need to see us as writers and risk takers. When they see us struggle for words and make mistakes, they know that it is acceptable for them to struggle with their writing and make mistakes. Poetry is all around us; we just need to stop and look for it.

Noah's Ark

by Peter Spier
Caldecott Medal Winner, 1978

READING

Before Reading

Story Summary

Noah's Ark begins with Spier's translation of "The Flood" by seventeenth-century Dutch poet Jacobus Revius. The poem fills one page and the remainder of the book is wordless. The poem recounts the story of the great flood in couplets, two lines of poetry that rhyme. The second two-page spread shows animals filing into the ark two by two and Noah's family members holding back the animals that will not get on the ark. As the water begins to rise, the animals that are left behind slowly disappear beneath the water. The trials and tribulations of living with and caring for an ark full of animals are depicted with humor and emotion. When the water recedes Noah, his family, and the animals clamor off the ark, leaving behind a colossal mess. The story continues on the endpapers with a glorious rainbow and Noah and his family farming the land and caring for the animals. Energetic, detailed illustrations created in line and watercolor washes portray a realistic account of life aboard the ark. Each time readers look at the intricate illustrations they discover something new as the illustrations of the interior of the ark depict daily life filled with mini-dramas (Silvey, 2002). Two other books about Noah's ark received Caldecott Honors. In *One Wide River to Cross*, Barbara Emberley (1966) adapted an American folk song about Noah's ark and Ed Emberley illustrated the book with woodcuts. Jerry Pinkney (2002) used detailed watercolor and pencil illustrations accompanied by powerful prose to tell the story of the great flood in *Noah's Ark*.

Activating Prior Knowledge

Show the students the cover of the book and read the title aloud. Ask the students what they know about Noah and the ark. Then, have one or two students retell the story.

During Reading

Read the poem aloud twice, sharing the illustrations with the students. Since the illustrations are small and detailed, this would work best with a small group of students or with several copies of the book for small groups to share. Explain that the poem is written in couplets, two lines of poetry that rhyme. Have the students read the poem

❖ ─────────────

Recommended Grade Levels

4–8

Standards for the English Language Arts

3, 4, 5, 6, 8

Information Literacy Standards for Student Learning

5, 8

Objectives

The students will:

- Carefully examine the detailed illustrations, and
- Write couplets using the illustrations for ideas.

───────────── ❖

❖ ─────────────

Author

Peter Spier was born in Amsterdam and attended the Royal Academy of Art. His family moved to Houston, Texas, in 1951, after he and his father visited the United States. In celebration of Spier's winning the Caldecott Medal, he received his father's collection of Randolph Caldecott works (Smedman, 1987). The collection consists of many first editions of Caldecott's books including one that Spier scribbled in with a red crayon when he was three years old. He received a Caldecott Honor for *The Fox Went Out on a Chilly Night* (Spier, 1961).

───────────── ❖

aloud with you so that they can see and hear the rhyming words. Read through the poem again having the students each read a couplet.

After Reading

Show the students how the poet lists the animals that clamored on board the ark but also gives some descriptions of them, such as "Good and mean, Foul and clean" or he describes their movements: "All that walked, crawled or stalked." As the students examine the illustrations, have them describe the "mini-dramas" in the illustrations. Ask them to close their eyes and imagine they are standing on the ark. "What would you hear? What would you smell?"

WRITING

Mini-lesson—Couplets

- Explain to the students that they are going to write their own couplets describing what they see in the illustrations.
- Write two of the poem's couplets on the board and point out the words that rhyme.
- Ask the students for other words that rhyme.
- Introduce the students to rhyming dictionaries such as *Merriam-Webster's Rhyming Dictionary* or *The Scholastic Rhyming Dictionary*.
- If Web access is available, show them Rhyme Zone located at http://www.rhymezone.com. On this Web site students can type in a word and find rhyming words, synonyms, and definitions.

Modeling

- Select a page of illustrations to use to model writing poems to go with the illustrations. For example, the left page of the seventh double page spread contains four small illustrations.
- Model for the students how to write couplets to describe what they see in each of the pictures.
- In the first illustration, Noah is feeding insects in jars. Therefore, your first line might be "Insects in jars" or "Bugs in jars."
- Then, brainstorm words that rhyme with jars.
- Try changing the first sentence to "Jars of bugs." What words rhyme with bugs?
- Try describing what is happening in the picture. Noah seems to be feeding them or watching them.
- As you write, tell the students what you are thinking and ask the students for suggestions as you work together to create couplets to accompany each picture.
- Once the students begin working on their poetry, you can continue working on your poem to make changes.
- You might end up with something like this:

Life on Noah's Ark

Noah caring,
Always sharing,
Dining on fish,

They're delish.
Lions curious,
Noah serious.
Standing pat,
Elephant and rat.

Writing Activity

- Place several copies of the book open to different illustrations on tables for the students to refer to as they work.
- As students finish writing about one set of illustrations encourage them to revise what they have written or select another set of illustrations as inspiration for additional couplets.
- Remind the students to consult the rhyming dictionaries.
- Finding rhyming words that make sense is sometimes difficult. Students who are struggling to find rhyming words can be reassured that it is acceptable to have lines that do not rhyme as it is more important that they write.

Conferencing

- During conferences, the students can read what they have written to the students seated near them and to themselves (Calkins, 1994).
- Reading poetry aloud helps writers determine which words sound just right and which words or parts of the poem to revise.
- Listening to other students' poems gives the students ideas for their own poems.
- Provide time for the students to read their poems to their classmates.

Time of Wonder

by Robert McCloskey
Caldecott Medal Winner, 1958

READING

Before Reading

Story Summary

This poem chronicles the adventures of two young girls as they spend the summer on an island in Maine. Shore birds, a foggy morning, the excitement of sailing, the quiet of the night, the sudden terror of a hurricane, and the peace of a Maine island are described in poetic language and vibrant, evocative watercolors. Realistic illustrations depict life's simple pleasures including soft, sudden, summer rain; fiddlehead ferns unfurling; sailing excursions; and swimming with friends. This book is available on audiocassette, videocassette, and CD.

Activating Prior Knowledge

McCloskey's love for the island off the coast of Maine where he lived is evident in this poem. He invites readers to share the experiences of two young girls as they explore

❖ ─────────────

Recommended Grade Levels

5–10

Standards for the English Language Arts

1, 2, 5, 6, 11, 12

Information Literacy Standards for Student Learning

4, 5

Objectives

The students will:

- Examine a poem of direct address, and
- Write a poem of direct address.

─────────────── ❖

❖ ————————————
Author

Robert McCloskey's stories come from his own life experiences (Isaac, 2004). He writes about events in his childhood or things that happened to his children. He grew up in a small town in Ohio and spent his adult life living on an island off the coast of Maine. These familiar settings are depicted in his stories and illustrations. Through his books readers come to know what mattered most to him, what inspired him, and what he valued (Isaac, 2004). He was the first artist to win the Caldecott Medal twice. He won it for *Time of Wonder* (McCloskey, 1957) and for *Make Way for Ducklings* (McCloskey, 1941). He received Caldecott Honors for illustrating *Journey Cake, Ho!* (Sawyer, 1953); and writing *One Morning in Maine* (McCloskey, 1952) and *Blueberries for Sal* (McCloskey, 1948). His wife, Margaret Durand, was a children's librarian and his mother-in-law, Ruth Sawyer, was a Newbery Medal–winning author (Silvey, 2002).

———————————— ❖

the island. The poem, written in second person, directly addresses readers. Sears (1990) calls this a "you" poem, which is a powerful means of personally involving readers in the poem. Janeczko (1994) refers to poetry written in the second person as a poem of direct address.

During Reading

By using the word "you" in this poem McCloskey directly addresses the readers and intimately involves them in the young girls' adventures. Readers feel as if they are on the coast of Maine with the girls as they explore the seashore and experience the weather changes. Before you read the poem aloud ask the students to listen closely so they can feel the summer rain splattering on them, feel the sand between their toes, and feel the warmth of the sun on their faces.

After Reading

Have the students examine the illustrations to see how McCloskey used color to depict the changes in the weather. Reread parts of the poem with the word "you" to help students understand how it encourages them to become personally involved with the adventures in the poem.

WRITING

Mini-lesson—Poem of Direct Address

- Poems of direct address or "you" poems are personal poems written to a specific audience, either a person or a thing, and they describe or tell about something that means a great deal to the writer.
- One way to start this mini-lesson is by reading other "you" poems such as the ones written by students in *Gonna Bake Me a Rainbow Poem* (Sears, 1990).
- Sharing these poems with the students provides them with additional models and ideas for writing their own poems.

Modeling

- Think about an event in your life that you would like to share with your students, such as a vacation or receiving a special birthday present.
- Write a short poem about the experience, using second person to have the students feel that they are present and the event is happening to them.
- As you write, have the students help you find just the right words to describe the experience.
- For example, this poem started with "The doorbell rings," which was replaced by the sounds of the doorbell. The box originally described as "brown" and was changed to "cardboard."
- Your poem might look something like this:

Package in the Mail

Brrrriing! Brrrriing! Brrrriing!
You open the door.
Thrust into your hands,
A small cardboard box.

Carefully you slice through the tape,
Inside a second box.
Curiosity rising,
You lift the lid,
You peek inside.
A tiny black velvet box.
You open it,
An opal ring.

Writing Activity

- Explain to the students that "you" poems require the poet to have an audience in mind, so they need to first decide on a particular person or a thing they will write to in their poem.
- Once they have determined their audience, they can decide what they are going to describe to that person.
- Janeczko (1994) suggests that the poem express feelings you have been keeping to yourself such as anger, admiration, respect, thanks, or bewilderment.
- Ask the students to brainstorm a list of things they might write about, such as a field trip, a special occasion, a surprising event, or a vacation. Brainstorming should lead them to topics they care about and find exciting.
- Share with the students that Robert McCloskey started his books with lots of ideas in his head, he imagined lots of pictures, and he wrote about his life experiences (Silvey, 2002).
- Explain to them that they want to write about something that actually happened to them or something they feel so that as they write they can stop and reflect on how they felt, what they saw, what they heard, and what they smelled.
- As they write, remind them to vividly capture the event or experience for their readers.

Conferencing

- Listen carefully as the students read their poems.
- Ask them to clarify things that do not paint a vivid picture in your mind or ask them questions about the event to help them determine what else needs to go into the poem.
- Remind them that each line in the poem should contain only one thought (Fletcher, 2002).
- Have the students read their poems aloud and listen for natural pauses to help them determine where to put in line breaks.

❖ ——————————

Recommended Grade Levels

1–4

Standards for the English Language Arts

3, 5, 6, 12

Information Literacy Standards for Student Learning

3, 4, 5, 9

Objectives

The students will:

- Examine a poem with a repeated refrain, and
- Write a free verse poem with a repeated refrain.

—————————— ❖

❖ ——————————

Author

Freelance writer Janice May Udry was a born in Jacksonville, Illinois. She lived with her husband, a teacher, and their two daughters in Chapel Hill, North Carolina. As a child she developed a love of reading.

—————————— ❖

❖ ——————————

Illustrator

Marc Simont was born in Paris, France, and spent his childhood in France, Spain, and the United States. His father was a magazine artist and this influenced Simont's decision to become an illustrator (Marcus, 2004). As an art student at New York's National Academy of Design he developed the lifelong habit of carrying a sketchbook and making quick sketches of people wherever he went (Marcus, 2004). He earned Caldecott Honors for *The Happy Day* (Kraus, 1949) and *The Stray Dog* (Simont, 2002). He illustrated Marjorie Weinman Sharmat's Nate the Great series.

—————————— ❖

A Tree Is Nice

by Janice May Udry
Illustrated by Marc Simont
Caldecott Medal Winner, 1957

READING

Before Reading

Story Summary

Udry invites readers to pause and consider all the benefits of trees such as limbs to climb, homes for birds, fruit to pick, shady retreats, sticks for writing, and shelter from the weather. The poem concludes with instructions for planting a tree and watching it grow. This free-verse poem with a repeated refrain explores the wonders of trees. The title appears throughout the poem as a repeated refrain, which gives the poem a predictable structure that students can model when they write their own poems. Watercolor illustrations alternate with black-and-white illustrations throughout the book, and young readers will find themselves and their families in the illustrations. This book is available on audiocassette.

Activating Prior Knowledge

Read the title of the book and ask the students why they think the author would write about why a tree is nice. Ask them to predict what the author will have to say about a tree.

During Reading

Invite the students to join you in reciting the repeated refrain as you read the poem. A refrain holds poems together (Janeczko, 1999) and provides structure to poems. Read the poem a second time and pause before each repeated refrain.

After Reading

Reread the stanza that begins with "A tree is nice because it makes shade." Write the stanza on the board or project a copy of the stanza for the students to see. Help the children recognize that the sentences that follow describe what happens in the shade of trees. The repeated refrain "A tree is nice" cues readers in to what is coming next in the poem.

WRITING

Mini-lesson—Free Verse with a Repeated Refrain

- Explain to the students that free verse is the easiest type of poetry to write. It does not have to rhyme and the lines vary in length, but free verse is not just writing down anything. It has a structure, which might include repetition, sound patterns, syllable counts, word stress, or rhyme (Livingston, 1991). This repetition sets up a structure to the poem that guides students as they write.

- Tell the students that, just as Udry did, they are going to select one object as the focus of their poem and brainstorm a list of attributes of the object.
- Refer back to the poem to show them again how the refrain sets the stage for what comes next about the tree.
- Caution the students that when using a refrain in a poem it should be something that is important to the poem or it could be boring (Janeczko, 1999).

Modeling

- Karla Kuskin (2004) suggests that you carefully study the object you have decided to write about and think about what makes that object special.
- Then, she suggests that you use words to paint a picture of the object.
- You might want to decide on an object and the title/repeated refrain before class begins in order to find something important to you to write about. For example, the Mississippi River is special to people who have spent time on the river and its banks.
- Show the students pictures of the river.
- Talk about times you spent on the river.
- Brainstorm a list of words to describe the river.
- Then, reread parts of *A Tree Is Nice* and try to model your sentences after Udry's.
- Your poem might look something like this:

The Mighty Mississippi

The mighty Mississippi is a muddy, brown river.
We sit on the banks and watch it flow past.
Water ripples.
The mighty Mississippi is a panorama of sights, sounds.
Tugboats push barges around the bend and out of site.
Whistle sounds.

Writing Activity

- Suggest to the students that they pick something they are familiar with and enjoy. This might be their pet, a favorite toy, or a special place.
- Ask the students to brainstorm a list of words to describe the object or the place they have decided on.
- Tell them to look at their list of words and decide on a repeated refrain to use in their poems.
- Remind them to use the repeated refrain as the title and throughout the poem as they write.
- Continue writing and revising your poem as the students begin writing theirs.

Conferencing

- After about ten minutes circulate through the classroom and help any students who are struggling with their poems.
- If several students are struggling you might have them join you at a round table where they can work together and help one another.
- After twenty minutes of sustained writing, ask the students to conference in small groups by reading their poems to each other.

- The students should respond to the poem by stating what they liked about the poem and what interested them.
- At the end of the conferences have each group select one poem to read aloud to the class. If the student who wrote the chosen poem does not want to read it aloud, ask if he or she will let another student from the group read it aloud.

The Spider and the Fly

by Mary Botham Howitt
Illustrated by Tony DiTerlizzi
Caldecott Honor Book, 2003

READING

Before Reading

Story Summary

Mary Botham Howitt's familiar 1829 poem is about a vain, innocent fly and the cunning, fiendish spider that lures her into his web with flattery. Howitt wrote the poem for her own children as a warning about those who use flattery to hide their real intentions. Ghostly remnants of past victims and a gruesome dinner table spread give readers clues as to the eventual fate of the hapless fly. The book concludes with a warning letter from the spider and information about the author and illustrator. Tony DiTerlizzi's black-and-white illustrations of the flapper fly and the dapper spider reflect his fascination with 1920s and 1930s classic horror movies.

Activating Prior Knowledge

Explain to the students that this poem is composed of sestets or six-line stanzas consisting of three couplets. The illustrator divided each stanza in two with the first four lines of the stanza on one two-page spread and the last two lines of the stanza on the next two-page spread. The rhythmic, lilting verse ensnares listeners just as the spider ensnares the fly, and the eerie black-and-white illustrations set just the right spooky, suspenseful tone for this tale of impending doom. Share the illustrations with the students to set the stage for reading the poem.

During Reading

Read the poem aloud with feeling and expression to lure the students into the poem and set up the suspense for the unfortunate ending. Suggest that they pay close attention to the details in the pictures to help them figure out how the poem will end. This is a great poem for students to perform. Divide the students into groups of three. One student will read the narrator's lines, one will read the spider's lines, and the third will read the fly's lines. Give them an opportunity to practice their lines and then let the groups perform for their classmates.

Recommended Grade Levels

6–12

Standards for the English Language Arts

1, 2, 3, 5, 6, 12

Information Literacy Standards for Student Learning

3, 5

Objectives

The student will:

- Critically examine the illustrations to predict the ending of the poem, and
- Write a poem with rhyming words.

After Reading

Rather than warn her children about the motives of people who flatter them and offer them compliments, Howitt wrote this cautionary poem. She did not lecture her children; instead she offered them a story about the evil that could befall them by listening to charming, cunning people who are intent on doing them harm. Notice that instead of using people she used animals that do harm to each other. If the students are familiar with fables, you might note that, like fables, this poem contains a cautionary message and has animal characters. Ask the students about warnings they have received from their parents, such as not talking to strangers, the harmful effects of smoking, staying away from drugs, or looking both ways before they cross the street.

WRITING

Mini-lesson—Rhyming Words

- Tell the students that poet Jack Prelutsky (2004) brainstorms rhyming words as a way to warm up before he begins writing.
- Demonstrate this to the students by having them help you brainstorm words that rhyme with the three pairs of rhyming words from the stanzas in the poem. For example, the rhyming words in the top line of the chart are from the first stanza of the poem.
- Draw a chart similar to the one in Figure 5-1 on chart paper or an overhead transparency and record the words the students brainstorm.

Modeling

- Show the students how they can write a variation of Howitt's poem by replacing some of her words with their own words.
- Ask the students to name animals that prey on other animals. For example, cats eat birds.
- Begin writing your poem and talk aloud to explain your thought processes and revisions to the students.
- For example, in the poem below the word "birds" was replaced with "jay" because it is an easier word to rhyme.
- Your poem might look something like this:

The Cat and the Blue Jay

"Welcome to my feeder," said the cat to the blue jay,

fly/spy	stair/there	vain/again
die	hair	lane
my	dare	stain
rye	mare	rain
sigh	rare	main

Figure 5-1. Rhyming Words

Author

Mary Botham Howitt was an English poet, author, and translator born in 1821. She translated Hans Christian Anderson's fairy tales (Silvey, 2002). Her translations made the fairy tales easier to read and understand, which led to changes in the style of writing used in children's books (Lancashire, 2003). Howitt and her husband William were both writers and they helped launch other writers, including John Keats. It is interesting to note that the illustrator, Tony DiTerlizzi, also helps other artists get started on their careers. Selected poetry and notes on her life are available on the Web at http://eir.library.utoronto .ca/rpo/display/poet171.html. Additional information on her and photographs of her former house are available at http://www.maryhowitt .co.uk/index1.htm.

Illustrator

As a child Tony DiTerlizzi dreamed of writing and illustrating his own book and today he helps other young artists fulfill their dreams by offering advice to them on his Web site, which is available at http://www.diterlizzi .com/. On his Web site, students can read his biography, which contains hyperlinks to additional information about his work. For example, clicking on the hyperlink for *The Spider and the Fly* takes students to an interactive mansion with different rooms. The drawing room contains early pencil sketches and concepts for the book. DiTerlizzi's work includes adult science fiction, and some of the pages on his Web site may not be appropriate for students.

"It has a tantalizing buffet,
Shiny, black sunflower seeds,
More than enough to suit your needs."
Squawked the jay, "You are a gracious host,
As I have often heard you boast."

Writing Activity

- Place several copies of the poem around the classroom for the students to refer to as they write.
- Tell the students to begin by thinking about animals in the food chain that they can incorporate into the poem.
- As they write, encourage them to return to the book if they cannot think of what to write.
- Mention to the students that sometimes poems are meant to rhyme and if they are meant to rhyme they start out rhyming (Stevens, 1997). You cannot force a poem to rhyme if it was not meant to rhyme.
- Hence, tell the students to just let the words flow and then try to revise them so they rhyme.

Conferencing

- Since the mini-lesson started with a reference to Jack Prelutsky, you might want to share his thoughts on revising during conferences with the students. Prelutsky (2004) revises at least once but usually four or five times.
- Willard (2001) offers this advice to poets: Sometimes poems need time to simmer. If the students are struggling with their poems, they may find it beneficial to put them in their writing folders and return to them later.

Recommended Grade Levels

2–5

Standards for the English Language Arts

2, 3, 5, 6, 12

Information Literacy Standards for Student Learning

3, 4, 5

Objectives

The students will:

- List family activities and holidays that occur during each month of the year, and
- Write poems with quatrains.

A Child's Calendar

by John Updike
Illustrated by Trina Schart Hyman
Caldecott Honor Book, 2000

READING

Before Reading

Story Summary

The poems in *A Child's Calendar* explore the months of the year through the eyes of children, focusing on events and activities that children will recognize. Set in New England, the vibrant, lively illustrations depict multicultural families as they play in the snow, watch flowers unfold, frolic on the beach, and jump in leaves. The book is a joyous celebration of the uniqueness of each month of the year. First published in 1965 with illustrations by Nancy Ekholm Burkert, this book contains updated versions of the poems and illustrations by Trina Schart Hyman. The pen, ink, and watercolor illustrations fill one page of the two-page spread and the poems share the other page with smaller illustrations. This book is available on audiocassette and CD.

Activating Prior Knowledge

Before reading this book, write the months of the year on the chalkboard and ask the children what things happen during each month. As they respond, write their ideas on the board next to the months. They will probably focus on holidays so you might ask them about what the weather is like and what they will be doing during that month. Children who live in areas without the distinct seasons noted in this book may describe similar activities throughout the year.

During Reading

Pause after reading each poem and have the students talk about the activities associated with that month. Help the students make connections to the families in the poems and the families' activities.

After Reading

After reading the poems, return to the lists on the board and ask the students what other activities they would like to add for the months of the year. When writing about the months of the year, Updike included information about the weather in the first stanza and then describes nature and activities, so help the students discover that pattern in the poetry. Reread one of the poems and ask the students to describe the weather in the poem and in the illustrations. Then, ask them about the different activities noted in the poem and in the illustrations.

WRITING

Mini-lesson—Quatrains

- Tell the students that the poems in this book are quatrains, four-line stanzas, with the second and fourth lines rhyming. Quatrains are the most used rhyming form and they often follow the pattern of the second and fourth lines rhyming (Livingston, 1991).
- Project one of the poems for the students to examine.
- Ask the students to count the number of stanzas in the poems. Each poem consists of four or five stanzas.
- Help the students determine the rhyming pattern in the poems.
- Point out to the students that the first stanza of the poem describes the weather and the other stanzas describe nature and the activities common to the month.

Modeling

- Tell the students that you are going to write a poem about the month in which you were born.
- Read aloud the ideas that the students have generated about the weather and the activities associated with that month.

Author

This prolific, talented writer, John Updike, is best known for his adult novels. However, he writes in a variety of genres including poems, essays, reviews, and short stories. His works reflect his interest in American middle-class families' inner lives, the common details of those lives, and the ordinary particulars of those lives such as fine, handmade furniture or a mowed field (Greiner, 1994). These details of American life are highlighted in this collection of poems celebrating the simple pleasures of a family, their friends, and their pets. Updike's father was a math teacher and his mother was an author.

Illustrator

Trina Schart Hyman grew up in a rural area outside of Philadelphia and now lives in New Hampshire, the setting for the illustrations in this book. When she is asked to illustrate a book set in a particular period she researches pictures of the period found in books in her personal library, the public library, and in bookstores. She works on only one book or book jacket at a time so that nothing intrudes on her imaginary world. Characters in her books are often family, friends, and neighbors. She uses a variety of media including Crayola crayons (Hyman, 2002). She has illustrated two other Caldecott books, *Little Red Riding Hood* (Grimm, 1983) and *Hershel and the Hanukkah Goblins* (Kimmel, 1989), and she won a Caldecott Medal for *Saint George and the Dragon* (Hodges, 1984). Additional information about Hyman is available at http://avatar.lib.usm.edu/~degrum/findaids/hyman.htm.

- Start your poem with a description of the weather; then describe what is happening in nature and any special holidays.
- Your poem might look something like this:

October in the South

Some days are sunny,
Soft breezes blow.
Most days are hot,
Grass we mow.

Leaves shrivel, die,
Flutter down.
No riotous colors,
Only brown.

Bears or hairy monsters,
We are not.
Halloween is much
Too hot.

Writing Activity

- Introduce the students to other poems about the months of the year and the seasons, such as *The Random House Book of Poetry* (Prelutsky, 1983) or *Pieces: A Year in Poems and Quilts* (Hines, 2001).
- Provide the students with a rhyming dictionary or access to http://www .rhymezone.com, to help them find just the right rhyming words.
- Have the students begin by deciding on the month they will write about in their poems.
- Then have them look at the list of activities the class generated for that month and encourage them to add to the list.
- If students are struggling to get the second and fourth lines to rhyme, encourage them to just write four-line stanzas without the rhymes.
- A group of fourth- and fifth-grade boys for whom English was a second language were struggling to find words that rhymed and to follow the patterns in the poems they read, so they collaborated with the teacher to compose this cautionary poem.
- Their triumph in composing the poem and sharing it with others was more important than whether or not they followed the pattern.

Conferencing

- As you conference with the students remind them that the poems in this book were originally published in 1965 and that they were updated and revised in 1999.
- Tell the students that even after their work is published authors continue to revise their writing.
- As you visit with the students share your revisions to your poem.

Don't Fly with a Witch

Flying in the sky at 12:00 at night
Riding on a yellow broom
to a haunted house
Rode a hairy, scary witch!

Holding to the broom
Was a black as night cat
Who was about to jump down to the roof
When the witch pushed him!

SPLAT!

That was the end of the cat!

Figure 5-2. Don't Fly with a Witch

Harlem: A Poem

by Walter Dean Myers
Illustrated Christopher Myers
Caldecott Honor Book, 1998

READING

Before Reading

Story Summary

Forceful words and powerful images portray the rich history of Harlem through images, sights, and sounds. Music, literature, and art; and hope, despair, pride, and determination tell the story of Harlem. The poem praises Harlem and recognizes it as a symbol of black American culture and community (Bishop, 1998). Paint, ink, and cut-paper collages depict life in Harlem and introduce readers to the men, women, and children who live there. The collages portray Christopher's perception of Harlem and

Recommended Grade Levels

4–12

Standards for the English Language Arts

1, 2, 5, 6, 9, 12

Information Literacy Standards for Student Learning

3, 5, 9

Objectives

The students will:

• Participate in a choral reading of the poem,

• Identify examples of personification in the poem, and

• Write poems with personification.

Author

Walter Dean Myers advocates looking to the past to make progress into the future (Silvey, 2002). Through his books, he creates windows into the world so that readers can share his images, feelings, thoughts, and delight (Myers, 2002). He grew up in Harlem and was raised by foster parents who instilled in him a love of reading. As he read, he imagined himself as the characters in the books (Myers, 2002). As he writes, characters in his books come to life in his imagination, and at times he talks aloud to them. He remembers that some of his teachers recognized his writing talent and encouraged him to write (Bishop, 1998). In school the other children teased him because of his speech impediment, and he eventually dropped out of school at seventeen and joined the army.

Illustrator

This book, written by his father, was Christopher Myers' picture book debut (Bishop, 1998). As a child, Christopher visited Harlem with his father, who shared his memories of growing up in Harlem. Those recollections and visits shaped the illustrations in the book. Christopher focused on portraying the architecture of Harlem with its red brick and fences (Bishop, 1998). He enjoys sharing his work with students and tells them about how he writes and illustrates what he knows. He wants to help readers understand Brooklyn, where he grew up, and Harlem, which is so much a part of his family (Merina, 2004).

he wants others to know and understand where he is coming from (Merina, 2004). This book is available on videocassette.

Activating Prior Knowledge

In this poem, Water Dean Myers writes about his own life experiences growing up in Harlem. His son Christopher introduces readers to the Harlem he knows through his collage illustrations. Through words and images, father and son have created a tribute to Harlem, a place they know well and want to share with others. Sharing books about the Harlem Renaissance can provide background information to help students understand the images in the poem. Consider sharing these books with the students: *Shimmy Shimmy Shimmy Like My Sister Kate: Looking at the Harlem Renaissance Through Poems* (Giovanni, 1996), *The Dream Keeper and Other Poems* (Hughes, 1993), *The Great Migration* (Lawrence, 1993), and *Harlem Stomp! A Cultural History of the Harlem Renaissance* (Hill, 2003).

During Reading

The rhythmic, song-like quality of this poem springs from the pages as you read it aloud, which lends the poem to dramatic presentations. Read the poem aloud to the students once and share the pictures with them. Additional readings of the poem can be by small groups or partners in the form of a choral reading. Each group or pair could practice and read one page from the poem. As the students practice, circulate among them to make sure they understand the meanings of the words they are reciting. The students can stand in their groups or with their partners lined up around the room to perform their readings.

After Reading

After reading the poem, encourage students to talk about the feelings the poem and the illustrations evoke. Did they understand the hope, despair, pride, and determination of the people described in the poem? Can they make connections between the lives of the people in Harlem and their own lives? What would they like to tell people about their own lives? What thoughts do they have about sharing their lives with others? After the discussion, the students can perform the poem again expressing the feelings they discussed.

WRITING

Mini-lesson—Personification

- Explain to the students that personification assigns human qualities to inanimate objects and brings a freshness to a poem that lets the imagination soar (Livingston, 1991).
- Tell the students that Myers uses personification to make the scenes he is describing come to life.
- Write examples of personification found in Harlem on the board. (See Figure 5-3.)
- Invite the students to look back in the poem and find other examples. Also, have them share other examples of personification that they remember from other texts.

> "Heavy hearted tambourine rhythms"
> "Colors loud enough to be heard"
> "A chorus of summer herbs"
> "Like a scream torn from the throat of an ancient clarinet"

Figure 5-3. Personification

Modeling

- Tell the students that the poet Janeczko (1999) uses these techniques for creating personification: begin by choosing an object and practice different ways to ascribe to it human body parts; describe it with verbs that depict human actions; or use a personal pronoun to refer to the object.
- Use a chart such as the one in Figure 5-4 to model how to create personification. Complete the chart using objects from memories about a place you lived in or visited during your childhood.

Writing Activity

- Ask the students to think about their own lives. What would they like to tell people about their lives and about their neighborhoods?

Objects	Ascribe human body parts	Verbs that depict human actions	Personal pronoun to refer to object
Corn Crib		Beckons you into the cool darkness	His dust suffocates me
Hay	Curling tendrils		He smells sweet
Blackberries	Thin, skinny fingernails scratch you	Oozing warm blue blood	She stains my fingers deep blue
Railroad Tracks	Like feet that move you forward	Sing as the train rumbles over	They slice through the property
Barbedwire Fence	Arms that reach out for you	Grabs you and holds you tight	He waits to snag my clothes

Figure 5-4. Creating Personification

- Provide each student with a personification chart such as the one in Figure 5-4, which is in the appendix.
- Tell the students that they do not have to complete all of the blanks in the chart.
- Once they have some ideas and words in the chart, they are ready to begin writing their free-verse poems.
- Remind the students that the lines do not have to rhyme, the length of the lines can vary, and that they should use personification sparingly.

Conferencing

- As the students are writing, circulate around the room and ask them if they need help creating personifications to use in their poems.
- As you circulate among the students you can also simply listen closely as they read what they have written. Sometimes all writers need is a person willing to listen to what they have written.

Zin! Zin! Zin! A Violin!

by Lloyd Moss
Illustrated Marjorie Priceman
Caldecott Honor Book, 1996

REACDING

Before Reading

Story Summary

Moss has readers counting along as he introduces the instruments of the orchestra and musical groupings. The exuberant musicians and the vibrant colors set the stage for a rollicking musical performance. In the background of the illustrations, readers follow the antics of two cats chasing a mouse. The confusion grows as a dog begins chasing the cats who are chasing the mouse around the stage. Colorful full-page illustrations and melodious verses introduce children to ten musical instruments and musical groupings. Descriptions, rhymes, alliteration, and rhythm introduce the instruments one by one. The text curls and swirls within the fluid, curving illustrations. The musicians' long limbs and postures mimic their instruments' shapes (Silvey, 2002). Marvin Hamlisch turned the poem into a symphony for children and at the symphony premiere, Lloyd Moss was the narrator. This book is available on audiocassette, videocassette, CD, and DVD.

Activating Prior Knowledge

If you have a recording of the symphony created from this book you can use it to introduce the story to the children. Another way to introduce the book is to have the students brainstorm a list of musical instruments. If the students are familiar with a variety of musical instruments you can have them sort them into groups such as woodwind or string.

❖ ─────

Recommended Grade Levels

1–4

Standards for the English Language Arts

3, 5, 6, 12

Information Literacy Standards for Student Learning

3, 5, 9

Objectives

The students will:

- Identify examples of onomatopoeia, assonance, and alliteration in the poem, and
- Write poems with alliteration.

❖

❖ ─────

Author

Lloyd Moss is an author, narrator, and actor, but is perhaps best known as the host of a classical music radio program in New York.

❖

Terms and Definitions	Examples	Examples from the book
Onomatopoeia — makes the sound of an action	Pop!	"Zin! Zin! Zin!"
Alliteration — repetition of initial constants	slinky, slithering snakes	"slender, silver sliver" "sings and stings its swinging song"
Assonance — repetition of vowel sounds	bounce trounce	"friend, extended" "clown, down" "descends and blends"

Figure 5-5. Onomatopoeia, Alliteration, and Assonance

During Reading

This is a fun poem to read aloud exuberantly. Young children can hold their fingers up as you count out the instruments. Before you read the poem a second time, tell the students to listen for the words that rhyme and for the terms that describe the musical groupings.

After Reading

Write the musical groupings on the board and have the students return to the poem to figure out the number that corresponds to the grouping. Moss weaves different elements of sound into the poem including onomatopoeia, assonance, and alliteration. A chart such as the one in Figure 5-5 helps students develop an understanding of these terms. A chart with the first two columns filled in is in the appendix. Younger students can complete the third column as a whole group activity and older students can complete the chart in small groups.

An example of onomatopoeia in the poem is the title "Zin! Zin! Zin!" Moss uses alliteration when he describes the flute as a "slender, silver sliver" and describes the actions of the trumpet as "sings and stings its swinging song." Assonance appears in the description of the cello with "friend, extended," in the description of the bassoon as "clown, down," and in the harp with "descends and blends." These are just some of the examples of the figurative language in the book.

WRITING

Mini-lesson—Alliteration

- Write "Peter Piper picked a peck of pickled peppers" on the board.
- Explain to the students that this is an example of alliteration because the initial consonant "p" is repeated in each word in the sentence.
- Tell the students that a repeating sound such as the initial consonant holds a poem together, sets up a pattern, and helps to craft a music (Livingston, 1991).
- Hold up an object such as a book and have the students brainstorm words that have the same initial consonant to describe the object such as big, bound, beautiful, and boring.

Illustrator

Marjorie Priceman lives in Lewisburg, Pennsylvania. Her vibrant, twirling watercolors with lines that swim across the pages bring an energy and excitement to the text. This author and illustrator cannot remember a time when she was not writing and reading (Silvey, 2002). Her illustrations are reminiscent of those of noted children's book illustrators Ludwig Bemelmans and Roger Duvoisin (Stevenson, 1999).

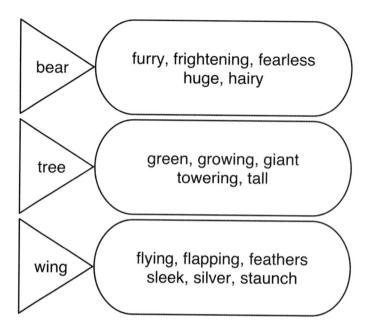

Figure 5-6. Alliteration

- Project a blank diagram like the one in Figure 5-6.
- Have the students suggest objects to write in the triangles and then have them suggest descriptive phrases using alliteration. (See Figure 5–6.)

Modeling

- Select some of the words from the chart and write a short poem with alliteration.
- Ask the students for suggestions as you write.
- Think aloud as you consider options for your poem. Remember that this poem is a quick model for the students, not a finished piece of work. So, just write and do not be concerned with the poem being a polished product.
- Your poem might look something like this:

Backyard Birds

Flocking to the feeder,
Flapping, flying, feathered wings.
Scrambling for seeds,
Seeking nourishment.

Writing Activity

- Give each student a blank chart such as the one in Figure 5–6 to brainstorm ideas for their poems.
- Tell the students that the poems can be very short; however, they should all have at least one example of alliteration.
- Remind the students that in this book, Moss uses a variety of the sound techniques but uses them sparingly.

Conferencing

- As you conference with the students, ask them to read the poem aloud.
- Then, ask them to point out the portions of the poem that contain alliteration.
- Encourage the students to try writing a short poem with onomatopoeia or assonance.

A Visit to William Blake's Inn: Poems for Innocent and Experienced Travelers

by Nancy Willard
Illustrated by Alice and Martin Provensen
Caldecott Honor Book, 1982

READING

Before Reading

Story Summary

This collection of poems transports readers to a magical, enchanted inn where animals and plants speak; a car flies; breakfast is served on the roof; and dragons, bears, angels, and rabbits tend to the guests' needs. Blake appears in the poems as the innkeeper of this wondrous, fanciful kingdom filled with unusual guests and employees. The illustrations beautifully depict the action in the poems in subdued colors that quietly highlight the detailed rooms of the inn. The illustrations and text blend to create a whole, although each is capable of standing on its own. William Blake was a British author, poet, painter, illustrator, and engraver who died in 1827. As a child, sick in bed with the measles, Nancy Willard first encountered poet William Blake's *Songs of Innocence and of Experience*, which is an illustrated book of poetry for children. Blake's poetry inspired Willard to write this book of poetry about a magical inn with Robert Blake as the innkeeper. A biography of Blake and links to some of his works are available at http://www.online-literature.com/blake. His poem "The Tyger," which captured the author's imagination as a child, is on this Web site.

Activating Prior Knowledge

Jennifer Coleman (2003), an elementary school librarian, likes to use props when she shares poetry with students. Before you read the poem to the students select a three-dimensional prop such as a stuffed dragon or a jar of marmalade to go with the book. Position the prop alongside of you as you introduce the book and ask the students to pay careful attention so that they can discover how the prop relates to the book.

During Reading

This is a collection of poems filled with excitement, anticipation, and surprise. As you read the poems, your voice inflections can mimic the excitement, anticipation, and surprise in the words.

❖ ─────────────

Recommended Grade Levels

6–10

Standards for the English Language Arts

1, 2, 3, 4, 6, 8, 12

Information Literacy Standards for Student Learning

3, 5, 8

Objectives

The students will:

- Identify metaphors in poems, and
- Write nonsense poems containing metaphors.

───────────── ❖

❖ ——————————————
❖ Author

Nancy Willard confesses that her writing muse is a wood stove (Willard, 2001). She compares lighting the stove to facing a blank sheet of paper. Keeping the flame going is important to both the cook and the writer. The most important part of the stove is the back burner, where pots slowly simmer and stew to perfection, occasionally being stirred and tended. And, so it is that writers put poems and stories that are going badly on the back burner, allowing them time to develop and to be transformed into the best that they can be. In the summer, her mother would row Nancy and her sisters to the middle of a lake where she would read to them as the boat drifted on the water (Willard, 2001). At age seven, she published her first poem. Making things with her hands starts her daydreaming and as she daydreams, she finds her stories (Linet, 2002). As she dreamed about the poems for this book, she constructed a six-foot-high inn of cardboard boxes. One day when her friend, a carpenter, was visiting, her cat jumped in the inn and it collapsed. Her friend replicated the inn in wood for her and it now resides in the rare book room at the University of Michigan library. One of the dedications at the front of this book is "For Ralph, who built the inn." This book was the first book of poetry to win the Newbery medal.

—————————————— ❖

After Reading

After reading the poems, you might begin the discussion by asking the students questions such as these:

- How does this prop relate to the poems?
- Who was your favorite character in the poems?
- What one thing at the inn would you like to have at your house?
- What would it be like to have a bear for a bed or a cloud for a bed?
- What would the plants in your house or yard say if they could talk?
- Where would you go if you had a car that could fly?

WRITING

Mini-lesson—Metaphor

- Explain to the students that a metaphor compares two unlike things. A good metaphor enables us to see our world from a different perspective (Livingston, 1991).
- Tell the students that metaphors challenge our imaginations but they are sometimes difficult to recognize. To help students understand metaphors, reread the description on page 17 where Willard compares the flying car to a wish.
- Challenge the students to reread the poems and look for other metaphors. Other examples they might find are on page 34 when Willard compares the fire to hissing tongues and on page 36 when she compares the Marmalade Man and the animals following behind him through the mist to a needle and thread.

Modeling

- Bring in a collection of different items such as a plant, a stuffed animal, a box, a birdhouse, and a clock.
- Pick up the different objects and suggest comparisons. For example, you could compare a box to a ship or compare a clock on the wall to the moon suspended in the air.
- Ask the students to help you think of metaphors and write them on the board.
- Pick one of the metaphors and write a short poem.
- Remember that you are simply modeling using metaphors for the students, not crafting great poetry. The students need to see your attempts and your revisions, and maybe your ultimate decision to put the poem away to come back to at another time.
- Just as Willard did, you too can create a nonsense poem. Your poem might look something like this:

The Clock

The clock a moon above my head,
Cast a light upon the floor,
As I lay upon my bed.
What next I wondered,
Would be my fate,
As the moon struck eight.

Writing Activity

- Present the students with a collection of objects for them to compare as they practice writing metaphors. Just as Willard used a model of the inn to write the poems, students can benefit from having objects to hold, to manipulate, and to engage their imaginations.
- Put the students in small groups or with partners, have them select one or two of the objects, and then brainstorm unlikely comparisons.
- Have the students write down the metaphors they create.
- Then, have the students work together to incorporate one of the metaphors into a nonsense poem.
- As they write encourage them to return to Willard's nonsense poems to gather ideas for their own poems.
- Mention to the students that writing metaphors is a skill that takes time to develop and that they will work on writing metaphors throughout the year.
- Encourage them to bring in any metaphors they find as they are reading other poems.

Conferencing

- As you conference with the students, ask them to point out the metaphors in their poems.
- Ask several of the students if they would be willing to read their poems aloud to their classmates toward the end of the class.

RESOURCES FOR LIBRARIANS AND TEACHERS

This section contains lists of poetry books, poetry reference books, and Web sites with resources for teaching poetry. The poets whose works are included in these lists have written many books of poetry and they can be located by an author search in your library catalog.

Caldecott Poetry Books

Baylor, Byrd. 1972. *The Desert Is Theirs*. Illustrated by Peter Parnall. New York: Scribner.
———. 1972. *When Clay Sings*. Illustrated by Tom Bahti. New York: Scribner.
———. 1978. *The Way to Start a Day*. Illustrated by Peter Parnall. New York: Scribner.
Cendrars, Blaise. 1982. *Shadow*. Translated and illustrated by Marcia Brown. New York: Simon & Schuster.
Chaucer, Geoffrey. 1989, 1958. *Chanticleer and the Fox*. Illustrated by Barbara Cooney. New York: HarperCollins.
Fleming, Denise. 1993. *In the Small, Small Pond*. New York: Holt.
Howitt, Mary Botham. 2002. *The Spider and the Fly*. Illustrated by Tony DiTerlizzi. New York: Simon & Schuster.
McCloskey, Robert. 1957. *Time of Wonder*. New York: Viking.
Moss, Lloyd. 1995. *Zin! Zin! Zin! A Violin!* Illustrated by Marjorie Priceman. New York: Simon & Schuster.
Myers, Walter Dean. 1997. *Harlem: A Poem*. Illustrated by Christopher Myers. New York: Scholastic.

❖ ━━━━━━━━━━━━━━━

Illustrators

As Alice and Martin Provensen worked on the illustrations for this book, they visited Willard's home and looked at the model of the inn housed in her living room (Linet, 2002). Willard realized that the model helped her write the poems, but that the model might hinder the illustrators in their work, and she wanted them to be free to create the illustrations in their own style. Alice and Martin Provensen worked so closely together that they cannot tell nor can their readers tell that two people did the work. When Martin died, Alice was not sure she could continue to write and illustrate without him. These prolific illustrators both had parents who supported their artistic endeavors (Marcus, 2001). They won the 1983 Caldecott award for *The Glorious Flight: Across the Channel with Louis Blériot*. Additional information on Alice Provensen is on this Web site: http://www.kidspoint.org/columns2 .asp?column_id=807&column_type= author.

━━━━━━━━━━━━━━━ ❖

Preston, Edna Mitchell. 1969. *Pop Corn & Ma Goodness*. Illustrated by Robert Andrew Parker. New York: Viking.

Spier, Peter. 1977. *Noah's Ark*. Garden City, NY: Doubleday.

Thayer, Ernest Lawrence. 2000. *Casey at the Bat: A Ballad of the Republic Sung in the Year 1888*. Illustrated by Christopher Bing. Brooklyn, NY: Handprint.

Udry, Janice May. 1956. *A Tree Is Nice*. Illustrated by Marc Simont. New York: HarperCollins.

Updike, John. 1999. *A Child's Calendar*. Illustrated by Trina Schart Hyman. New York: Holiday House.

Willard, Nancy. 1981. *A Visit to William Blake's Inn: Poems for Innocent and Experienced Travelers*. Illustrated by Alice and Martin Provensen. New York: Harcourt Brace.

Poetry Books, Books on Writing Poetry, and Reference Books

Bauer, Caroline Feller. 1995. *The Poetry Break: An Annotated Anthology with Ideas for Introducing Children to Poetry*. New York: Wilson.

Blake, William. 1970, 1967. *Songs of Innocence and of Experience*. New York: Oxford.

Bryan, Ashley. 1997. *ABC of African-American Poetry*. New York: Atheneum.

Fletcher, Ralph. 2002. *Poetry Matters: Writing a Poem from the Inside Out*. New York: HarperCollins.

Florian, Douglas. 1999. *Winter Eyes*. New York: Greenwillow.

Graves, Donald. 1996. *Baseball, Snakes, and Summer Squash: Poems about Growing Up*. Honesdale, PA: Boyds Mills.

Grimes, Nikki. 2005, 1997. *It's Raining Laughter*. Honesdale, PA: Boyds Mills.

Heide, Florence Parry. 2000. *Some Things Are Scary*. Cambridge, MA: Candlewick.

Hines, Anna Grossnickle. 2001. *Pieces: A Year in Poems and Quilts*. New York: Greenwillow.

Hopkins, Lee Bennett. 1998. *Pass the Poetry, Please!* 3rd ed. New York: HarperCollins.

———. 2004. *Alphathoughts: Alphabet Poems*. Honesdale, PA: Wordsong.

Janeczko, Paul B., compiler. 1994. *Poetry from A to Z: A Guide for Young Writers*. New York: Bradbury.

———. 1999. *How to Write Poetry*. New York: Scholastic.

———, compiler. 2002. *Seeing the Blue Between: Advice and Inspiration for Young Poets*. Cambridge, MA: Candlewick.

———. 2003. *Opening a Door: Reading Poetry in the Middle School Classroom*. New York: Scholastic.

———. 2005. *A Kick in the Head: An Everyday Guide to Poetic Forms*. Illustrated by Chris Raschka. Cambridge, MA: Candlewick.

Kelley, True. 2005. *School Lunch*. New York: Holiday House.

Livingston, Myra Cohn. 1991. *Poem-Making: Ways to Begin Writing Poetry*. New York: HarperCollins.

———. 1996. *Festivals*. Illustrated by Leonard Everett Fisher. New York: Holiday House.

Merriam-Webster's Rhyming Dictionary. 2002. Springfield, MA: Merriam-Webster.

Nye, Naomi Shihab, selector. 2000. *Salting the Ocean: 100 Poems by Young Poets*. New York: Greenwillow.

O'Neill, Mary. 1989. *Hailstones and Halibut Bones*. Illustrated by John Wallner. New York: Doubleday.

Paschen, Elise, editor. 2005. *Poetry Speaks to Children*. Naperville, IL: Sourcebooks.

Prelutsky, Jack, selector. 1983. *Random House Book of Poetry for Children*. New York: Random.

———. 1984. *The New Kid on the Block*. Illustrated by James Stevenson. New York: Greenwillow.

———. 2004. *If Not for the Cat*. Illustrated by Ted Rand. New York: Greenwillow.

———, selector. 2005. *Read a Rhyme, Write a Rhyme*. Illustrated by Meilo So. New York: Alfred A. Knopf.

The Scholastic Rhyming Dictionary. 1996. New York: Scholastic.

Sears, Peter. 1990. *Gonna Bake Me a Rainbow Poem*. New York: Scholastic.

Silverstein, Shel. 1974. *Where the Sidewalk Ends*. New York: HarperCollins.

Wong, Janet S. 2003. *Knock on Wood: Poems and Superstitions*. Illustrated by Julie Paschkis. New York: Margaret K. McElderry.

Yolen, Jane. 2005. *Water Music*. Honesdale, PA: Boyds Mills.

Web Sites

Academy of American Poets
www.poets.org/npm
This Web site contains information and resources for celebrating National Poetry Month in April.

Giggle Poetry
http://www.gigglepoetry.com/
Online poetry activities, interviews with poets, poetry contests to enter and resources for educators and students are on this site.

Mama Lisa's House of Nursery Rhymes
http://www.mamalisa.com/house/index.html
Favorite nursery rhymes accompanied by humorous illustrations and sounds that delight the youngest poets are on this Web site.

The Poetry Zone: The Teaching Zone
http://www.poetryzone.ndirect.co.uk/teacher.htm
Download *How to Write Poems* (Stevens, 1997) from this site. The book is for children ages eight to twelve. The site also contains useful resources for librarians and teachers.

Poetry4Kids
http://www.poetry4kids.com
Poetry lessons, poems to read, poetry contests to enter, and links to Web sites about children's poets are featured here.

Writing with Writers: Poetry
http://teacher.scholastic.com/writewit/poetry/
Three children's poets offer students workshops on writing poetry and invite them to publish their poetry online. The workshops are designated for different grade levels.

Books about Harlem

Giovanni, Nikki, editor. 1996. *Shimmy Shimmy Shimmy Like My Sister Kate: Looking at the Harlem Renaissance Through Poems*. New York: Holt.

Hill, Laban Carrick. 2003. *Harlem Stomp! A Cultural History of the Harlem Renaissance!* Boston: Little, Brown.

Hughes, Langston. 1993. *The Dream Keeper and Other Poems*. New York: Knopf.

Lawrence, Jacob. 1993. *The Great Migration*. New York: HarperCollins.

RESOURCES FOR STUDENTS

Students interested in reading other books by the authors and illustrators in this chapter might consider reading these books.

de Regniers, Beatrice Schenk, Eva Moore, Mary M. White, and Jan Carr, selectors. 1990. *Sing a Song of Popcorn*. New York: Scholastic.

DiTerlizzi, Tony. 2001. *Ted*. New York: Simon & Schuster.

Grimm, Jacob W. 1983. *Little Red Riding Hood*. Illustrated by Trina Schart Hyman. New York: Holiday House.

Hodges, Margaret. 1984. *Saint George and the Dragon*. Illustrated by Trina Schart Hyman. Boston: Little, Brown.

Kimmel, Eric. 1989. *Hershel and the Hanukkah Goblins*. Illustrated by Trina Schart Hyman. New York: Holiday House.

Kraus, Ruth. 1949. *The Happy Day*. New York: Harper.

McCloskey, Robert. 1941. *Make Way for Ducklings*. New York: Viking.

———. 1952. *One Morning in Maine*. New York: Viking.

———. 1976, 1948. *Blueberries for Sal*. New York: Viking.

Moss, Lloyd. 2001. *Our Marching Band*. New York: Putnam.

———. 2003. *Music Is*. New York: Putnam.

Myers, Christopher. 1999. *Black Cat*. New York: Scholastic.

———. 2000. *Wings*. New York: Scholastic.

———. 2001. *Fly*. New York: Hyperion.

Myers, Walter Dean. 1993. *Brown Angels*. New York: HarperCollins.

———. 2000. *The Blues of Flats Brown*. New York: Holiday House.

———. 2003. *Blues Journey*. Illustrated by Christopher Myers. New York: Holiday House.

Petersham, Maud, and Miska Petersham. 1945. *The Rooster Crows: A Book of American Rhymes and Jingles*. New York: Simon & Schuster.

Prelutsky, Jack. 1991. *For Laughing Out Loud: Poems to Tickle Your Funnybone*. Illustrated by Marjorie Priceman. New York: Knopf.

Provensen, Alice. 1990. *The Buck Stops Here: The Presidents of the Untied States*. New York: Harper & Row.

———. 2003. *A Day in the Life of Murphy*. New York: Simon & Schuster.

Provensen, Alice, and Martin Provensen. 1983. *The Glorious Flight: Across the Channel with Louis Bleriot*. New York: Viking.

———. 2001, 1978. *The Year at Maple Hill Farm*. New York: Simon & Schuster.

Sawyer, Ruth. 1953. *Journey Cake, Ho!* Illustrated by Robert McCloskey. New York: Viking.

Simont, Marc. 2001. *The Stray Dog*. New York: HarperCollins.

Spier, Peter. 1980. *People*. Garden City, NY: Doubleday.

———. 1985. *The Book of Jonah*. Garden City, NY: Doubleday.

———. 1994, 1961. *Fox Went out on a Chilly Night: An Old Song*. Garden City, NY: Doubleday.

Udry, Janice May. 1993. *Is Susan Here?* Illustrated by Karen Gundersheimer. New York: HarperCollins.

———. 2000. *Thump and Plunk*. Illustrated by Geoffrey Hayes. New York: HarperCollins.

Updike, John. 1965. *A Child's Calendar*. Illustrated by Nancy Ekholm Burkert. New York: Knopf.

Willard, Nancy. 1997. *Cracked Corn and Snow Ice Cream: A Family Almanac*. New York: Harcourt.

———. 2001. *The Moon and Riddles Diner and the Sunnyside Café*. Illustrated by Chris Butler. New York: Harcourt.

———. 2003. *Cinderella's Dress*. New York: Blue Sky.

———. 2003. *The Mouse, the Cat, and Grandmother's Hat*. Boston: Little, Brown.

IDEAS FOR PARENTS AND CAREGIVERS

Poet Naomi Shihab Nye wakes her son up each morning by reading a poem to him rather than shouting at him to get up (Lesesne, 1998b). Poetry can be read at bedtime rather than a story. Bauer (1995) suggests parents and caregivers keep a favorite poem in their purse or pocket to read to the children when waiting in a line or at a traffic light. Parents and caregivers can recite nursery rhymes or favorite poems as they drive and have the children recite them too. Poems can be stuck in unexpected places, such as lunch boxes, sock drawers, or the bathroom mirror. Adults can write poems with children using their favorite poems as models for their writing. Since poems do not have to rhyme, do not have to be written in complete sentences, and can contain nonsense words, they lend themselves to shared writing experiences.

REFERENCES

Bauer, Caroline Feller. 1995. *The Poetry Break: An Annotated Anthology with Ideas for Introducing Children to Poetry*. New York: Wilson.

Bishop, Rudine Sims. 1998. "Following in Their Fathers' Paths." *Horn Book* 74, no. 2 (March/April): 249–255.

Brightman, Marcia. 1998. "Practically Speaking." *School Library Journal* 44, no. 10 (October): 52–54.

Calkins, Lucy McCormick. 1994. *The Art of Teaching Writing*. Portsmouth, NH: Heinemann.

Certo, Janine L. 2004. "Cold Plums and the Old Men in the Water: Let Children Read and Write 'Great' Poetry." *The Reading Teacher* 58, no. 3 (November): 266–271.

Coleman, Jennifer. 2003. "The Prop Connection: Bringing Books to Life." *Library Media Connection* 22, no. 3 (November): 26–27.

Collins, Billy. 2004. "How to Read a Poem Out Loud." [Online] Available: http://www.loc.gov/poetry/180/ [cited 13 October 2004].

Emberley, Barbara. 1966. *One Wide River to Cross*. Illustrated by Ed Emberley. Upper Saddle River, NJ: Prentice-Hall.

Greiner, Donald J. 1994. "John Updike." *Dictionary of Literary Biography, Volume 143: American Novelists Since World War II, Third Series*. Farmington Hills, MI: Thomson Gale.

Higashi, Chris. 1998. "How to Plan a Moveable Feast of Poetry." *American Libraries* 29, no. 2 (February): 52–54.

Hyman, Trina Schart. 2002. "How I Do My Work." [Online] Available: http://www.ortakales.com/illustrators/Hyman3.html [cited 31 October 2004].

Isaac, Megan Lynn. 2004. "Remembering a Legend: The Life and Works of Robert McCloskey." *Children and Libraries* 2, no. 1 (Spring): 31–34.

Janeczko, Paul B., compiler. 1994. *Poetry from A to Z: A Guide for Young Writers.* New York: Bradbury.

Kuskin, Karla. 2004. "Poetry Writing with Karla Kuskin." [Online] Available: http://teacher.scholastic.com/writewit/poetry_home.htm [cited 13 October 2004].

Lancashire, Ian. 2003. "Selected Poetry of Mary Howitt (1799–1888)." [Online] Available: http://www.eir.library.utoronto.ca/rpo/display/poet171.html [cited 1 November 2004].

Lesesne, Teri. 1998a. "The Poetry Zone According to Mel Glenn." *Emergency Librarian* 25, no. 3 (January/February): 58–59.

———. 1998b. "Honoring the Mystery of Experience." *Teacher Librarian* 26, no. 2 (November/December): 59–61.

Linet, Valerie. 2002. "Talking with Nancy Willard." *Book Links* 11, no. 5 (April/May): 30–34.

Livingston, Myra Cohn. 1991. *Poem-Making: Ways to Begin Writing Poetry.* New York: HarperCollins.

Marcus, Leonard S. 2001. "A Collaborative Effort." *Publishers Weekly* 248, no. 29 (6 July): 84–87.

———. 2004. "Marc Simont's Sketchbook: The Art Academy Years: 1935–1938." *Horn Book* 80, no. 2 (March/April): 130–143.

Merina, Anita. 2004. "Wow You Really Wrote That?" *NEA Today* 22, no. 5 (February): 32–33.

Miguez, Betsy Bryan. 2005. "Bring Back Poetry." *Teacher Librarian* 32, no. 4 (April): 26–29.

Myers, Walter Dean. 2002. "Voices of the Creators." In *Children's Books and Their Creators*, edited by Anita Silvey. Boston: Houghton Mifflin.

"Nancy Willard." 2002. *Contemporary Authors Online.* Farmington Hills, MI: Thomson Gale.

Pinkney, Jerry. 2002. *Noah's Ark.* New York: North-South.

Potts, Cherly. 2004. "National Poetry Month." *LibrarySparks* 1, no. 8 (April): 14–19.

Prelutsky, Jack. 2004. "Poetry Writing with Jack Prelutsky." [Online] Available: http://teacher.scholastic.com/writewit/poetry/jack_home.htm [cited 1 November 2004].

Routman, Regie. 2000. "Kids' Poems." *Instructor* 109, no. 7 (April): 22–24.

———. 2001. "Everyone Succeeds with Poetry Writing." *Instructor* 111, no. 1 (August): 26–30.

Schliesman, Megan. 2004. "Words to Share: Poetry for Children." *LibrarySparks* 1, no. 8 (April): 2–3.

Sears, Peter. 1990. *Gonna Bake Me a Rainbow Poem.* New York: Scholastic.

Silvey, Anita, editor. 2002. *The Essential Guide to Children's Books and Their Creators.* Boston: Houghton Mifflin.

Silvey, Anita, and Mary M. Burns. 1993. "Booklist: Picture Books." *Horn Book* 69, no. 5 (September/October): 584–585.

Smedman, M. Sarah. 1987. "Peter Spier." In *Dictionary of Literary Biography, Volume 61: American Writers for Children Since 1960: Poets, Illustrators, and Nonfiction Authors,* edited by Glen E. Estes. Farmington Hills, MI: Thomson Gale.

Stevens, Roger. 1997. *How to Write Poems.* [Online] Available: http://www.poetryzone.ndirect.co.uk/howto.htm [cited 1 November 2004].

Stevenson, Deborah. 1999. "Rising Star: Marjorie Priceman." [Online] Available: http://www.alexia.lis.uiuc.edu/puboff/bccb/0799rise.html [cited 1 November 2004].

Timblin, Carol. 1998. "Using a Team Approach in Teaching Children's Poetry." *School Library Media Activities Monthly* 13, no. 7 (March): 17–18.

Willard, Nancy. 2001. "Put It on the Back Burner." *Writer* 114, no. 6 (June): 24–27.

6 ❖ FANTASY

Fantasy invites readers to use their imaginations to experience things that are not real (Krapp, 2004). Fantasy has just enough reality to make readers feel like these things could possibly happen, just enough reality to enable readers to suspend disbelief. The main elements of fantasy include: the description of a fantasy world, the events occurring there, the meaning of those events, and the description of the events (Nodelman, 1996). These elements work together to present readers with a context for believing and accepting the fantasy. Fantasy may have animal characters that act like humans, but whether the characters are animals or humans their actions must be believable.

Fantasy provides us another perspective for looking at the real world and imagining possibilities. Imagining possibilities fosters creativity by altering the way readers look at the world. *Tuesday* (Wiesner, 1991), with its frogs flying on magic carpet lily pads, forever changes the way readers look at frogs and lily pads. After reading the book, when readers see frogs and lily pads they wonder what it would be like to see them take flight. Inventors and scientists look at ordinary things in different ways and imagine possibilities. Fantasy helps children develop scientific attitudes including curiosity, habits of observation, awareness of rules, variations of rules, skepticism, and forward-looking ideas (Raymo, 1996). Science writer Chet Raymo contends that any Suessian invention, such as the wondrous fish in *McElligot's Pool* (Seuss, 1947), can find its equal in nature.

Wordless or nearly wordless fantasy books help reluctant readers develop their oral and written skills as they read and retell the stories. Parents and caregivers who may not be proficient readers can share wordless books with the students. They can look at the pictures and make up their own stories using familiar vocabulary and any language. In his Caldecott acceptance speech, David Wiesner (1992) mentioned that teachers who have English as a second language like his wordless picture books because they give the students opportunities to express their thoughts in English without having to complete literal translations.

The authors illustrated all of the books highlighted in this chapter, so it is not surprising that they often start their books with visual images. Wiesner explores the images and derives his stories from them. When writing about fantasy worlds the author must believe in them and do research to make sure that the laws that govern the worlds ring true (Yolen, 1996). Writers have to provide the readers with supporting details, so that the readers believe in the fantasy world (Yolen, 1996). In order for readers to accept a fantasy they need a believable narrator who convinces them that the fantasy world exists (Nodelman, 1996). Fantasy requires well-developed plots, characters, and settings in order to help readers believe the impossible. Fantasy writers draw upon their imaginations and the ideas they gather from reading fantasy (Fischer, 2004). Writer Fraser Sherman (1994) suggests that writing fantasy requires reading fantasy written in different styles and by different authors. After reading a variety of fantasy, start thinking about possible stories. He cautions authors that in order for the fantasy to be believable it needs to be realistic. Introducing students to a variety of fantasy titles ensures they have sufficient ideas to incorporate into their writing.

Kitten's First Full Moon

by Kevin Henkes
Caldecott Medal Winner, 2005

READING

Before Reading

Story Summary

Seeing a full moon in the night sky, Kitten thinks it is bowl of milk. She leaves the safety of the porch and sets out for the giant bowl of milk. Her attempts to lap up the moon lead to a series of mishaps that leave her tired and hungry. She slowly makes her way back to the porch to find a bowl of milk awaiting her return. The text features recurring refrains and the illustrations feature a recurring circle motif. "Poor Kitten!" and "Still, there was the little bowl of milk, just waiting" are the repeated refrains. The recurring circle motif encompasses the full moon in the sky, the flowers in the garden, the lights of the fireflies, and the eyes of the cat. Each time the refrain or the circles appear it reminds readers of the earlier recurrences, which creates a familiar, rhythmic pattern to the book. The black-and-white illustrations with their thick lines accompanied by bold sans serif font on soft, creamy paper set just the right mood for this nighttime adventure.

Activating Prior Knowledge

Kitten sees what she thinks is a bowl of milk but try as she may she just cannot reach it. Ask the students to share their experiences about not being tall enough to reach things they want or need. They can also share stories of their mishaps as they try to reach things that are just beyond their reach.

During Reading

As you read, the youngest children will chime in with the "Poor Kitten!" refrain. Children who are a little older will be chiming in to add "Still, there was the little bowl of milk, just waiting." As they listen to the story, ask the children to try to remember all of the different ways that Kitten attempts to reach the moon and the outcomes of the attempts.

After Reading

A discussion of the story can focus on the cause-and-effect pattern. Figure 6-1 shows a diagram of the cause-and-effect pattern in this story.

WRITING

Mini-lesson—Repeated Refrain

- To ensure that the students understand the repeated refrain "Poor Kitten! Still, there was the little bowl of milk, just waiting," write it on the board or chart paper and have them read it aloud with you.

❖ ─────────────────

Recommended Grade Levels

1–4

Standards for the English Language Arts

3, 4, 5, 6, 12

Information Literacy Standards for Student Learning

3, 5

Objectives

The students will:

- Deduce the cause-and-effect pattern in the story,

- Recognize the repeated refrain in the story,

- Use a cause-and-effect chart to organize their writing, and

- Incorporate a repeated refrain in their writing.   ❖

❖ ─────────────────

Author

Kevin Henkes lives in Madison, Wisconsin, with his wife and son. As a child, he made regular visits to the public library and the local art museum. In high school, one of his teachers encouraged him to develop his writing skills (Op de Beeck, 1996). After his first year of college, he traveled to New York City with a portfolio of his work, determined to obtain a book contract. His meeting that week with Greenwillow editor Susan Hirschman resulted in his first book contract when he was only nineteen. Henkes won a Caldecott Honor for *Owen* (Henkes, 1993) and a Newbery Honor for *Olive's Ocean* (Henkes, 2003). More information about Henkes and his work is on his Web site at http://www.kevinhenkes.com/.   ❖

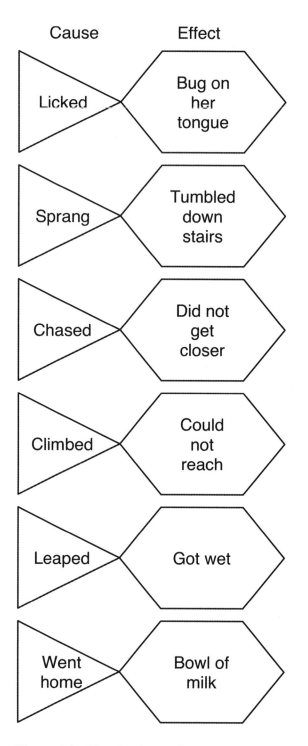

Figure 6-1. *Kitten's First Full Moon* **Cause and Effect**

- Explain to the students that a repeated refrain is a phrase or a sentence that appears throughout the story.
- Then, show them how the refrain appears just after each of Kitten's unsuccessful attempts to get to the bowl of milk.

Modeling

- In order to model how to use the repeated refrain in writing, begin by asking the students for other ideas about how Kitten can get to the bowl of milk in the sky.
- Use one of their ideas as you model writing with a repeated refrain.
- Your writing might look something like this:

So, she raced to a tall building, took the elevator to the top floor, and ran out on the roof.
But Kitten could not reach the bowl of milk.
"Poor Kitten!"
"Still, there was the little bowl of milk, just waiting."

Writing Activity

Younger students

- Ask the students to think of other ways kitten could try to get to the bowl of milk.
- Write their ideas on the board.
- Give them a blank sheet of paper with the repeated refrain written at the bottom and ask them to draw a picture showing how Kitten could reach the bowl of milk.

Older students

- Give the students a blank cause-and-effect chart such as the one in the appendix.
- Tell the students to think of something they have failed to do after repeated attempts or something they have seen someone else make several attempts to do.
- Ask them to complete the cause-and-effect chart diagramming the different attempts.
- Once the chart is completed have the students decide on a repeated refrain to include in the story.
- The students may find it helpful to work with a partner as they think of a repeated refrain.
- When the chart is completed and they have decided on a repeated refrain, they are ready to begin writing their stories.
- Encourage the students to return to the book and examine Henkes's text structure if they are unsure of how to proceed.

Conferencing

- When you conference with the students ask them to show you how they incorporated their cause-and-effect charts into their writing.
- Encourage them to check off the items in the diagram as they include them in their writing.

My Friend Rabbit

by Eric Rohmann
Caldecott Medal Winner, 2003

❖

Recommended Grade Levels

2–5

Standards for the English Language Arts

3, 5, 6, 12

Information Literacy Standards for Student Learning

3, 5

Objectives

The students will:

- Predict the events in the story,
- Analyze the structure of a circle tale, and
- Write a circle tale.

Author

Eric Rohmann lives in Chicago. As a child, he remembers reading *Where the Wild Things Are* (Sendak, 1963), *The Snowy Day* (Keats, 1962), some of Dr. Seuss's books, and comic books (Rohmann and Scales, 2003). He writes and illustrates children's books and teaches drawing and printmaking. He received a Caldecott Honor for *Time Flies* (Rohmann, 1994).

READING

Before Reading

Story Summary

Rohmann hooks readers at the very beginning of the book by describing rabbit as a friend whom "trouble follows." This foreshadowing tells readers that adventure and trouble are not far behind. Rabbit quickly gets mouse's new airplane stuck high in a tree. No sooner is the plane stuck than rabbit hatches a plan to retrieve the plane. He prods and pulls an assortment of animals into a living ladder that collapses just as mouse reaches his stranded airplane. Just as the angry animals plot their revenge, mouse flies down to rescue rabbit, only to have the grateful if overzealous rabbit cause mouse's airplane to once again get stuck in the treetop. But, rabbit declares he has a plan. Before Rohmann settled on using hand-colored relief prints to create the illustrations for this story, he tried pencil sketches, pastels, watercolors, woodcuts, linocuts, collage, pen and ink and scratchboard, and little paper sculptures. Rohmann, noted for his trademark oil paints, decided that the thick dark outlines filled in with bold watercolors best suited the story he was telling in this book (Rohmann and Scales, 2003).

Activating Prior Knowledge

A circle tale begins where it ends and that is what happens in this amusing look at friendship. A balsa wood airplane or a folded paper airplane flown across the library or classroom would be a great way to introduce this book. Having the plane land on top of a tall shelf or cabinet could begin a brainstorming session about creative ways to retrieve the airplane.

During Reading

As you read the story, pause and let the students predict which animal rabbit is going to enlist to help next. Then, pause and have the students figure out why the ducks are running around squawking. Last, have them predict what is going to happen when mouse and rabbit escape from the angry animals.

After Reading

In his Caldecott acceptance speech, Rohmann notes that the text and the illustrations are incomplete without the reader. Children are visually aware and curious about their world; they see things in the book that the author/illustrator leaves out (Rohmann, 2003). So, start a discussion of this book by having the students talk about what they think of the book and maybe what they learned from it. The idea is to get them talking about it to each other and then to just listen to what they have to say about the book.

WRITING

Mini-lesson—Circle Tale

- To show the students how a circle tale begins and ends at the same place, draw a large circle on the board or an overhead transparency.
- In the middle of the circle write the title of the book.
- At the top of the circle write "Plane stuck in tree."
- Next, show the students that at the beginning of the book and at the end of the book the plane is stuck in the tree.
- Now flip through the pages of the book and let the students write the story events on the circle. (See Figure 6-2.)

Modeling

- In order to model writing a circle tale, start with a blank circle on the board or on an overhead transparency. There is a blank circle map in the appendix.
- Think about an incident or an event that you remember that could have begun and ended in the same way.
- Write the beginning and ending event at the top of the circle.
- Share with the students that you are basing the story on a real event and making up some parts of the story.

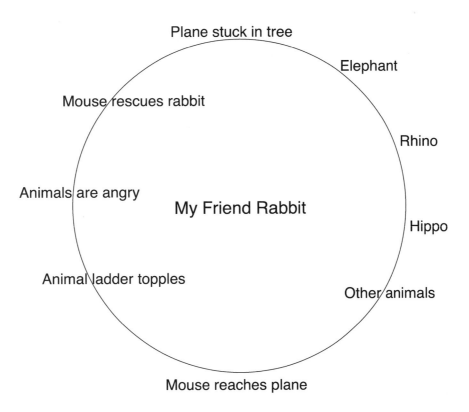

Figure 6-2. *My Friend Rabbit* **Circle Map**

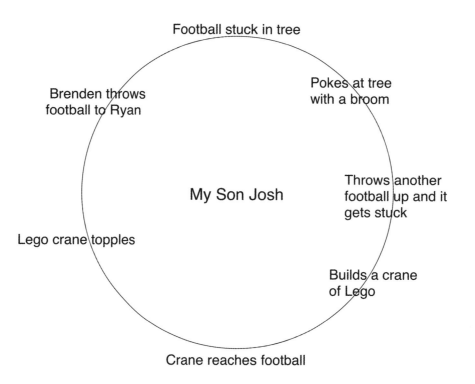

Figure 6-3. My Son Josh Circle Map

- Invite the students to help you think up details to include in your story.
- Your circle map might look something like the one in Figure 6-3.

Writing Activity

- Give the students blank circle maps to plan their stories.
- If some of the students have ideas for their circle tales, allow them to begin.
- Remind the students that tale begins and ends with the same event.
- For students who are not sure what they are going to write about, ask them to think about times when they got toys stuck in high places or over fences or lost in their rooms.
- Then, ask them to brainstorm creative ways to retrieve their toys.
- Remind them that this is a fantasy so they can make up impossible ways to accomplish their goals.
- Once the students have their circle maps completed and they begin writing, start writing your circle tale.

Conferencing

- As you conference with the students, ask them to tell you their stories using their circle maps.
- When they finish, ask them if they included any details in their oral retelling that they want to include in the written versions.

Tuesday

by David Wiesner
Caldecott Medal Winner, 1992

READING

Before Reading

Story Summary
Nine carefully chosen words set the day and the time of this fanciful frog adventure. One magical Tuesday evening a squadron of frogs flies off on lily pads to visit the town. They spy on a late-night snacker, tangle with laundry left on clothes lines, watch late-night television, encounter a dog, and as the sun rises shed their lily pads and return to their pond. The policemen and the television crew are left to ponder the lily pad–strewn street until next Tuesday, when strange happenings are once again occurring. Computer graphics were used to enhance some of the detailed watercolor illustration sequences (Hurst, 1993).

Activating Prior Knowledge
The double page spread toward the end of the book with the policemen and the television crew trying to figure why the lily pads are strewn across the road gets students thinking and predicting what will happen in the story they are about to read. The idea for this illustration came from Wiesner's editor Dorothy Briley (Marcus, 1998). After the students have made their predictions, show them the cover of the book, which includes partial views of frogs riding on the lily pads. You might have to help them discern that there are frogs on lily pads on the edges of the cover illustration. Then, ask the students for additional predictions about what they think is going to happen in the story.

During Reading

Wordless picture books let children interpret the stories in their own words, which builds their understanding of story structure, enhances their comprehension, and encourages their creativity. In wordless books, readers can each tell their own version of the story and hence the reader becomes the storyteller (Wiesner, 1992). As you share this story with the students let them describe what is happening in each illustration. When you get to the second-to-last page, with the shadow of the flying pigs on the barn and the tail of one pig barely visible in the top right corner of the illustration, ask the children to predict what is going to happen next.

After Reading

As you discuss this story with the students, you will want to return to the illustrations and focus on details they may have missed during the first reading of the book. You might ask them questions such as:

- What are the turtles and the fish in the pond thinking as the frogs take flight?
- How do you think the birds felt when the frogs disturbed their slumber?

❖ ——————————————

Recommended Grade Levels

1–4

Standards for the English Language Arts

2, 4, 5, 6, 8

Information Literacy Standards for Student Learning

3, 4, 5, 8

Objectives

The students will:

- Make predictions about the story,
- Critically analyze the story illustrations,
- Construct a plot of the story structure using *Kidspiration* software,
- Construct a storyboard or a story structure for their own story using *Kidspiration* software, and
- Write a story based on their storyboard or their story structure.

—————————————— ❖

❖ ───────────────

Author

David Wiesner revealed that inspiration for his wordless books comes from Lynd Ward's adult wordless picture book *Mad Man's Drum*. This allegorical novel tells its story in 130 woodcuts (Wiesner, 1992). Ward's book *The Biggest Bear* won a Caldecott Medal in 1953. In his Caldecott acceptance speech, Wiesner (1992) explained the process of elimination he used to decide on the just the right day for the setting. Friday, Saturday, and Sunday had too many connotations. He did not want Monday as that was the first day of work and he did not like the spelling of Wednesday. That left Tuesday and Thursday. He decided on Tuesday as it has an "ooze" quality that seemed to fit with frogs. Wiesner also won the Caldecott Medal for *The Three Pigs* (Wiesner, 2001), and he won Caldecott Honors for *Sector 7* (Wiesner, 1999) and *Free Fall* (Wiesner, 1988). To learn more about David Wiesner and his work, visit his Web pages at http://www.houghtonmifflinbooks.com/authors/wiesner/home.html or http://www.childrenslit.com/f_wiesner.html. ❖

───────────────── ❖

- What is the snacker thinking as the frogs fly past his window and wave?
- At the end of the book, what is the snacker telling the news crew?
- What does the news crew think of the snacker's story?
- How do you think the frogs got free of the laundry?
- Why did the frogs fly through the window?
- Notice the frog with the television remote control. What channel is he looking for? What would frogs watch on late-night television?
- The lady is asleep in front of her television but her cat is not. What can you tell from the look on the cat's face?
- What happened with the dog? Did the dog scare the frogs or did the frogs scare the dog?
- Why do you think the lily pads fell to the ground as the sun came up?
- What are the policemen thinking?
- What are the policemen saying to each other?
- What could the cat and dog tell them about the lily pads?
- What kind of adventures are the pigs going to have as they fly through the night sky?
- What is causing these animals to fly?
- Why are the animals only flying on Tuesday nights?

WRITING

Mini-lesson—Story Structure

- Tell the students that at first glance, the story may seem to be a series of silly pictures.
- Show them that if they look closely at the illustrations they will discover that there is a beginning, an end, and in between there is a series of events that move the story along. However, the story is open to a variety of creative interpretations.
- Share with them that Wiesner (1992) cautions that in order to make a story from a series of funny pictures, the pictures have to be developed carefully to move the story forward. At http://www.houghtonmifflinbooks.com/authors/wiesner/process/process.shtml, students can see how he went from the original rough sketches for *Tuesday* to the storyboard thumbnails to the final watercolor paintings. The storyboard thumbnail drawings are also in *A Caldecott Celebration* (Marcus, 1998).
- With the book and the writing component of *Kidspiration* software, have the students help you plot the story structure as shown in Figure 6-4, or simply write the structure on the board.

Modeling

The idea for this book came from a *Cricket* magazine cover Wiesner illustrated that featured flying frogs on magic carpet lily pads (Marcus, 1998). After looking at the flying frogs in his illustration, he wondered what came before and what came after the scene. While flying on an airplane he got to thinking about the flying frogs and wondered what it would be like if he were a flying frog (Wiesner, 1992). Where would he go and what would he do? The last illustration in the book shows the pigs in flight and this is a great place to start a fantasy.

Tuesday _____

Beginning: Frogs fly _____

Event 1: Scare the birds _____

Event 2: Fly past man snacking _____

Event 3: Fly through clothesline _____

Event 4: Watch television _____

Event 5: Meet dog _____

Event 6: Return to pond _____

Event 7: Policemen and news crew _____

End: Pigs fly _____

Figure 6-4. Story Structure

- Tell the students that they are going to write the sequel to the story describing what happens when the pigs take flight.
- Ask the students to brainstorm answers to the same questions Wiesner asked himself when he wrote *Tuesday*.
- Write these questions on the board leaving room for the students' responses: "What would it be like to be a flying pig? Where would a flying pig go? What would a flying pig do?"
- Write their answers on the board so they can refer to them for ideas for their own stories.
- As the students respond to the questions, you may need to remind them that for readers to suspend disbelief the fantasy has to be grounded in reality. One way Wiesner did this was by placing the flying frogs in the familiar context of a slumbering neighborhood.
- When the students have finished responding to the questions, use some of their responses to create a structure for your story similar to the one in Figure 6-5.

Writing Activity

- Give the students the option of starting their stories by drawing rough sketches to turn into a storyboard or to create a written story structure using *Kidspiration* software. There is a blank story structure in the appendix.
- Suggest that the students use the ideas the class wrote down in response to the questions or to think up their own pig adventures.

Pigs Flying

Beginning: Pigs fly

Event 1: Scare chickens

Event 2: Fly past farmer getting ready for bed

Event 3: Fly past drive through window of fast food restaurant

Event 4: Chase cows

Event 5: Return to barnyard

Event 6: Policemen and news crew

End: Dogs fly

Figure 6-5. Pigs Flying Story Structure

- Assure the students that it is acceptable for them to use the same ideas, as their stories will vary based on the writer.
- Less proficient writers may prefer to draw pictures and just put a few words under each drawing, hence creating their own, almost wordless storybook.

Conferencing

- As the students work, encourage them to quietly conference with one another to try out ideas and to ascertain that their fantasy is grounded in reality.
- Suggest to them that one way to do this is to ask one another if the events they describe are believable. Can the reader suspend disbelief and imagine that the events could happen?

The Polar Express

by Chris Van Allsburg
Caldecott Medal Winner, 1986

READING

Before Reading

Story Summary

On Christmas Eve an old-fashioned steam train transports a young boy to the North Pole to witness Santa giving the first gift of Christmas. When the boy is selected to receive the first gift, he asks for a sleigh bell from the reindeers' harness, which he puts in his bathrobe pocket. As he boards the train for home, he realizes the bell has slipped out through the hole in his pocket. On Christmas morning, he finds the bell nestled inside a small package under his tree with a note from Mr. C. The boy rings the bell but his parents do not hear it ring. He realizes that only those who believe in Santa can hear the bell. Oil pastel illustrations with muted colors, fuzzy forms, and sparse scenes receive light from windows and an unseen moon (Marantz, 1985). This book is available on audiocassette and CD. The animated movie based on the book is available on videocassette and DVD. Resources for incorporating this book into the classroom are available at http://www.houghtonmifflinbooks.com/features/thepolarexpress/educators.shtml.

Activating Prior Knowledge

Introduce this book to students by asking if they have ever had a dream that seemed so real, it was hard to believe that it was a dream. In this story, the narrator is an adult who shares his personal recollection of a very special Christmas Eve fantasy by capturing the magic of the event to share with others.

During Reading

Ask the children to listen carefully as you read the story aloud and Van Allsburg's words paint pictures in their minds.

After Reading

Questions such as these engage students in a discussion of the story and the illustrations. Your role in the discussion should be to continually direct the students back to the text and to encourage them to offer multiple explanations as they interpret the text (Lenihan, 2003).

- Van Allsburg does not come out and tell us that the narrator of the story is an older person thinking back on his childhood. How does he convey this information to the readers?
- How old do you think the narrator was when he rode the train? How old do you think he is now? Can you support your answers by information in the text or in the illustrations?
- How do the illustrations help to set the mood for the story?
- Van Allsburg's artistic style is "surrealistic fantasy." What do you think "surrealistic fantasy" means?

Recommended Grade Levels

2–6

Standards for the English Language Arts

2, 3, 4, 5, 6, 12

Information Literacy Standards for Student Learning

4, 5, 9

Objectives

The students will:

- Identify the similes in the story,
- Practice writing similes, and
- Write a description of a real or a fantasy trip.

❖ ────────────────

Author

Chris Van Allsburg has won numerous awards for his stunning collection of picture books. His stories are full of mystery and intrigue told from different perspectives. They blend fantasy and reality, leaving readers wondering about what really happened. The mysterious stories linger in readers' minds and they return to them again and again searching for answers. Van Allsburg looks for the child within himself and to his own two daughters for stories that reflect childhood experiences, feelings, and memories. Fragments of pictures form in his mind and from these pictures he creates his stories (Silvey, 2002). Van Allsburg (2002) writes that the idea for *The Polar Express* began as an image of a young boy who discovers a train in his front yard. He and the boy took several trips on the train before it headed to the North Pole. Van Allsburg began college with plans to be a lawyer, but those plans changed as he first studied sculpture and then illustration. Whereas he finds sculpting easy, illustrations become tedious and boring, as it takes so many to make a book. Van Allsburg won a Caldecott Medal for *Jumanji* in 1982 and a Caldecott Honor for *The Garden of Abdul Gasazi* in 1980. Additional information about Chris Van Allsburg is available at http://www.eduplace .com/author/vanallsburg.

──────────────── ❖

- Why do you think the boy selected the bell for a present?
- What would you have selected for the first present of Christmas? Why would you have selected that?

WRITING

Mini-lesson—Simile

- Explain to the students that similes and metaphors compare things readers may not be familiar with to things that are familiar. Similes use "like" or "as" to make the comparison whereas metaphors make a broader connection without using "like" or "as."
- Tell the students that metaphors and similes are one way to communicate and express abstract thoughts and feelings. These comparisons help the readers visualize the scene and set the mood for the story.
- Write some of the similes on the board and discuss them with the students. (See Figure 6-6.)

Modeling

- Before you begin writing, think aloud about trips you have taken, trips you would like to take, and modes of transportation.
- Ask the students which trip they think you should turn into a fantasy adventure.
- On chart paper or an overhead transparency make some brief notes about what you might include in your story.
- Look over your notes and then write a few sentences down on chart paper or the overhead.
- Your fantasy adventure might begin something like this.

Balloon Adventure

With the balloon inflated and the burner fired, we lifted off. Directly above us was a bank of clouds, but we knew that once we popped through the clouds the skies would be calm and blue. We knew that the quiet calm of the morning would provide us a smooth uneventful flight. Momentarily, we were engulfed in white, damp clouds. We passed through the clouds, and quickly discovered that this would not be an uneventful flight.

- Stop and look at the sentences and ask the children if they can help you think up a simile or a metaphor to add to your description of the event.

"...nougat centers as white as snow."
"...cocoa as thick and rich as melted chocolate bars."
"... rolling over peaks and through valleys like a car on a roller coaster."
"They looked like the lights of a strange ocean liner..."

Figure 6-6. Similes

- These are some possible similes to include in the story:

  engulfed in clouds as wet as just-washed sheets
  clouds as wet as dog licks

- Changing "Momentarily, we were engulfed in white, damp clouds" to read, "As we ascended we were surrounded by clouds as wet as dog licks" is one way to incorporate a simile into the story.

Writing Activity

Younger Students

- Have younger students collaborate with you to write a class story about a magical trip.
- Interactive writing enables the whole class to write collaboratively about a shared experience on chart paper (Pinnell and Fountas, 1998).
- The librarian or the teacher models the writing process and focuses the children's attention on the sounds and spelling patterns in the words they write.
- Over time, as the students' writing skills develop, the librarian or the teacher shares the pen with the children by inviting them to come up and write down letters and words.

Older Students

- Give the students time to talk quietly in small groups about trips they have taken or would like to take.
- Once they decide on where they will go and how they will get there, they can discuss ideas for what will happen on the trip. Not only does collaboration produce assignments that are more authentic, it also results in greater student achievement (Baskin, 2003).
- As the students talk encourage them to briefly write down ideas to include in their stories.
- Have the students go back over their written ideas and number them in the order they will appear in their stories.
- As the students begin writing, continue writing your story.

Conferencing

- Once the students have their drafts written they can conference with a partner or in small groups to brainstorm similes they can include in their fantasies.
- As you move between the groups, ask some of the students to write their similes on the board to share with their classmates.
- Not all of their stories will lend themselves to including similes.

Jumanji

by Chris Van Allsburg
Caldecott Medal Winner, 1982

❖ ———————————————

Recommended Grade Levels

3–8

Standards for the English Language Arts

3, 4, 5, 6, 11, 12

Information Literacy Standards for Student Learning

2, 5, 6

Objectives

The students will:

- Examine the illustrations and infer the perspective,

- Critically examine the illustrations and generate an understanding of the effect of perspective,

- Locate action verbs in the story and consider their impact on the story, and

- Incorporate strong action verbs in their writing.

——————————————— ❖

READING

Before Reading

Story Summary

When Judy and Peter's parents leave them home alone, they head for the park where they discover a jungle adventure board game. The simple instructions come with a cautionary note that once you begin the game you have to finish it. When a ferocious lion appears and begins chasing Peter around the house, Judy realizes that in order for the lion to disappear they have to finish the dangerous game. Rampaging monkeys, a monsoon, a rhinoceros stampede, a slithering python, and an erupting volcano must all be overcome before the horrendous game ends and the animals disappear. When the games ends, the children quickly return the game to its box and take it back to the park where the Budwig boys who "never read instructions" grab the game. The story hovers on the edge of fantasy and reality, and readers are never really sure which is which in this board game adventure. The idea for this story came from an art assignment Chris Van Allsburg gave his students at the Rhode Island School of Design (Healy, 2004). The assignment was to draw a room and then populate it with wild animals. Whereas the movie may be too scary for younger students, older students delight in the action and suspense. Older students who are interested in learning more about the computer-generated animals in the movie enjoy Robertson's (1996) article in *Computer Graphics World*. The Teacher's Guide Library, at http://www.houghtonmifflinbooks.com/features/thepolarexpress/educators.shtml, contains guides, lesson plans, and classroom activities for Van Allsburg's books. Van Allsburg created the black-and-white illustrations using Conté dust and Conté pencil and the illustrations drawn from different perspectives pull readers into the harrowing tale. *Zathura: A Space Adventure* (Van Allsburg, 2002) tells the story of the Budwig boys' board game experience.

Activating Prior Knowledge

How would you get rid of a lion resting on top of your piano, monkeys wreaking havoc in your kitchen, rhinos charging through your living room, or a python wrapped around your clock? Students who are familiar with either the book or the movie know they have to finish the game to get rid of the animals. What if the game ends and the animals are still there? What would you do? These intriguing questions can start the students thinking before you read the book.

During Reading

As you read, encourage the children to look at the illustrations and try to determine the perspective. Ask them to think about where in the room or the park they would have to be to see things from the perspective shown in the illustrations. To get the students started on this activity, show them the first illustration, of Peter kneeling in the chair. Ask them where they would have to be in the room to see Peter from the angle depicted in the illustration. Their responses might be sitting or lying on the floor looking up.

After Reading

When you finish reading the story, examine the illustrations and ask the students about why they think the illustrations were drawn from different perspectives. The varying perspectives draw readers into the story, make some objects appear very large (the monkeys), and sometimes give readers a bird's-eye view. The altered perspectives keep readers off balance as reality and fantasy blend together in this jungle journey.

Discussions of this story could also focus on the importance of finishing things you start, the children's self-reliance as they realized that adults could not help them, cooperation as they worked together to finish the game, and things that might happen when you stay home alone.

WRITING

Mini-lesson—Action Verbs

- Explain to the students that the turmoil in the illustrations combined with the strong action verbs in the text take readers on a roller coaster ride of adventure.
- Reread the portions of the text where Peter runs from the lion and rhinos stampede through the house.
- If possible, project copies of the text and ask the students to examine it and locate the action verbs.
- As the students identify the action verbs, ask them to write the verbs in a column on the board or a large piece of chart paper.
- Label the column strong action verbs and add a second column that you label weaker verbs. (See Figure 6-7.)

Author

Chris Van Allsburg was born in Grand Rapids, Michigan. He lives in Providence, Rhode Island, with his wife Lisa, a former elementary school art teacher, and his two daughters. Children often ask why *Jumanji* has black-and-white illustrations and the reason is that when the author was in art school he did not study color (Marcus, 1998). Lisa, David Macaulay, and Macaulay's editor thought that Chris's drawings would appeal to children and with that encouragement came *The Garden of Abdul Gasazi*. Van Allsburg won a Caldecott Honor for *The Garden of Abdul Gasazi* in 1980 and a Caldecott medal for *The Polar Express* in 1986. Additional information about Chris Van Allsburg and other noted children's authors is at http://www .readingrockets.org/books/authorinter views.php. This Web site contains an interview with Van Allsburg that includes the story of Fritz, the bull terrier, featured in *The Garden of Abdul Gasazi,* who makes cameo appearances in other books.

Strong Action Verbs	Weak Verbs
roared	shout, growl
knocked	fell, pushed
squeeze	crawl
scrambled	rushed
slammed	shut, closed
charged	ran
crushing	breaking

Figure 6-7. Verb Chart

- Then, ask the students to suggest weaker verbs that are synonyms for the action verbs. A thesaurus, or www.thesaurus.com, can be used to locate weaker verbs and to find additional strong action verbs.

Modeling

- Share a piece of your writing with the students and ask them for suggestions about strong action verbs that you could use to replace verbs you have included in the piece.
- As they suggest verbs, you might have them write the verbs on the chart so that they can refer to them when they are writing.
- For example, here is a piece of writing that was revised by adding some strong action verbs. The original verbs are in parentheses.

Morning Walk

Early every morning, Blanco, our retired racing greyhound, toured (walked around) the pine tree–filled backyard to make sure that nothing had changed since his trip around the yard the evening before. Assured that nothing was amiss he sprinted (ran) to the patio on long, thin, powerful legs. There he pranced (stood) until someone slid open the glass door.

Writing Activity

- Before the students begin writing, offer them some options such as writing about what happens when the game ends and the animals do not disappear, or what might happen to the Budwig boys if they played Jumanji.
- The students might also be given the option of creating their own board game and then writing about what happens when two children play the game.
- Tell the students that one way to organize their writing would be to draw a board game and in each space write down what will happen if they land on that square. Then, they could actually roll dice, move markers, and write about what happens as the game is played.
- When they have completed their drafts, ask them to go back and underline the verbs in their writing.

Conferencing

- When the students have finished underlining the verbs in their writing, have them conference with a partner to determine if they used strong action verbs.
- The students can work together and use a thesaurus to find strong action verbs that more accurately portray what they are trying to say.

Where the Wild Things Are

by Maurice Sendak
Caldecott Medal Winner, 1964

READING

Before Reading

Story Summary

Max has had a busy evening getting into mischief. When his mother reaches the end of her patience, she calls him a "Wild Thing." Max retorts, "I'll eat you up!" and is banished to his room without supper. Alone in his room, Max's imagination takes flight and he sails to a make believe land where wild beasts cavort and he is in control. His anger and energy spent, he returns from his fantasy to find a warm dinner awaiting him in his bedroom. Max escapes from the real world of his bedroom to the fantasy world he creates in his mind. Once he calms down, he is ready to return to the real world where he knows he is loved. Sendak is a picture book illustrator who understands that the text, the illustrations, and the design of the book must all work together. The text describes what the colored pen-and-ink illustrations cannot and the illustrations do not repeat what the text tells us. The illustrations increase and decrease in size, as do the imaginary creatures when Max's fantasy and feelings intensify and lessen (Sonheim, 1997). An opera and a ballet have been written based on this storybook.

Activating Prior Knowledge

What does "mischief" mean? In this book, Max is sent to his room for "making mischief." What happens when you make mischief? Another way to introduce the book is to ask the students about how relatives greet them when they come to visit. Maurice Sendak's inspiration for the wild things was his Brooklyn relatives, who greeted him by pinching his cheeks as they leaned over him displaying bad teeth and hairy noses and threatening to eat him up because he was so cute (Lanes, 1980). *Where the Wild Things Are* (Sendak, 1963), *In the Night Kitchen* (Sendak, 1970), and *Outside Over There* (Sendak, 1981) form a trilogy of books that explore children's fantasies and feelings. All three books have engendered controversy over their themes and illustrations. If the students are familiar with *When Sophie Gets Angry—Really, Really Angry* (Bang, 1999) you can help them make connections between the two texts as both texts are about dealing with feelings and emotions.

During Reading

As you read the book you might want to mention to the students how the illustrations change to match Max's feelings. On the wordless double-page spreads pause long enough for the students to view the details in the illustrations.

After Reading

Use questions such as these to begin a discussion of the story:

- Why was Max's mother mad? You can find the reasons for her anger in the illustrations where Max is seen chasing the dog with a fork, standing on books, and cracking the wall as he hammers a large nail.

❖ ─────────────

Recommended Grade Levels

1–4

Standards for the English Language Arts

2, 4, 5, 6, 8, 12

Information Literacy Standards for Student Learning

5, 8, 9

Objectives

The students will:

- Utilize a story map to diagram the real and the fantasy portions of the story, and

- Draw a picture of their fantasy world or create a story map to organize their writing.

───────────── ❖

❖ ─────────────

Author

Maurice Sendak was born in Brooklyn, New York, the youngest of three children. His parents were Polish immigrants and Sendak credits the fantastic stories his father told as important sources for his own stories. As a young child he was very sick and spent a great deal of time in bed, looking out of his window and sketching the children he saw playing outdoors. In 1955, Sendak created a dummy book titled *Where the Wild Horses Are* and put it away until 1963, when it eventually evolved into *Where the Wild Things Are* (Marcus, 1998). Recognizing how difficult it is to become a children's book illustrator, after he won the Caldecott medal he devoted himself to helping other illustrators get started (Sonheim, 1997). Maurice Sendak won Caldecott Honors for *A Very Special House* (Krauss, 1953), *What Do You Say, Dear?* (Joslin, 1958), *The Moon Jumpers* (Udry, 1959), *Little Bear's Visit* (Minarik, 1961), *Mr. Rabbit and the Lovely Present* (Zolotow, 1962), *In the Night Kitchen* (Sendak, 1970), and *Outside Over There* (Sendak, 1981). In 1970, he became the first American to receive the Hans Christian Anderson Award in recognition for his entire body of work.

───────────── ❖

- Why does Max escape to his fantasy world?
- Why does he come back?
- What do the Wild Things remind you of?
- Describe the Wild Things.
- Describe Max's fantasy world. Why might it be a good place to visit? Why might you not want to visit?
- What parts of Max's fantasy world seem real? What parts of his world are not real?
- How do you know Max is in charge in his fantasy world?
- Why is it important for Max to be in charge?
- Have you ever felt like a Wild Thing?
- When you feel like a Wild Thing what do you do to calm yourself down?

WRITING

Mini-lesson—Real and Fantasy

- Ask the students which parts of the story are real and which parts are fantasy. Sendak first sets the problem in the real world, transports Max to his fantasy world, and in the end returns Max to his own world (Sonheim, 1997).
- Create the story map with *Inspiration* software and project a copy of the blank story map in the appendix, or draw the story map on chart paper.
- Work with the children to complete the story map as shown in Figure 6-8.

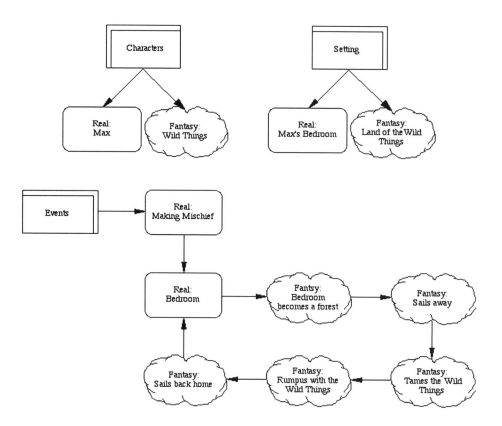

Figure 6-8. *Wild Things* **Story Map**

Modeling

- Tell the students that when he is alone in his room, Max closes his eyes and imagines a fantasy world where he can take control of his feelings and his actions. Escaping to his fantasy world allows Max to relax and calm down.
- Explain to the students that when they get angry, frustrated, or scared they can do as Max does and create their own fantasy world.
- Tell the students that sometimes going to the dentist to get a tooth filled can be a scary experience. So, when they are in the dentist's office they can create a fantasy place to escape to in their mind.
- Project a blank story map to use to organize your writing.
- As you complete the story map share your thoughts with the students.
- Your story map might look something like the one in Figure 6-9.

Writing Activity

- Ask the students to close their eyes and imagine a place they can escape to when they are feeling angry, frustrated, or scared.
- The students can then draw a picture of their fantasy place just as Sendak uses two-page spreads to show the fantasy world rather than describe it in words.
- Give the students blank story maps to help them organize their writing.
- Have the students write about their adventures using the notes on their story maps.

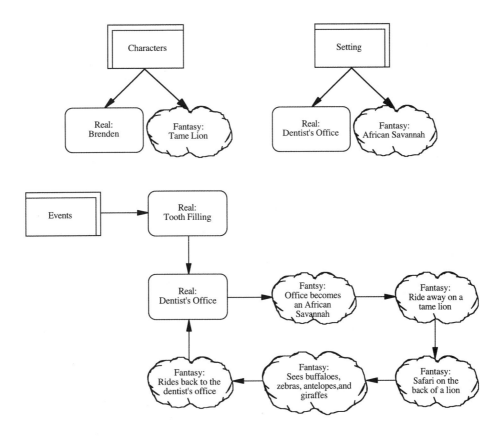

Figure 6-9. African Savannah Story Map

Conferencing

- Allow the students to conference in small groups and ask them to read their stories to each other.
- Remind the students to listen very carefully to be sure they understand the stories.
- When the author finishes reading, the other group members offer positive feedback and suggestions to the author.

McElligot's Pool

by Dr. Seuss (Theodor Seuss Geisel)
Caldecott Honor Book, 1948

READING

Before Reading

Story Summary

Anyone who has ever spent time fishing dreams of catching that special fish. When the farmer tells Marco that he will never catch a fish in McElligot's Pool, Marco begins dreaming about that special fish he just might catch. Marco decides that an underground stream might feed the pool and who knows where that stream begins. In Marco's imagination there are all sorts of wondrous fish that could be swimming toward his hook this very minute. Readers get swept away with Marco's enthusiasm and join in believing that unusual, never-before-seen fish are swimming his way.

Activating Prior Knowledge

Sharing experiences about going fishing sets the stage for this fantasy fishing outing. For students who are familiar with the imaginative animals in Dr. Seuss's books, you can show them the cover of the book and ask them to predict what kinds of interesting creatures might be lurking in the waters of McElligot's Pool.

During Reading

The rhyme, repetition, and rhythm of the text and the creative illustrations enchant readers, who are grateful the book is as long as it is. As you read, pause occasionally to let the students predict what kind of sea creature will appear next.

After Reading

Rather than having a whole class discussion of this book, you can put the children in small groups with crayons and drawing paper and let them discuss the book as they draw their own imaginative sea creatures. Students who have difficulty creating their own sea creatures can return to Dr. Seuss's illustrations and draw their own variations of his creatures. Students can also use *Exploring the Deep, Dark Sea* (Gibbons, 1999) and *Down, Down, Down in the Ocean* (Markle, 1999) to get ideas for their own special sea creature. As the students draw, the librarian and the teacher can move among the groups and answer questions about the story.

❖

Recommended Grade Levels

1–6

Standards for the English Language Arts

1, 4, 5, 6, 12

Information Literacy Standards for Student Learning

2, 3, 4, 9

Objectives

The students will:

- Predict what kinds of interesting creatures might be lurking in the waters of McElligot's Pool,
- Draw imaginative sea creatures,
- Examine books with sea creatures to gather ideas for designing their own sea creatures, and
- Write metaphors to describe their sea creatures.

❖

WRITING

Mini-lesson—Metaphor

- Return to the illustrations in the book and show the students how Dr. Seuss created a dogfish that looks like a dog and a catfish that looks like a cat.
- Explain to the students that we do not usually think of fish as looking like dogs or cats, but they do in Dr. Seuss's imagination. He has compared two unlike things, which is a metaphor.

Modeling

- Ask one of the students to let you share his or her drawing of the sea creature with the rest of the class.
- Hold the drawing up for the other students to see.
- Ask the students to help you think of a metaphor to describe the sea creature.
- Remind the students that a metaphor compares two unlike things.
- The drawing and sentence in Figure 6-10 shows a shark compared to a football.

Writing Activity

- Encourage the students to work in small groups to help each other create metaphors to describe their sea creatures.
- Suggest to the students that they return to the text and adapt Dr. Seuss's words and sentence patterns to create their metaphors.
- Just as Dr. Seuss places his words inside of the illustrations, the students can write their final descriptions on their illustrations.
- Their fanciful illustrations and descriptions can be displayed on the bulletin board or combined into a class book.

Conferencing

- Have the students conference in small groups to share their illustrations and their metaphors.
- Challenge them to help each other think up other metaphors to describe their sea creatures.

I might catch a shark
that looks like a football.

Figure 6-10. Shark

Author

Theodor Seuss Geisel was born in Springfield, Massachusetts. His mother read to Ted and his sister and his mother encouraged his drawing. His father taught him to be a perfectionist (Ford, 2003), a trait commented on by those who worked with him at Random House (Roback and Maughan, 1991). Prejudice against his German heritage and his family's brewery led to Ted Geisel being bullied by his schoolmates (Krull, 2004). He did not share his parents' fondness for rifle shooting and he avoided athletic endeavors, but he loved to draw. The zoo was only a few blocks from his home and his father was superintendent of parks, so Ted spent many hours at the zoo observing and drawing the animals. His lively, imaginative books have been credited with ridding the world of the deadly, boring stories of Dick, Jane, and Spot (Bandler, 1987). Dr. Seuss won Caldecott Honors for *If I Ran the Zoo* (Seuss, 1950) and *Bartholomew and the Oobleck* (Seuss, 1949). Additional information about Dr. Seuss and his work is at http://www.seussville.com/.

RESOURCES FOR LIBRARIANS AND TEACHERS

Here are the books discussed in this chapter and some other fantasy Caldecott Medal and Honor books.

Falconer, Ian. 2000. *Olivia.* New York: Lectorum.

Henkes, Kevin. 1993. *Owen.* New York: Greenwillow.

———. 2003. *Olive's Ocean.* New York: Greenwillow.

———. 2004. *Kitten's First Full Moon.* New York: Greenwillow.

Joslin, Sesyle. 1958. *What Do You Say, Dear?* Illustrated by Maurice Sendak. New York: Harper.

Krauss, Ruth. 1953. *A Very Special House.* Illustrated by Maurice Sendak. New York: Harper.

Lehman, Barbara. 2004. *The Red Book.* Boston: Houghton Mifflin.

Minarik, Else H. 1961. *Little Bear's Visit.* Illustrated by Maurice Sendak. New York: Harper.

Rohmann, Eric. 1994. *Time Flies.* New York: Crown.

———. 2002. *My Friend Rabbit.* Brookfield, CT: Roaring Brook.

Sendak, Maurice. 1963. *Where the Wild Things Are.* New York: HarperCollins.

———. 1970. *In the Night Kitchen.* New York: Harper.

———. 1981. *Outside Over There.* New York: Harper.

Seuss, Dr., pseud. (Theodor Seuss Geisel). 1947. *McElligot's Pool.* New York: Random.

———. 1949. *Bartholomew and the Oobleck.* New York: Random House.

———. 1950. *If I Ran the Zoo.* New York: Random House.

Udry, Janice May. 1959. *The Moon Jumpers.* Illustrated by Maurice Sendak. New York: Harper.

Van Allsburg, Chris. 1979. *Garden of Abdul Gasazi.* Boston: Houghton Mifflin.

———. 1981. *Jumanji.* Boston: Houghton Mifflin.

———. 1985. *The Polar Express.* Boston: Houghton Mifflin.

Ward, Lynd. 1952. *The Biggest Bear.* Boston: Houghton Mifflin.

Wiesner, David. 1988. *Free Fall.* New York: Lothrop.

———. 1991. *Tuesday.* Boston: Houghton Mifflin.

———. 1999. *Sector 7.* New York: Clarion.

Willems, Mo. 2003. *Don't Let the Pigeon Drive the Bus.* New York: Hyperion.

Zolotow, Charlotte. 1962. *Mr. Rabbit and the Lovely Present.* Illustrated by Maurice Sendak. New York: Harper.

Resource Books

Bang, Molly. 1999. *When Sophie Gets Angry—Really, Really Angry.* New York: Scholastic.

Gibbons, Gail. 1999. *Exploring the Deep, Dark Sea.* Boston: Little, Brown.

Keats, Ezra Jack. 1962. *The Snowy Day.* New York: Viking.

Markle, Sandra. 1999. *Down, Down, Down in the Ocean.* New York: Walker.

RESOURCES FOR STUDENTS

Students interested in reading other books by the authors and illustrators in this chapter might consider reading these books.

Grimm, Wilhelm (Trans. Ralph Manheim). 1988. *Dear Mili: An Old Tale.* Illustrated by Maurice Sendak. New York: Farrar Straus Giroux.

Henkes, Kevin. 1990. *Julius, the Baby of the World.* New York: Greenwillow.

———. 1991. *Chrysanthemum.* New York: Greenwillow.

———. 1996. *Lilly's Purple Plastic Purse.* New York: Greenwillow.

———. 2000. *Wemberly Worried.* New York: Greenwillow.

Kushner, Tony. 2003. *Brundibar.* Illustrated by Maurice Sendak. New York: Hyperion.

Marshall, James. 1999. *Swine Lake.* Illustrated by Maurice Sendak. New York: HarperCollins.

Rohmann, Eric. 1997. *The Cinder-Eyed Cats.* New York: Crown.

Sendak, Maurice. 1962. *Chicken Soup with Rice: A Book of Months.* New York: Harper & Row.

———. 1993. *We Are All in the Dumps with Jack and Guy: Two Nursery Rhymes with Pictures.* New York: HarperCollins.

Seuss, Dr., pseud. (Theodor Seuss Geisel). 1948. *Thidwick, the Big-Hearted Moose.* New York: Random.

———. 1954. *Horton Hears a Who!* New York: Random.

———. 1957. *The Cat in the Hat.* New York: Random.

———. 1957. *How the Grinch Stole Christmas.* New York: Random.

———. 1960. *Green Eggs and Ham.* New York: Random House.

———. 1972. *Marvin K. Mooney, Will You Please Go Now!* New York: Random.

———. 1990. *Oh, the Places You'll Go.* New York: Random.

Van Allsburg, Chris. 1984. *The Mysteries of Harris Burdick.* Boston: Houghton Mifflin.

———. 1993. *The Sweetest Fig.* Boston: Houghton Mifflin.

———. 1995. *Bad Day at Riverbend.* Boston: Houghton Mifflin.

———. 2002. *Zathura: A Space Adventure.* Boston: Houghton Mifflin.

Wiesner, David. 1990. *Hurricane.* New York: Clarion.

———. 1992. *June 29, 1999.* New York: Clarion.

———. 2001. *The Three Pigs.* New York: Clarion.

IDEAS FOR PARENTS AND CAREGIVERS

Wordless and almost wordless picture books allow parents and caregivers, no matter what their reading ability, to share stories with their children. If the parents and caregivers do not speak English or speak English as a second language they can share the wordless books in their first language. Some of the books in this chapter have movie versions and parents and caregivers can watch them with the students. After they read the books and watch the movies, parents, caregivers, and children can then discuss which version they liked better and make comparisons between the versions. Using movie reviews in the newspaper as models, the family can write their own reviews of the movies they watch together.

REFERENCES

Bandler, Michael J. 1987. "Seuss on the Loose." *Parents Magazine* 62, no. 9 (September): 116–120, 229–230.

Baskin, Kenda. 2003. "What Literature Has to Tell Us." *Library Media Connection* 21, no. 4 (January): 24–27.

Caroff, Susan F., and Elizabeth B. Moje. 1992/1993. "A Conversation with David Wiesner: 1992 Caldecott Medal Winner." *The Reading Teacher* 46, no. 4 (December/January): 284–289.

Coutot, Marilyn. 2004. "David Wiesner." [Online] Available: http://www.childrenslit
.com/f_wiesner.html [cited 3 May 2005].

Drennan, Mirian. 1999. "David Wiesner: Telling the Story with Pictures." [Online]
Available: http://www.bookpage.com/9909bp/david_wiesner.html [cited 3
May 2005].

Fischer, David Marc. 2004. "Flights of Fantasy." *Scholastic Scope* 53, no. 4/5 (18
October): 16–19.

Ford, Carin T. 2003. *Dr. Seuss: Best-Loved Author.* Berkeley Heights, NJ: Enslow.

Healy, John W. 2004. "Curriculum that Works: Artful Author Studies." *Teaching
PreK–8* 35, no. 3 (November/December): 34–35.

Hurst, Carol Otis. 1993. "Five 'Sure Things' Books for Not-So-Sure Times."
Teaching PreK–8 24, no. 1 (August/September): 76–79.

Inspiration. Version 7.5. Portland, OR: Inspiration Software.

Kidspiration. Version 2.1. Portland, OR: Inspiration Software.

Krapp, JoAnn Vergona. 2004. "So Many Books: Genres of Children's Fiction."
School Library Media Activities Monthly 21, no. 2 (October): 44–45.

Krull, Kathleen. 2004. *The Boy on Fairfield Street: How Ted Geisel Grew Up to
Become Dr. Seuss.* New York: Random.

Lanes, Selma G. 1980. *The Art of Maurice Sendak.* New York: Abrams.

Lenihan, Greg. 2003. "Reading with Adolescents: Constructing Meaning Together."
Journal of Adolescent and Adult Literacy 47, no. 1 (September): 8–12.

Marantz, Kenneth. 1985. "Review of *The Polar Express.*" *School Library Journal* 32,
no. 10 (October): 164–165.

Marcus, Leonard S. 1998. *A Caldecott Celebration: Six Artists and Their Paths to
the Caldecott Medal.* New York: Walker.

Nodelman, Perry. 1996. "Some Presumptuous Generalizations about Fantasy." In
Only Connect: Readings on Children's Literature, 3rd ed., edited by Sheila
Egoff, Gordon Stubbs, Ralph Ashley, and Wendy Sutton. Toronto, ON:
Oxford.

Op de Beeck, Nathalie. 1996. "A Talk with Kevin Henkes." *Publisher's Weekly* 243,
no. 33 (12 August): 26.

Pinnell, Gay Su, and Irene C. Fountas. 1998. *Word Matters: Teaching Phonics and
Spelling in the Reading/Writing Classroom.* Portsmouth, NH: Heinemann.

Raymo, Chet. 1996. "Dr. Seuss and Dr. Einstein: Children's Books and Scientific
Imagination." In *Only Connect: Readings on Children's Literature,* 3rd ed.,
edited by Sheila Egoff, Gordon Stubbs, Ralph Ashley, and Wendy Sutton.
Toronto, ON: Oxford.

Roback, Diane, and Shannon Maughan. 1991. "Dr. Seuss Remembered." *Publishers
Weekly* 238, no. 47 (25 October): 32–33.

Robertson, Barbara. 1996. "*Jumanji*'s Amazing Animals." *Computer Graphics World*
19, no. 1 (January): 28–34.

Rohmann, Eric. 2003. "Caldecott Medal Acceptance." *Horn Book* 79, no. 4
(July/August): 393–400.

Rohmann, Eric, and Pat Scales. 2003. "Eric Rohmann Crawled Out on a Limb to
Create the Caldecott Medal–Winning *My Friend Rabbit.*" *School Library
Journal* 49, no. 7 (July): 52–54.

Sherman, Fraser. 1994. "Off to See the Wizards." *Writer* 107, no. 11 (November):
18–20.

Silvey, Anita, editor. 2002. *The Essential Guide to Children's Books and Their
Creators.* Boston: Houghton Mifflin.

Sonheim, Amy. 1997. "Maurice Sendak." In *Twayne's United States Authors on
CD-ROM.* New York: G. K. Hall.

Van Allsburg, Chris. 2002. "Voices of the Creators." In *Children's Books and Their Creators,* edited by Anita Silvey. Boston: Houghton Mifflin.

Wiesner, David. 1992. "Caldecott Acceptance Speech." *Horn Book* 68, no. 4 (July): 416–422.

Yolen, Jane. 1996. "Turtles All the Way Down." In *Only Connect: Readings on Children's Literature,* 3rd ed., edited by Sheila Egoff, Gordon Stubbs, Ralph Ashley, and Wendy Sutton. Toronto, ON: Oxford.

7 ❖ INFORMATION

Information or nonfiction books contain facts about real things, people, and events. Reading information books and writing about real things, people, and events gives children a powerful motivation to learn and actively engage in inquiry. Information books have an unlimited scope, provide children with information on topics of interest to them, and satisfy children's curiosity about the world. Using information books as models for writing ensures that students learn about specific topics and gain a deeper understanding of the structure of expository texts (Moss, 2004). Observations of students reading information books in their classrooms showed that many of the books were too difficult for them to read on their own, so they simply looked at the pictures (Palmer and Stewart, 2003). When teachers incorporate information books, magazine articles, media, and Internet resources into their curriculum, librarians are invaluable resources as they can locate materials that have the appropriate concept load for the students and that match the students' reading levels.

Debbie Abilock, a librarian, and Molly Lusignan, a science teacher (1998), found that when they collaborated their collective wisdom improved their teaching, and that when they worked together they were able to provide each other support as they taught the students information literacy skills to use as they researched their topics. Librarians and teachers can form powerful partnerships when they work together to teach students how to research and write information texts. Teachers know their students' abilities and they know their curriculum, whereas librarians know how to teach information literacy skills and how to integrate the skills into the curriculum (Riedling, 2004). Additionally, Riedling notes that collaboration takes time, trust, and understanding. Gross and Kientz (1999) contend that collaborating with teachers to integrate information literacy skills into the curriculum provides students with a meaningful context for learning. Through her collaboration with teachers Virginia Rankin (1996) discovered that starting with brief interesting text, modeling the writing for the students, and giving the students time to practice writing in pairs before they wrote individually resulted in high-quality, original student writing.

Snowball (1995) and Furr (2003) found that students who struggled to write fiction flourished when writing information texts. Before writing, the students read and examined nonfiction books on topics of their own choosing. The teachers read nonfiction books aloud and discussed how the information in the books was organized. These books provided the students with models for their own writing and gave them ideas for presenting material not only with text but also with graphs, charts, illustrations, and diagrams. The students selected their own informational writing topics based on their personal interests. Writing on personally interesting topics allows the students' voices to come through in their writing. Modeling their writing on the structure of a familiar information text enables students to focus on the content rather than the organization. Moss (2004) suggests that you first model for the students how to use the structure of the text to organize their writing and then have them write using the structure.

Nonfiction writer James Cross Giblin (1994) suggests that you write about something that interests you. He collects newspaper and magazine articles about topics that interest him. When he begins to write he starts with the articles he has and then he begins researching his topic. He will use only some of the material he gathers, but he feels that the knowledge he gains from his research gives his writing credibility and authenticity. Before he begins writing, he reads and rereads his notes; then when he writes he does not have to refer to his notes, and his writing flows freely. Giblin revises each paragraph until it sounds just right and he strives to make his writing speakable, as his books are frequently read aloud. He notes that writing nonfiction is difficult because you have to read a great deal of information and then write about it in a clear, readable, entertaining style.

Ferrell's (1999) suggestions for adult authors interested in writing nonfiction for young readers are also helpful for young writers who are writing nonfiction. She suggests that authors study the nonfiction books of other authors, show the readers that you have fascinating things to tell them such as unusual facts and anecdotes, keep your audience in mind as you write, use action verbs, address the senses, use an interesting lead, and include newspaper headlines, dialogue, and pictures to break up the text and to hold the readers' interest.

So You Want to Be President?

by Judith St. George
Illustrated by David Small
Caldecott Medal Winner, 2001

READING

Before Reading

Story Summary
The premise of the book is that anyone can grow up to be president, but there are some factors that might help you become president, such as being born in a log cabin or being named James. Using a comparison and contrast format, St. George shares a fascinating collection of anecdotes and trivia about the presidents of the United States. She compares their sizes, their occupations, their personalities, their ages, and their spending habits. The book reveals the presidents' abilities and their faults showing them as the fallible human beings they are (Small, 2001). At the end of the book are the presidential oath, a list of the presidents found in each of the illustrations, a very brief biography of each of the presidents, and a bibliography. This extensively researched book is a historical journey into the United States presidency, filled with comical anecdotes and humorous illustrations. While it is written for children, the book's clever nuances about the presidents and the humorous illustrations appeal to young adults and adults as well (Giorgis and Johnson, 2001/2002). Comical caricatures of the presidents fill the illustrations, rendered in ink, watercolor, and pastel chalk. This book is available on audiocassette, videocassette, CD, and DVD.

Activating Prior Knowledge
Before reading the book put the students in small groups and have them spend five minutes writing down the names of as many presidents as they can and any facts they remember about each president.

❖ ———————————
Recommended Grade Levels

5–10

Standards for the English Language Arts

1, 2, 4, 6, 7, 11, 12

Information Literacy Standards for Student Learning

1, 2, 3, 6, 8, 9

Objectives

The students will:

- Critically analyze the text,

- Complete a compare-and-contrast chart of presidential traits,

- Research the lives of famous Americans,

- Fill in a fact-gathering chart, and

- Compile the information from the fact-gathering chart into a class book.

——————————— ❖

❖ ─────────────────────

Author

Former teacher Judith St. George was born in Westfield, New Jersey. She remembers that as a child she loved to read and to receive books for Christmas presents. She enjoys doing research and looking into the past to find interesting people to write about. St. George saves all of her research notes. She delved into her boxes of notes as part of her research for this book and she consulted a book of statistics on the presidents. Her research on the presidents' lives uncovered a collection of fascinating presidential anecdotes (Margolis, 2000). Additional information about Judith St. George is available at http://www.judithstgeorge.com/. ❖

─────────────────────

During Reading

As you read the book use a different voice inflection for the presidential quotes to call students' attention to the quotes, or if there are multiple copies of the books invite the students to read the presidential quotes.

After Reading

St. George includes a variety of revealing quotes from the presidents in the book. Return to the book, read the quotes aloud, and have the students discuss the quotes and what they reveal about the presidents' thoughts and personalities. If you are using the book with younger students focus the discussion on the presidents they are most familiar with such as George Washington and Abraham Lincoln.

WRITING

Mini-lesson—Compare and Contrast

- Explain to the students that St. George used a compare-and-contrast organization for the book.
- Project a comparison chart such as the one in Figure7-1 to show the students how St. George compared and contrasted the presidential traits by grouping the related traits in a logical way.

Modeling

- Tell the students that they will be completing a similar chart as they collect information on a group of people in order to write an informative book modeled on *So You Want to Be President?* (St. George, 2000).

Presidents	Sizes	Ages	Pets
George Bush			Dog
Jimmy Carter			Cats
Bill Clinton			Dog, Cat
Benjamin Harrison			Goat
Herbert Hoover			3 Dogs
Abraham Lincoln	Tallest		
James Madison	Shortest		
Ronald Regan		Oldest	
Franklin Roosevelt			Dog
Theodore Roosevelt		Youngest	Dogs, Cats, Mice, Rats, Guinea Pigs, Badgers, Raccoons, Parrots, Shetland Pony
William Howard Taft	Biggest		

Figure 7-1. Comparing the Presidents

- Have copies of *So You Want to Be an Inventor?* (St. George, 2002), *So You Want to Be an Explorer?* (St. George, 2005), and *The Buck Stops Here: The Presidents of the United States* (Provensen, 1990) available in the classroom to give the students additional books to use as models for their writing.
- Let the class decide on the group of people they will research. You might suggest astronauts, scientists, famous African Americans, famous women, or technology visionaries.
- Working together, the librarian and the teacher can locate book series such as Internet Biographies published by Enslow, Great Minds of Science published by Enslow, or Colonial Leaders published by Chelsea House for the students to use as resources. Additional resources are in the teacher resource section at the end of this chapter and information can be located on the Internet.
- Using bulletin board paper, create a large chart (see Figure 7-2) for the class to use to gather information on the people they will include in their book.
- As they begin gathering information, encourage them to suggest other columns to add to the chart.
- As the students are completing the chart encourage them to locate interesting facts and quotes about the people and to make comparisons such as the ones St. George made in her books.
- A chart for technology visionaries might look like the one in Figure 7-2. There is a blank copy of this chart in the appendix.
- As the students are gathering information for the chart, have them create a bibliography of the resources they consulted to put at the end of the book.

Writing Activity

- Invite the students to return to *So You Want to Be President?* (St. George, 2000), *So You Want to Be an Inventor?* (St. George, 2002), *So You Want to Be an Explorer?* (St. George, 2005), and *The Buck Stops Here: The Presidents*

❖ ───────────────
Illustrator

David Small was born in Detroit, Michigan, and spent summers in rural Indiana. He did extensive research for the illustrations in this book, which included, among other things, examining official presidential portraits, studying photographs of the presidents, a visit to Monticello, and research on the architecture of the White House (Giorgis and Johnson, 2001/2002). In his Caldecott acceptance speech Small noted that in this book he was able to combine his years of experience as an editorial artist and his experience as a children's book illustrator (Small, 2001). In his speech he decried the lack of art programs in many of the nation's schools, because the art classes he attended in school gave direction to his life (Small, 2001). He illustrates his own books and books for other authors including his wife, Sarah Stewart. David Small received a Caldecott Honor for *The Gardener* (Stewart, 1997). Additional information about David Small is available at http://www.nccil.org/small.html.
─────────────── ❖

Visionary	Birthday	Birthplace	Company	Partners	Other Jobs
Jeff Bezos	1/12/64	New Mexico	Amazon.com		Programmer
Steve Case	8/21/58	Honolulu, Hawaii	America Online		Pizza Hut Manager
Esther Dyson	7/14/51	Zurich, Switzerland	EDVenture Holdings		Reporter, Analyst
Larry Ellison	8/17/44	New York	Oracle Corporation	Bob Miner Ed Oates	Programmer
Bill Gates	10/28/55	Seattle, Washington	Microsoft Corporation	Paul Allen	Programmer
Steve Jobs	2/24/55	California	Apple Computer	Steve Wozniak	Video Game Designer

Figure 7-2. Fact-Gathering Chart

of the United States (Provensen, 1990) to use as models as they write short blurbs about the similarities and differences among the visionaries.

- Have the students post their blurbs on a bulletin board.
- After the students read the blurbs let them decide which ones will be included in the class book.
- Assign one group of students to type the blurbs into a word processing program or a desktop publishing program.
- Assign another group of students to edit and proofread the text.
- Students in the class who enjoy drawing can be assigned to create illustrations to accompany the blurbs.

Conferencing

- As you conference with the students, encourage them to carefully examine the information in the chart and look for unusual things about the visionaries that might lend themselves to comparisons.
- Rather than tell the students about comparisons they should make, ask questions about their research to help them discover the comparisons.

White Snow, Bright Snow

by Alvin Tresselt
Illustrated by Roger Duvoisin
Caldecott Medal Winner, 1948

❖ ─────────────

Recommended Grade Levels

2–5

Standards for the English Language Arts

1, 2, 4, 11, 12

Information Literacy Standards for Student Learning

3, 5, 9

Objectives

The students will:

- Complete a cause-and-effect chart on the impact of the snowstorm,
- Create a cause-and-effect chart based on an event in their lives, and
- Use the information in the chart to organize their writing about an event in their lives.

─────────────── ❖

READING

Before Reading

Story Summary

The story begins with rhyming couplets describing falling snow blanketing the earth. Then, readers join the postman, the farmer, the policeman, the policeman's wife, the rabbits, and the children as they anticipate the approaching snowstorm, contend with the snow, and search for signs of spring as the snow melts. Tresselt and Duvoisin also collaborated on *Hide and Seek Fog*, which won a Caldecott Honor in 1966 and is another example of a book with a cause-and-effect structure.

Activating Prior Knowledge

Introduce this book to the students using the note at the end of the book that tells how Tresselt's mother always complained that her big toe hurt before a snowfall. Ask the students how they know when the weather is going to change.

During Reading

As you share the book with the students point out that the author uses a cause-and-effect structure to organize the information about the winter storm. Tell the students to listen carefully to learn what the characters do when a snowstorm blankets the town.

After Reading

One way to discuss the events in the story is to complete a chart on the impact of the storm on each of the characters. The chart in Figure 7-3 shows how the characters reacted to the snowstorm.

The chart can be adapted depending on the ages and ability levels of the students. Some students might need to complete the chart as a whole group activity, others might work in small groups to complete the chart, and some students might focus on only one or two of the characters.

Author

Alvin Tresselt says that he wrote his nature stories in poetic prose to help children develop an appreciation for the feeling of words and language. He was born in Passaic, New Jersey, in 1916 and died in 2000. The University of Minnesota houses some of his original manuscripts (Tresselt, 2001). Tresselt's wife, Blossom Budney, also wrote children's books.

Characters	Snowstorm coming	Snow begins to fall	That night	Next day	Signs of Spring
Postman	looks like snow	put on his rubbers	slipped and fell	put on his high boots	delivered mail
Farmer	smells like snow	got his snow shovel	dug a path to the barn	milked his cows	let his cows out of the barn
Policeman	feels like snow	buttoned his coat	got his feet wet and soaked them	stayed in bed with a chill	felt better and walked in the park
Wife	big toe hurt	found the cough mixture	made a mustard plaster	knitted a scarf	looked for snowdrops and crocuses
Rabbits	scurried in the leaves	hid under ground	stirred in their sleep	made rabbit tracks	hopped in the warm world
Children	watched and waited	laughed and danced	dreamed of playing in the snow	played in the snow	watched for the first robin

Figure 7-3. Snowstorm Cause and Effect

❖ ────────────────

Illustrator

Roger Duvoisin was born in Switzerland in 1904. He was a prolific American author and illustrator. He illustrated the Happy Lion series authored by his wife, Louise Fatio. His father, an architect, and his godmother, a painter, encouraged him to pursue his interest in drawing (Silvey, 2002). He came to America to work for a textile design firm that closed during the Great Depression. He then began illustrating magazines and children's books. During his lifetime, he wrote and illustrated over forty books and illustrated over 100 books. When he was a child his parents worried because he spent so much time reading. He liked to visit the zoo and the traveling circus because that gave him opportunities to practice drawing animals. Many of the books he illustrated feature animals as the main characters. ❖

────────────────

WRITING

Mini-lesson—Cause and Effect

- Select a familiar event in nature such as a hurricane, a tornado, a snow-storm, or a thunderstorm.
- Project a copy of a cause-and-effect chart to record your experiences. There is a blank cause-and-effect chart in the appendix.
- Have the students help you add details to complete the chart. (See Figure 7-4.)

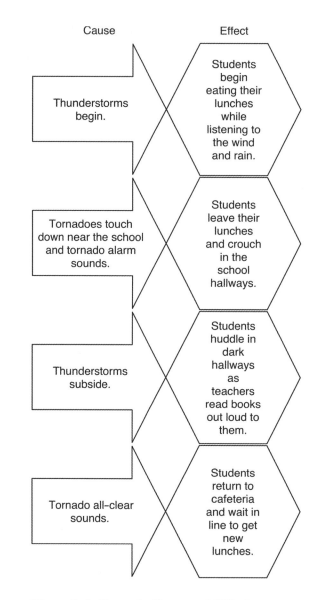

Figure 7-4. Tornado Cause and Effect

Modeling

- Use the information in the chart to begin writing your story.
- As you write, describe aloud what you are thinking and feeling.
- Your story might look something like this:

Tornado

Howling wind whipped around the cafeteria as rain pelted down on the roof while 130 hungry fourth graders made their way through the lunch line. Suddenly the lights flickered and then darkness engulfed the cafeteria. Before the startled children and teachers could react the tornado siren pierced the air. Pandemonium broke out and the teachers scurried to get the students into the safety of the schools' inner hallways.

Writing Activity

Younger Students

- Project a blank copy of the cause-and-effect chart.
- Remind the students of a recent event in the school or a local event that they experienced.
- Work together as a class to complete the cause-and-effect chart.
- Then, as a class write a story using the information in the chart.

Older Students

- Give each student a blank copy of the cause-and-effect chart.
- Provide the students with time to talk to each other to share ideas about the topics for their stories.
- As they decide on a topic ask them to write it at the top of the page and begin filling in their charts.
- Once the students complete the charts they are ready to begin writing their stories.
- Remind them to check off each cause and effect in their charts as they include it in their stories.
- As the students write continue writing your story.

Conferencing

- As you conference with the students bring along your own writing and have them ask you questions about your writing.
- During a conference ask questions about the writer's choices or questions that arise from the writing rather than offering direct advice to the author (Wolf and Wolf, 2002).

Recommended Grade Levels

2–8

Standards for the English Language Arts

1, 4, 6, 7, 8, 11, 12

Information Literacy Standards for Student Learning

1, 2, 3, 6

Objectives

The students will:

- Discover the unique features of the animal's body parts,

- Access print and electronic resources to research animals,

- Use *Inspiration* software to create webs of information on animals, and

- Write informative pieces with interesting leads.

Authors

Steve Jenkins and Robin Page are a husband-and-wife team and this book is based on an idea Robin had. Steve and Robin collaborated on *Animals in Flight* (Jenkins and Page, 2001). They live with their three children in Boulder, Colorado.

What Do You Do with a Tail Like This?

by Steve Jenkins and Robin Page
Illustrated by Steve Jenkins
Caldecott Honor Book, 2004

READING

Before Reading

Story Summary

Captured within the pages of this book is a terrific animal guessing game. Not only do students have to guess which body parts belong to which animal; they have to guess how the animals use the body parts. From mouths that suck blood to eyes that squirt blood and from sticky feet to noses that dig, this is an informative, enticing look at the animal kingdom. Clear instructions at the beginning of the book tell readers to look carefully at each animal part and try to figure out which animal it belongs to and how it uses it. The book begins with five very distinct noses spread across two pages. The following two-page spread has a complete illustration of the animals and a brief description of how they use their noses. This format is followed throughout the book as students examine the ears, tails, eyes, feet, and mouths of a variety of animals. At the end of the book is a picture glossary with additional information about the animals featured in the book and answers to questions that might arise about the animals while reading the book. Cut-paper collage illustrations with a three-dimensional look and feel draw readers into the book.

Activating Prior Knowledge

Show the students the cover of the book and read the title. Explain to the students that the authors have used an intriguing question for the book title and there are intriguing questions throughout the book to grab the readers' attention and hook them into reading to discover the answers. Then ask the students to describe how cats, dogs, cows, horses, and lizards use their tails.

During Reading

As you read, pause and allow the children time to guess which animals the body parts belong to and what is unique about each body part.

After Reading

After reading let the children talk about what was the most interesting animal fact they learned. Then, ask them which animal they would like to research.

WRITING

Mini-lesson—Questions as Leads

- Explain to the students that they are going to research animals and write about the animals using a question as their lead or beginning.

- Tell the students that they are going to turn the most unusual or interesting fact about their topic into a question that becomes the first sentence in their text.
- The second sentence is going to be a general statement that invites readers to continue reading. Furr (2003) finds this pattern particularly helpful for his struggling fifth-grade readers who can immediately start writing after they conduct their research, as they know exactly how to begin their papers.
- Explain to the students that they are going to create webs to help them collect their information and to organize their papers.

Modeling

- Before modeling the activity for the students, gather a collection of books with information about different animals and select one animal to use to model the writing activity.
- Demonstrate for the students how to create a web using *Inspiration* software to organize the information you found on an animal. (See Figure 7-5.)
- Once the web is completed ask the students to help you select the most interesting fact to use as a strong lead.
- Ask the students to help you turn the interesting fact about the animal into a question.
- Remind the students that the sentence after the lead should be a general statement that invites their readers to continue reading.

Barred Owls

Who cooks for you? Who cooks for you all? You hear this call of the barred owls as evening falls and they begin to hunt their prey.

Writing Activity

- Introduce the students to the print and electronic resources available for their research about animals.

Illustrator

Steve Jenkins's father Alvin is a physicist and Steve always believed he would be a scientist like his father (Jenkins, 1999). His father encouraged Steve's interest in nature and supported his artistic endeavors. In college, rather than pursue a science degree, he majored in design. The children's books he writes and illustrates enable him to combine his interest in science with his art career. The topics for some of his books come from the questions his children ask (Silvey, 2002). Steve and his father collaborated on *Next Stop Neptune: Experiencing the Solar System* (Jenkins, 2004). Additional information about Steve Jenkins is available at http://www.childrenslit.com/f_stevejenkins.html.

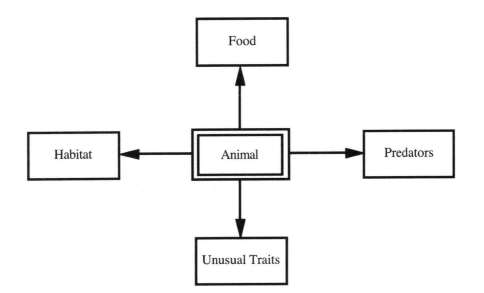

Figure 7-5. Animal Web

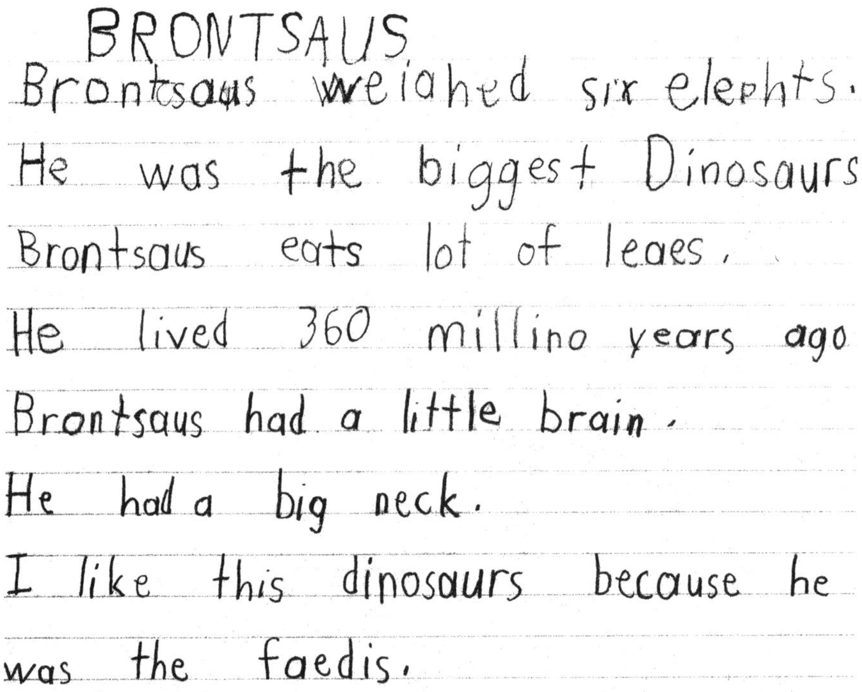

BRONTSAUS

Brontsaus weighed six elephts.

He was the biggest Dinosaurs

Brontsaus eats lot of leaes.

He lived 360 millino years ago

Brontsaus had a little brain.

He had a big neck.

I like this dinosaurs because he

was the faedis.

Figure 7-6. Brontosaurus

- Provide the students with a blank web to record their information. There is a blank animal web in the appendix.
- Have the students work with a partner to decide which fact about their animal is the most interesting and to turn the fact into a question to use as the lead for their report.

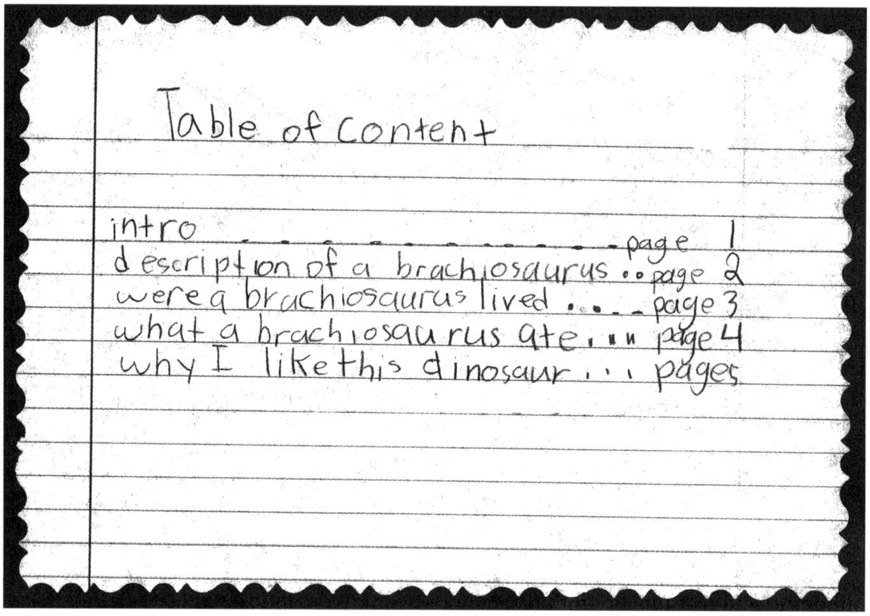

Table of Content

intro .... page 1
description of a brachiosaurus .. page 2
were a brachiosaurus lived ... page 3
what a brachiosaurus ate ... page 4
why I like this dinosaur ... page 5

Figure 7-7. Brachiosaurus Table of Contents

- After researching Brontosaurus a second grader began his report with the most interesting thing he learned, as shown in Figure 7-6.
- Another second grader in the same class created a book about Brachiosaurus complete with a table of contents, paper trimmed with fancy edges, and illustrations. Figure 7-7 is her table of contents and Figure 7-8 is the information she learned about his habitat with an illustration.

Figure 7-8. Brachiosaurus Habitat

Conferencing

- As you conference with the students, ask them to show you their webs and have them point out the one most interesting fact they learned about the animals they researched.
- Then, ask them to read you the questions they used for their leads and the general statements they wrote to invite their readers to continue reading.

❖ —————————————————————

Recommended Grade Levels

1–3

Standards for the English Language Arts

4, 5, 6, 12

Information Literacy Standards for Student Learning

4, 5, 6

Objectives

The students will:

- Dramatize action verbs, and
- Write sentences with action verbs.

—————————————————————— ❖

❖ —————————————————————

Author

After reading children's books to her daughter, Indigo, Denise Fleming decided that making books was something she needed to do (Fleming, 2002). She experimented with different styles of writing and art techniques until she found her own style. Her books begin with a rough idea and then she begins sketching. She carefully searches for the right words and likes words that feel good when you roll them around in your mouth. Her husband, who is also an artist, and her daughter help create her books. They live in Toledo, Ohio, with seven cats and a dog named Warfy. Her Web site at http://www.denisefleming.com contains information on the papermaking process she uses in her books.

—————————————————————— ❖

In the Small, Small Pond

by Denise Fleming
Caldecott Honor Book, 1994

READING

Before Reading

Story Summary

In this colorful, lively book, Fleming depicts a frog's-eye view of life in a pond. Changing seasons, the cycles of nature, pond animals, alliteration, rhyming words, and action verbs are all introduced in this colorful, lively picture book. Most of the pages of this rhyming text have four words on the double-page spreads. The book begins in the spring with tadpoles wiggling in the pond and ends with winter as the frog burrows into the mud at the bottom of the pond to wait for spring to come again. The colors in the illustrations change to reflect the seasons from the bright yellows and greens of spring and summer to the browns and oranges of fall to the white freeze of winter. *In the Tall, Tall Grass* (Fleming, 1995) is also a model for students to use to explore alliteration and action verbs. Fleming created the distinctive full-page illustrations by pouring colored cotton pulp through hand-cut stencils (Silvey and Burns, 1993). This book is also available on audiocassette, videocassette, and CD.

Activating Prior Knowledge

Alliteration and action verbs create a lively, rhyming poem that captivates young audiences and gives them a chance to participate as they wiggle and jiggle and waddle and wade along with the animals in the pond ecosystem. The words in the book are as much fun to say as they are to demonstrate, so have the students join you in wiggling, jiggling, waddling, and wading before your read the book.

During Reading

As you read, point out the frog splashing or lurking on every page of the book. This brief rhyming text is fun to read more than once. On subsequent readings point out how the colors on the pages change as the seasons change and how the activity in the pond changes as the seasons change.

After Reading

While young writers may not recognize the term "action verbs," they quickly learn wiggle, jiggle, waddle, shiver, twirl, sweep, and the other action verbs used in the poem. So as you discuss the book allow the children to demonstrate the animals' actions.

WRITING

Mini-lesson—Action Verbs

- Write "hop" on the board and have the students read it aloud with you.
- Next, ask one of the students to demonstrate a hop.
- Then, ask the students to think of a sentence about an animal that hops.
- Write the sentence on the board and have the students read the sentence with you.
- Ask the students to think of other action verbs that describe animals' movements, have them demonstrate the actions, and write sentences about the animals and their actions.

Modeling

- To demonstrate how action verbs make writing lively and interesting you can use an ecosystem the students have studied such as a rainforest or a desert.
- Have the students brainstorm and complete a chart on the animals and their actions such as the one in Figure 7-9.
- Just as Denise Fleming searches for just the right word, show the children how to search for just the right word.
- At this time you can introduce the students to the thesaurus to model selecting just the right word, or use http://www.thesaurus.com to find synonyms for the actions in the chart.
- Model for the students how to turn their lists of words into phrases or sentences to create a poem modeled on the text in the book.
- Your poem might look something like this:

In the Hot, Hot Desert
In the hot, hot desert . . .
scamper, scramble, lizards scurry
float, fly, hawks glide

Desert Animals	Actions
Hawk	fly, soar, hover, glide, skim, float
Coyote	run, chase, slink, hunt, race
Lizard	creep, scamper, scramble, slither, scurry

Figure 7-9. Desert Animals and Action Verbs

Writing Activity

- When you finish modeling the process, have the children work in groups to add additional animals and actions to the chart. There is a copy of a blank chart in the appendix.
- As they complete their charts, circulate around the room to answer any questions.
- The students can work together to write their texts using the information in their charts.

Conferencing

- Listen carefully as they read their writing by focusing on the content of what the students are reading. Does their writing reflect the content they learned about the ecosystem? Are there misconceptions in their understanding that you can clarify? Do they know more than they have included in their writing?
- Conferences such as these provide an informal assessment of the students' learning.

Freight Train

by Donald Crews
Caldecott Honor Book, 1979

Recommended Grade Levels

K–2

Standards for the English Language Arts

4, 5, 6, 12

Information Literacy Standards for Student Learning

4, 5, 6

Objectives

The students will:

- Match the colors of the freight train cars with the colors of their clothing,
- Predict the contents of the freight train cars, and
- Write descriptive phrases.

READING

Before Reading

Story Summary

This bright, colorful concept book uses short, descriptive sentences to introduce colors and the different kinds of cars on a freight train. The cars blur as the train begins moving, gathers speed, travels through the night into the daylight, and then disappears from the page. *Inside Freight Train* (Crews, 2001) is a sturdy, interactive board book that lets young readers peek inside the freight cars to see what each is carrying. In 2000, *Freight Train* was named one of the 100 books that shaped the twentieth century.

Activating Prior Knowledge

This concept book introduces the different cars on a freight train and introduces the colors red, orange, yellow, green, blue, purple, and black. Say each of the colors out loud and ask the students to stand up or raise their hands if they are wearing one of the colors that you mention. Students can also share their experiences in sitting at railroad crossings waiting for trains to pass.

During Reading

As you read the book increase the tempo as the train begins to move and disappear from the pages.

After Reading

When you finish reading the book, ask the children to predict what might be in each of the freight train cars. If you have a copy of *Inside Freight Train* (Crews, 2001), you can share that with the students after they have made their predictions. As you talk about the book, mention that modern freight trains do not have cabooses, tenders, and steam engines.

WRITING

Mini-lesson—Descriptive Phrases

- Crews uses brief, descriptive phrases throughout the book to describe the cars and the moving train.
- He describes each car first by its color and then its name, which is an easy writing pattern for young children to model.
- Tell the students to think about automobiles traveling down the highway. Rather than write about freight train cars moving down the railroad tracks, tell them they are going to write about cars on the highway.
- To help the students with their writing, have them make a color chart with the color words written next to the colors, or label different colored objects in the room with their colors.
- Ask the students to name different types of cars and write them on the chalkboard for them to refer to as they write.

Modeling

- Begin by quickly sketching your car. The idea is to quickly draw your car, as you want to focus on the writing.
- When you finish the sketch, tell them that first you are going to write down the color of your car and then you are going to write down the kind of car.
- Above the sketch, write a descriptive phrase about your car, writing first the color and then the name. (See Figure 7-10.)

Writing Activity

- Give the children blank sheets of paper and crayons or markers.
- Tell them to first draw a picture of a car.
- Magazine pictures of cars or photographs of cars will give them additional ideas for drawing and writing.

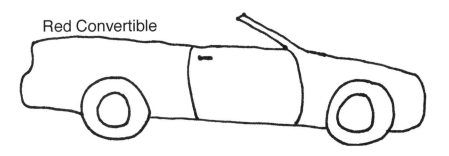

Figure 7-10. Red Convertible

Author

Donald Crews was born in Newark, New Jersey, and he has been drawing since he was a child. His mother was a dressmaker and she involved Donald and his three siblings in art projects. Trains were an important part of Crews' childhood as his father worked for the railroad and each summer Crews road the train to visit his grandparents in Cottondale, Florida, where he sat on the porch and watched the freight trains traveling through the countryside (Crews, 2002). In his books Crews emphasizes the pictures rather than the words and his brief stories end with a twist (Bodmer, 1998). Crews's wife Ann Jonas is an author and illustrator as is their daughter Nina Crews. *Truck* (Crews, 1981) received a Caldecott Honor. Additional information about Donald Crews is available at http://www.nccil.org/dcrews.html.

- Once the students have their car drawn tell them to write down the color of the car and the kind of car to form a descriptive phrase. Remind them to refer to the color words and the names of the cars written on the board.
- As they write their descriptive phrases, encourage them to use invented spellings if they do not know how to spell a word, instead of asking the teacher to spell the word for them. Using invented spellings helps children write with ease and think creatively (Neuman, 2004).

Conferencing

- As you conference with the students, ask them to read their descriptive phrases.
- The students can also conference with each other by sharing their pictures and reading their descriptive phrases.
- Laminate the drawings and bind them together to create a class book to send home with the students on a rotating basis for them to read with their parents.

The Desert Is Theirs

by Byrd Baylor
Illustrated by Peter Parnall
Caldecott Honor Book, 1976

READING

Before Reading

Story Summary
The interdependence of the Papago Indians and the other inhabitants of their desert environment are the focus of this picture book. This lyrical poem contains a great deal of information about the relationship between desert inhabitants and their environment. The desert dwellers' respect for the land, the animals, and the resources engenders in readers an appreciation of the desert environment and an understanding of the importance of respecting and protecting the environment. The Indians recognize that they do not own the land; they share it with the desert plants and animals. The people and the animals share the fruit of the cactus, the mesquite beans, and all of the desert resources. When the rain comes the people, the animals, and the plants all rejoice. This is one of several books that Baylor and Parnall have collaborated on about the American Southwest.

Activating Prior Knowledge
Introduce this book by having the students spend two minutes making lists of everything they know about the desert. Then, have several of the students read their lists aloud.

During Reading

Tell the students to listen carefully as you read because when you finish they are going to spend three minutes adding to their lists of things they know about the desert. The

---

❖ ─────────────
Recommended Grade Levels

5–8

Standards for the English Language Arts

1, 2, 4, 5, 6, 7, 9, 11, 12

Information Literacy Standards for Student Learning

1, 2, 3, 5

Objectives

The students will:

- Compile a list of characteristics of the desert and inhabitants of the desert,
- Discuss the interdependence of the desert inhabitants,
- Use the text structure as a model for their own writing, and
- Write their own text.

─────────────── ❖

peaceful harmony of this desert environment is reflected in the quiet, respectful tone of the writing. When read out loud, this is a book that can relax and quiet students after a rousing recess or exhausting field trip. The lyrical prose is for savoring and for reading more than once.

After Reading

When you finish reading the book, ask the students to spend three minutes adding to their lists of things they know about the desert. Begin your discussion of the book by having the students share the additional items they wrote on their lists. Ask the students to return to the text and find examples of how the inhabitants are dependent on one another and share the desert's resources. Examples from the story include the coyotes spreading the cactus's seeds and the people and the rats sharing the mesquite beans.

WRITING

Mini-lesson—Text Structure

- Closely examining the text structure helps students understand how to use the text as a model for their own writing.
- Make an overhead transparency of a page of the text. Begin by reading the page aloud as the students follow along.
- Ask them questions about the sentence beginnings, the content, and the layout of the text on the page. For example, page 15 begins, "Papagos try not to anger. . . ." On this page, the author tells what actions the Papagos take to avoid making the animals angry.
- Point out how several of the sentences begin with the word "They" and have a similar structure.
- The sentence content reveals that snakes, foxes, spiders, and ants are all desert inhabitants.
- The text hugs the left side of the two-page spread and each line is broken up into phrases.
- Toward the end of the page the author repeats the word "share" three times for emphasis.
- Explain to the students that these writing techniques are ones they can emulate in their own writing. Literature provides models for students as they adapt the authors' sentence patterns to their own writing (Barnitz, 1998).

Modeling

- If the students are familiar with another ecosystem, such as the rainforest, they can use that as the topic of their writing.
- The students can also write about their playground.
- If possible, take the students outside to the playground to quietly walk around and observe the plants and bugs.
- Call their attention to any litter on the playground or other signs that the playground is not being cared for properly.
- Ask the students to brainstorm a list of words about the playground to use in their writing.
- Model for the students how to write about their playground using the same text structure that Byrd Baylor used.

Author

Byrd Baylor grew up in the American Southwest including Arizona, Texas, and Mexico. Her books stress the importance of realizing our connections to the natural environment and the culture of Native Americans. Her quiet message of the importance of respecting the environment and living in harmony with the plants and animals is a powerful one reflected in many of her books. She writes about things that she cherishes and her passion for her topics shows in her writing.

Illustrator

Peter Parnall's stunning detailed illustrations of the natural world reflect the places he has lived, including the Mojave Desert, the Big Bend country in Texas, and the rugged coast of Maine (Silvey, 2002). He has written several short chapter books in addition to numerous picture books. As a child he developed a love of animals and went to college to become a veterinarian. However, he recognized that he would rather draw animals than take care of them so he began studying art. Parnall received Caldecott Honors for *Hawk, I'm Your Brother* (Baylor, 1977) and *The Way to Start a Day* (Baylor, 1978).

- Your writing might look something like this:

The Playground is Theirs
Students try
not to anger the creatures
on their playground.
They don't
knock over
the ant's home.
They don't
disturb
the bird's nest
in the tree.
We share.
We share
the playground
with other creatures.

Writing Activity

- As the students begin writing, encourage them to use the structure Baylor used and keep a sample of the text projected for them as they write.
- Baylor's structure provides a way for students to organize their thoughts and the information they have gathered.
- Reluctant writers benefit from having a structure to follow. More proficient writers in the class may want to branch off and decide on their own structure for their writing.
- The students will need time to experiment with their writing and those who are not comfortable writing poetry can write in a style that suits them.

Conferencing

- As you conference with the students ask them to read you a line and then tell you more about the line.
- As they talk, listen carefully so you can offer suggestions for additional details to include in their writing.

RESOURCES FOR LIBRARIANS AND TEACHERS

Here are the books discussed in this chapter and some other informational Caldecott Medal and Honor books.

Baylor, Byrd. 1972. *When Clays Sings*. Illustrated by Tom Bahti. New York: Scribner.
———. 1975. *The Desert Is Theirs*. Illustrated by Peter Parnall. New York: Scribner.
———. 1976. *Hawk, I'm Your Brother*. Illustrated by Peter Parnall. New York: Scribner.
———. 1978. *The Way to Start a Day*. Illustrated by Peter Parnall. New York: Scribner.
Crews, Donald. 1978. *Freight Train*. New York: Greenwillow.
———. 1980. *Truck*. New York: Greenwillow.
Feelings, Muriel. 1971. *Moja Means One: Swahili Counting Book*. Illustrated by Tom Feelings. New York: Dial.

———. 1974. *Jambo Means Hello: A Swahili Alphabet Book.* Illustrated by Tom Feelings. New York: Dial.

Fleming, Denise. 1993. *In the Small, Small Pond.* New York: Henry Holt.

Jenkins, Steve, and Robin Page. 2003. *What Do You Do with a Tail Like This?* Boston: Houghton Mifflin.

Kerley, Barbara. 2001. *The Dinosaurs of Waterhouse Hawkins.* Illustrated by Brian Selznick. New York: Scholastic.

Macaulay, David. 1973. *Cathedral.* Boston: Houghton Mifflin.

Musgrove, Margaret. 1976. *Ashanti to Zulu: African Traditions.* Illustrated by Leo and Diane Dillon. New York: Dial.

St. George, Judith. 2000. *So You Want to Be President?* Illustrated by David Small. New York: Philomel.

Tresselt, Alvin. 1947. *White Snow, Bright Snow.* Illustrated by Roger Duvoisin. New York: Lothrop.

———. 1965. *Hide and Seek Fog.* Illustrated by Roger Duvoisin. New York: Lothrop, Lee & Shepard.

Resource Books

Provensen, Alice. 1990. *The Buck Stops Here: The Presidents of the United States.* New York: Harper & Row.

Roy, Jennifer Rozines. 2002. *You Can Write a Report.* Berkeley Heights, NJ: Enslow.

RESOURCES FOR STUDENTS

Students interested in reading other books by the authors and illustrators in this chapter might consider reading these books.

Baylor, Byrd. 1986. *I'm in Charge of Celebrations.* Illustrated by Peter Parnall. New York: Scribner.

———. 1992. *One Small Blue Bead.* Illustrated by Ronald Himler. New York: Scribner.

Crews, Donald. 1984. *School Bus.* New York: Greenwillow.

———. 1992. *Shortcut.* New York: Greenwillow.

———. 1998. *Night at the Fair.* New York: Greenwillow.

———. 1999. *Cloudy Day/Sunny Day.* New York: Greenwillow.

———. 2001. *Inside Freight Train.* New York: HarperCollins.

Fleming, Denise. 1991. *In the Tall, Tall Grass.* New York: Henry Holt.

———. 1998. *Mama Cat Has Three Kittens.* New York: Henry Holt.

———. 2002. *Alphabet under Construction.* New York: Henry Holt.

———. 2003. *Buster.* New York: Henry Holt.

Jenkins, Alvin. 2004. *Next Stop Neptune: Experiencing the Solar System.* Illustrated by Steve Jenkins. Boston: Houghton Mifflin.

Jenkins, Steve. 1998. *Hottest, Coldest, Highest, Deepest.* Boston: Houghton Mifflin.

———. 1999. *The Top of the World: Climbing Mount Everest.* Boston: Houghton Mifflin.

———. 2001. *Slap, Squeak, & Scatter: How Animals Communicate.* Boston: Houghton Mifflin.

———. 2004. *Actual Size.* Boston: Houghton Mifflin.

Jenkins, Steve, and Robin Page. 2001. *Animals in Flight.* Boston: Houghton Mifflin.

Kerley, Barbara. 1995. *Songs of Papa's Island.* Boston: Houghton Mifflin.

————. 2002. *A Cool Drink of Water.* Washington, DC: National Geographic Society.

————. 2004. *Walt Whitman: Words for America.* Illustrated by Brian Selznick. New York: Scholastic.

Ryan, Pam Muñoz. 1999. *Amelia and Eleanor Go for a Ride.* Illustrated by Brian Selznick. New York: Scholastic.

————. 2002. *When Marian Sang: The True Recital of Marian Anderson.* New York: Scholastic.

Small, David. 1992. *Ruby Mae Has Something to Say.* New York: Crown Books for Young Readers.

————. 2000, 1985. *Imogene's Antlers.* New York: Random House.

St. George, Judith. 1997. *Betsy Ross, Patriot of Philadelphia.* Illustrated by Sasha Meret. New York: Henry Holt.

————. 1997. *Sacagawea.* Illustrated by Peter and Connie Roop. New York: Putnam.

————. 2000. *The Boy of a Thousand Faces.* New York: Laura Geringer.

————. 2002. *So You Want to Be an Inventor?* Illustrated by David Small. New York: Philomel.

————. 2004. *You're On Your Way, Teddy Roosevelt!* New York: Philomel.

————. 2005. *So You Want to Be an Explorer?* Illustrated by David Small. New York: Philomel.

Tresselt, Alvin. 1991, 1951. *Wake Up, Farm!* Illustrated by Carolyn Ewing. New York: Lothrop, Lee & Shepard.

————. 1992. *The Gift of the Tree.* Illustrated by Henri Sorensen. New York: Lothrop, Lee & Shepard.

Wells, Rosemary. 2002. *Wingwalker.* Illustrated by Brian Selznick. New York: Hyperion.

IDEAS FOR PARENTS AND CAREGIVERS

As children progress through the grade levels they read more information books in their classrooms. Parents and caregivers can familiarize the children with the structure of information books and help them learn to enjoy information books by including them when they read to the children. For example, children who are interested in dinosaurs prefer to be read books about dinosaurs, rather than stories. After reading the book parents and caregivers can talk about the information in the book and provide the children with pencils, crayons, markers, and paper so they can draw pictures and write about what they learn. (See Figure 7-11.)

Figure 7-11. Dinosaur

REFERENCES

Abilock, Debbie, and Molly Lusignan. 1998. "Teacher-Librarian Collaboration in Practice." *Book Report* 17, no. 2 (September/October): 42–45.

"Alvin Tresselt." 2001. *Contemporary Authors Online.* Farmington Hills, MI: Thomson Gale.

Barnitz, John. 1998. "Revising Grammar Instruction for Authentic Composing and Comprehending." *The Reading Teacher* 51, no. 7 (April): 608–611.

Bodmer, George. 1998. "Donald Crews: The Signs and Times of an American Childhood—Essay and Interview." *African American Review* 32, no. 1 (Spring): 107–117.

"Donald Crews." 2002. *Contemporary Authors Online.* Farmington Hills, MI: Thomson Gale.

Ferrell, Nancy Warren. 1999. "Writing Nonfiction for Young Readers." *Writer* 114, no. 4 (April): 14–16.

Fleming, Denise. 2002. "Denise Fleming: Authors Up-Close Movie Transcript." [Online] Available: http://www.TeachingBooks.net [cited 31 October 2004].

———. 2004. "Bio: A Visit with Denise Fleming." [Online] Available: http://www.denisefleming.com [cited 31 October 2004].

Furr, Derek. 2003. "Struggling Readers Get Hooked on Writing." *The Reading Teacher* 56, no. 6 (March): 518–525.

Giblin, James Cross. 1994. "Writing Nonfiction for Children: Questions and Answers." *Writer* 107, no. 4 (April): 18–20.

Giorgis, Cyndi, and Nancy J. Johnson. 2001/2002. "2001 Caldecott Medal Winner: A Glimpse into the Art of David Small." *The Reading Teacher* 55, no. 4 (December/January): 386–390.

Gross, June, and Susan Kientz. 1999. "Developing Information Literacy: Collaborating for Authentic Learning." *Teacher Librarian* 27, no. 1 (October): 21–24.

Inspiration. Version 7.5. Portland, OR: Inspiration Software.

Jenkins, Steve. 1999. "Boston Globe-Horn Book Award Acceptance Speech." [Online] Available: http://www.houghtonmifflinbooks.com/catalog/authordetail.cfm?textType=interviews&authorID=1643 [cited 5 March 2004].

"Judith St. George." 2001. *Contemporary Authors Online.* Farmington Hills, MI: Thomson Gale.

Margolis, Rick. 2000. "Hail to the Chief: A Children's Book Casts a Droll Eye on the Presidency." *School Library Journal* 46, no. 11 (November): 43–45.

Maughan, Shannon. 2001. "The Dinosaurs of Waterhouse Hawkins." *Publishers Weekly* 246, no. 43 (22 October): 24.

Moss, Barbara. 2004. "Fabulous, Fascinating FACT BOOKS." *Instructor* 113, no. 8 (May/June): 28–30.

Neuman, Susan B. 2004. "Introducing Children to the World of Writing." *Early Childhood Today* 18, no. 4 (January/February): 34–38.

Palmer, Rosemary G., and Roger A. Stewart. 2003. "Nonfiction Trade Book Use in Primary Grades." *The Reading Teacher* 57, no. 1 (September): 38–48.

Rankin, Virginia. 1996. "Get Smart." *School Library Journal* 42, no. 8 (August): 22–26.

Riedling, Ann. 2004. "Grappling with Teachers' Lack of Research Skills." *Teacher Librarian* 31, no. 4 (April): 54.

Selznick, Brian. 2002. "From Scrapbook to Picture Book." *Book Links* 11, no. 4 (February/March): 16–22.

Silvey, Anita, editor. 2002. *The Essential Guide to Children's Books and Their Creators.* Boston: Houghton Mifflin.

Silvey, Anita, and Mary M. Burns. 1993. "Booklist: Picture Books." *Horn Book* 69, no. 5 (September/October): 584.

Small, David. 2001. "Caldecott Medal Acceptance." *Horn Book* 77, no. 4 (July/August): 411–419.

Snowball, Diane. 1995. "Building Literacy Skills through Nonfiction." *Teaching PreK–8* 25, no. 8 (May): 62–63.

Wolf, Shebly Anne, and Kenneth Paul Wolf. 2002. "Teaching True and to the Test in Writing." *Language Arts* 79, no. 3 (January): 229–240.

8 ❖ LETTERS AND DIARIES

Letters and diaries can be expressions of our most personal thoughts, which may be read by others or read only by the writer. With the ease and accessibility of electronic communication, letters may be sent via e-mail rather than the postal service and diaries may be kept in an electronic format rather than using pen and paper. Web sites such as http://ePALS.com connect educators and students from around the world in a safe, monitored environment (McCaffrey and Minkel, 2002). Blogs and Web logs contain personal diaries, political commentary, and links to interesting Web sites. As teachers and students explore different forms of electronic communication, they rely on librarians to locate resources and provide support as they learn to use the Internet in a safe, effective manner. The books in this chapter examine the power of letters to persuade, letters as a form of communication when family members are separated, and a journal as a means of recording observations and experiences to share with others.

Personal letters have the power to enhance learning, reading, and writing. Donald Graves observed that students' brief, lifeless journal responses to books became lively, thoughtful responses when they began exchanging personal letters with their teachers and other students (Graves, 1990). The students now had an authentic reason for writing, a real audience, and they knew they would get a response to their letters. In the letters, the teachers asked questions about the books, questions that they did not know the answers to, and questions that would help the children relate what they were reading to their own lives. The students answered the questions in their next letter to the teacher. They also wrote letters to other students about what they were reading. Responding to students' letters can be overwhelming if only the teacher is responding, but working collaboratively with a librarian can lessen the burden. Additionally, as students finish reading a book the librarian can offer suggestions for other books that the students can read.

Berrill and Gall (1999) describe a pen-pal program between preservice teachers and first and second graders. The children gathered on the carpet as either they or the teacher read aloud the letters from their pen pals. As the letters were read aloud the teacher took the opportunity to point out the conventions of letter writing, such as the parts of a letter, asking and responding to questions, sharing experiences, and writing on topics of interest to both parties. By sharing all of the letters with all of the children they were exposed to a range of possible writing strategies and conventions, such as different ways to close a letter. Sharing time together on the carpet established for the children the value of the written word and the benefits of coming together as a community of learners. These pen-pal exchanges gave the students a real audience and authentic reasons for writing and improving their writing skills.

Pen pals can be students in other grade levels at your school, nursing home residents, high school students, students in other parts of the country, or students in foreign countries. Pen pals provide a real reason to write and provide students with responses that will encourage them to continue writing. When second graders in Ohio became pen pals with first graders in Arizona the students quickly learned that capitalization, punctuation, grammar, and penmanship were important if they wanted their pen pals to be able to read their letters (Lemkuhl, 2002).

The terms "diaries" and "journals" are frequently used interchangeably. For some a diary is a daily record of the events in a person's life. There are different types of journals including subject area, reading response, interest, dialogue, and writing. Students use subject-area journals to summarize and reflect on their learning and to collect their thoughts as they solve problems. In reading-response journals readers write reflections, describe characters, and record interesting sentences or words. Interest journals focus on one topic and provide students a forum for exploring topics with other students as they share their opinions, ask questions, and respond to each others' writings (Bromley and Powell, 1999). Hannon (1999) introduced dialogue journals to her kindergarten students by offering to write responses to their journal writing. Writers keep journals to record observations, thoughts, feelings, ideas that intrigue them, quotes from books or articles, and to practice their writing.

Miriam Sagan (2002) advocates that writers give themselves writing assignments to complete in their journals. For example, assignments could be to describe an event in their lives using their five senses or to write a poem every day. Writers use journals to practice their writing, trigger new ideas, or sustain inspiration (Johnson, 2002). Matthewson (2004) finds that writing down the thoughts floating through her head allows her to sort them out and she uses her journal to practice her writing skills. She finds that the thoughts and words she records find their way into her short stories, personal essays, and creative nonfiction. Anne Frank planned to write a book using the ideas she collected in her diary (Johnson, 2002).

Lynn Caggiano (2004) describes how her reluctant writers enjoyed creating picture journals. Gradually, she transitioned the students from drawing pictures on paper and writing sentences about their pictures to drawing pictures in their minds and writing about those pictures. Caggiano knew she had succeeded when one student commented that he did not want to read; he would rather write because he had so much he wanted to share. Adding pictures to their journals is not just for children; adults can include pictures to record the weather, animals, and sights (Hostetter, 2004). In addition to writing, journals can include photos, newspaper clippings, phrases, dreams, or lists.

Journals can be a place for writers to practice their craft by spontaneously writing their ideas and experimenting with their writing. Journals should not be graded and should only be read if the students want to share them (Barlow, 2001). Students might write for five to ten minutes at the beginning of class every day. Offer suggestions for their writing but also give them the choice of writing about anything that interests them. During conferences talk to the students about any journal entries they think can become a longer piece of writing (Montgomery, 2001).

Donna Pitino's (2004) eighth-grade students write for five minutes every day in their journals and she does not read what they write. After the death of a teacher, the students asked to write for longer periods. Students also expressed their grief through poems, which were compiled in a book for the teacher's daughter and mother. The students talked about the impact of the teacher's death on her fifteen-year-old daughter and from that sprang an impromptu writing assignment where the students wrote letters to their own parents. The students also wrote one or two sentences about the teacher and what she meant to them, which were published in the local paper.

Click, Clack, Moo: Cows That Type

by Doreen Cronin
Illustrated by Betsy Lewin
Caldecott Honor Book, 2001

READING

Before Reading

Story Summary

When Farmer Brown's cows begin typing letters trouble is sure to follow. The cows and hens have a cause they are passionate about and hence a reason to write persuasive letters. The barn is cold and they demand electric blankets. When Farmer Brown does not meet their demands, they go on strike. There will be no more milk or eggs until they get electric blankets. A neutral party, Duck, steps in to resolve the standoff in exchange for the typewriter. Once the cows and hens are satisfied, the ducks type up a demand of their own. This barnyard menagerie demonstrates the power of the written word, the art of negotiation, and the art of compromise. Bold watercolor washes and brushed black lines convey the emotions and hilarity of the situation. This book is available on videocassette, audiocassette, and CD. In *Giggle, Giggle, Quack* (Cronin, 2002), Duck, with pencil in hand, wreaks havoc when Farmer Brown goes on vacation leaving his brother in charge. In *Duck for President* (Cronin, 2004), Duck wins a barnyard election to replace Farmer Brown and then sets out to become president.

Reading other books with persuasive letters gives students additional models for their letter writing. *Dear Mrs. LaRue: Letters from Obedience School* (Teague, 2002) contains humorous letters written by a dog to his owner, trying to convince her that the doggy resort spa obedience school is really a prison and that she needs to spring him. *Mr. Lincoln's Whiskers* (Winnick, 1999) tells the story of eleven-year-old Grace Bedell, who persuaded Abraham Lincoln to grow a beard so that he would not look so sad. She reasoned that if he did not look so sad more people would vote for him. *Thank You, Sarah!!!: The Woman Who Saved Thanksgiving* (Anderson, 2002) relates the story of Sarah Hale who spent thirty-eight years writing letters to four different presidents and finally convinced President Lincoln to proclaim Thanksgiving a national holiday. This determined woman persisted because she was passionate about her cause.

Activating Prior Knowledge

Readers may be familiar with cows, hens, and ducks but they probably have never encountered ones as smart as these. Not only do these barnyard animals type, they type persuasive letters seeking to improve their living conditions. This is a humorous look at the power of writing to accomplish goals and change lives. Introduce this book by asking the students if they have ever tried to convince their parents to buy them a new pair of brand name tennis shoes or have written a letter to Santa.

During Reading

After you read each "Click, clack, moo" refrain, pause and have the students predict what the animals are writing in their letters.

❖ ─────────────

Recommended Grade Levels

3–6

Standards for the English Language Arts

1, 2, 4, 5, 6, 7, 8, 12

Information Literacy Standards for Student Learning

1, 2, 3, 5, 6

Objectives

The students will:

- Examine the contents of a persuasive letter,
- Decide on a topic that matters to them, and
- Write a persuasive letter.

───────────── ❖

❖ ─────────────

Author

It is probably not surprising that a collector of old typewriters, Doreen Cronin, would have a typewriter play an important role in one of her books (*USA Today,* 2002). The words "Click, clack, moo" rattled around in her head until one morning, unable to sleep, she sat at her computer and the story poured out. When she finished, she laughed aloud—something she had not done since her father's death two months earlier. She knew that this manuscript was different from her other children's book manuscripts that had been rejected. Cronin claims to have enough rejection letters to fill an attic (*USA Today,* 2004).

───────────── ❖

❖ ───────────────

Illustrator

Author and illustrator Betsy Lewin travels the globe with her author and illustrator husband Ted. Books such as *Gorilla Walk* (Lewin and Lewin, 1999) and *Elephant Quest* (Lewin and Lewin, 2000) reflect their travels. She recalls a childhood spent listening to her mother, a kindergarten teacher, read her picture books. She wrote her own illustrated stories and her parents, recognizing her talent, encouraged her. However, they thought that a career as an artist would be impractical (Silvey, 2002).

─────────────── ❖

After Reading

As you discuss the book focus on the letters to show the students how the animals presented their ideas and then told the farmer what they expected him to do. Project a copy of each letter using either transparencies or a document camera as you begin discussing them. Show the students how the animals first determined their audience, Farmer Brown. They knew he would be the one who could meet their demands. In the first sentence the animals stated a problem and in the second sentence the animals told Farmer Brown what they expected him to do to solve their problem, or, a call to action. When Farmer Brown did not meet their demands, the animals went on strike until their demands were met. Ask the students to brainstorm other ways the animals might have gotten Farmer Brown to meet their demands, rather than go on strike. What could the animals might included in their letters to support their demands? For example, instead of simply stating their request and their demand they could have listed facts to support their request and given reasons why meeting their demands would benefit Farmer Brown.

WRITING

Mini-lesson—Persuasive Letters

- The best time to introduce students to persuasive letters is when there is something they are passionate about, as you want the letters to be personally meaningful to the students (Wollman-Bonilla, 2004). The writers need to first find a topic they care about and then determine their audience.
- Tell the students that their audience is the person or group of people who can make the change they request, and have the students decide on their audience.
- Have the students make a list of facts to support their position and write their facts on the board.
- Once the students compile their list of facts have them arrange the facts in order of importance.
- Explain to the students that they will want to either begin their letter with the most important fact or end their letter with the most important fact.
- Then, have the students create a list possible objections to their requests.
- Next to each objection the students should write their responses to the objections.

Modeling

- At the end of the book, the ducks have typed up their own letter to Farmer Brown requesting a diving board because their pond is boring.
- The book does not tell us what is in the letter, so tell the students that they are going to help you write the letter for the ducks.
- Use a chart such as the one in Figure 8-1 to have the students brainstorm ideas to include in the letter.
- Read the ideas in the chart and have the students select one or two ideas to include in the letter.
- Have the students help you compose the letter.

Request: diving board
Audience: Farmer Brown

Supporting Facts and Opinions	Possible Objections	Responses to Objections
pond is quite boring		

Figure 8-1. Ideas for Ducks' Letter

Writing Activity

- To write effective letters the students need to have a real concern and a real audience. Are there changes in the library routine or classroom routine that they could persuade you to adopt? Are there topics of particular interest that they could persuade you to include in the curriculum? Are there books they can persuade you to add to the library collection?
- Suggest topics to the students and let them suggest their own topics.
- After students have decided on their topics have them draw a chart such as the one in Figure 8-2 on blank paper. The chart helps them organize their thoughts before they begin writing.
- Once the students have the chart completed they are ready to begin writing their letters.

Conferencing

- As the students finish their letters have them read their letters to each other and offer suggestions.
- Wollman-Bonilla (2004) finds that peer conferences work best for persuasive letters, because the students can anticipate the readers' perspectives, can provide additional ideas to support the requests, and can help the writers formulate responses to possible objections.

Opinion _____

Audience _____

Supporting Facts and Opinions	Possible Objections	Responses to Objections

Figure 8-2. Persuasive Letter Chart

Tibet: Through the Red Box

by Peter Sís
Caldecott Honor Book, 1999

Recommended Grade Levels

5–10

Standards for the English Language Arts

1, 2, 3, 4, 5, 6

Information Literacy Standards for Student Learning

3, 4, 5, 6

Objectives

The students will:

• Record observations using their five senses, and

• Write about their observations.

READING

Before Reading

Story Summary

Peter Sís's father, Vladimir, was a documentary filmmaker in Czechoslovakia. In the mid-1950s, he was drafted to teach the Chinese army to make films. Their project was to document the construction of a road through the Himalayas that would open Tibet to China. Vladimir and his cameraman became separated from the construction crew by a landslide. They made their way to the city of Lhasa to warn the Dalai Lama of the construction of the road that would change the lives of the Tibetan people. Vladimir recorded his adventures in Tibet in a diary that he kept in a red box. A two-month assignment turned into a fourteen-month adventure. The book is more than a diary; it contains the story of young Peter who missed his father, the wonderful tales his father told on his return, and the story of a grown man coming to understand his father through a diary and intricate illustrations.

Activating Prior Knowledge

Ask the students if they write in diaries or journals. If you keep a diary or journal, you can talk to the students about why you keep a journal, what you write about, and perhaps share a passage from the journal with them (Manning and Raymond, 2001). This book contains a diary that Peter Sís's father kept while in Tibet. *Tibet* (Kummer, 2003) contains useful background information to help students comprehend the information in this diary.

During Reading

This is a book to read over several days to enjoy and to appreciate the complex story. When you have finished reading a portion of the book place it in an accessible spot for the students to peruse. Children who enjoyed the tales interspersed through the diary might also enjoy *All the Way to Lhasa: A Tale from Tibet* (Berger, 2003).

After Reading

Begin a discussion of the book by having the students work with partners or in small groups with large blank sheets of paper to sketch and write down everything they learned about Tibet. Then, have the students discuss what they sketched and wrote. Focus on the diary entries and the margin notes that record observations and information about Tibet, the people, the climate, and the culture. For example, "Everywhere you look, you see mountains," and "Everybody here carries a prayer wheel."

WRITING

Mini-lesson—Observations

- Miriam Sagan (2002) advocates that writers give themselves writing assignments to complete in their journals such as selecting one thing, observing it every day, and recording their observations.
- Students can select something to observe every day and record their observations in their journals. They can observe aquarium fish, scenes outside of a school window, students in the library, the buses lining up at the end of the school day, or students checking out books in the library.
- As they record their observations, a chart such as the one in Figure 8-3 may help them remember to use their five senses to gather as much information as possible.

Author

Born in Prague, Czechoslovakia, Peter Sís immigrated to America and became a citizen. He is a writer, artist, television animator, and filmmaker. He began his artistic career as a young child by drawing on everything in the house and drawing during school. He decorated chairs for his favorite people and recalls one visitor who, after sitting on her newly painted chair, left with part of his picture on her clothing (Sís, 2003). His parents gave him drawing assignments with deadlines. These assignments helped to develop his creative abilities and the deadlines provided him with discipline that would be useful later in life (Silvey, 2002). At the suggestion of a friend, he sent some of his artwork to Maurice Sendak, who was impressed with Sís's work and introduced him to a children's book editor. Sís received a Caldecott Honor for *Starry Messenger* in 1997. His Web site is at http://www.petersis.com/index2 .html.

	What I Saw	What I Tasted	What I Smelled	What I Heard	What I Felt
Day 1					
Day 2					
Day 3					
Day 4					
Day 5					

Figure 8-3. Observation Record

Modeling

- As you model recording and writing about observations, focus on something in the library that the children can see, such as someone feeding aquarium fish or students looking for books in the library.
- Create an observation chart on the board and have the children help you complete the chart.
- Once the chart is completed begin writing your observations, which might look something like this:

  The flakes of fish food felt smooth as I crumbled them between my fingers. When I dropped food in the fish bowl, the four goldfish silently swam to the top and hungrily gobbled the flakes. Some flakes slowly slipped to the bottom of the bowl while the fish swam around trapping the flakes in their mouths. As I leaned over to observe them, I smelled the water in the fish bowl and realized that it would soon need cleaning.

Writing Activity

- This activity works best if the students have opportunities to record their observations over several days, spending five minutes each day observing and recording their observations.
- If this is not possible have the students observe an activity for ten minutes.
- Give the students five-senses charts to use to record their observations. (See Figure 8-3.) There is a copy of the chart in the appendix.
- As the students record their observations they will want to talk to the other students about them. They will each see different things and learn from each other about seeing from another person's perspective.
- When the observations are finished, have the students begin writing about what they observed.

Conferencing

- As you conference with the students listen carefully as they read their entries. Graves (1990) stresses the importance of listening to students during the writing conference because by listening to their students, teachers learn more about what their students know.
- Ask the children to point out the different senses they used to describe what they observed.

The Gardener

by Sarah Stewart
Illustrated David Small
Caldecott Honor Book, 1998

READING

Before Reading

Story Summary
During the Great Depression, ten-year-old Lydia Grace Finch moves from the country to the city to live with her dour uncle until her father can find work. She boards the train to the city with two suitcases and seeds from her grandmother's garden. While living in the city, she transforms a bleak rooftop into a flowering garden. The story unfolds in letters first to her uncle and then to her parents and grandmother. Lydia is a resilient young girl who sets out to surprise her somber uncle and make him smile. While he never does smile, when it is time for Lydia to return home he engulfs her in a warm, loving hug. Three two-page spreads are wordless and the illustrations speak more eloquently than words. Students who share a special relationship with their grandmothers will recognize the bonds the young girl and her grandmother share through their common interest in gardening. Stewart enjoyed spending time in her grandmother's gardens and those special times resound in *The Gardener* (Stewart, 1998). Finely detailed colored-pencil illustrations fill each two-page spread. This book is available on audiocassette and videocassette. *The Journey* (Stewart, 2001) chronicles an Amish girl's experiences in Chicago through diary entries, which could be used in conjunction with this book.

Activating Prior Knowledge
Set in the depression era, this story develops through the letters a young girl writes to her family while temporarily separated from them. Students may need a brief introduction to the Great Depression, but most will be able to relate to separation from family and friends who live in other states or other countries. Students may be more familiar with making telephone calls and sending e-mail than sending letters as ways of communicating when separated from family members.

During Reading

As you read, include the dates of the letters because they mark the passing of Lydia Grace's time in the city. When you encounter the wordless double-page spreads pause and let the students enjoy the impact of the illustrations on the story. The first two show gloom and despair, whereas the last one is a glorious riot of colorful flowers filled with joy and excitement.

After Reading

When we write personal letters our voices come through (Spandel, 2001) just as Lydia Grace's voice comes through in the letters she writes. When we are excited about what we are writing, our voices come through naturally (Spandel, 2001). In personal letters, we reveal ourselves to our readers, they know how we feel and what we are thinking,

❖ ─────────────
Recommended Grade Levels

1–4

Standards for the English Language Arts

2, 4, 5, 6, 9, 12

Information Literacy Standards for Student Learning

3, 4, 5

Objectives

The students will:

• Examine letter writing conventions, and

• Write a personal letter.
─────────────── ❖

❖ ─────────────
Author

Sarah Stewart was born and raised in Texas. She began keeping a diary when she was about seven or eight years old and carried it with her everywhere (Stewart, 2002). Although she remembers beginning to write stories and poems at a young age, it was not until she was older and married to David Small that she realized that writing was her true vocation (Silvey, 2002). She relishes silent places, so gardens and libraries are special places for her to enjoy the quiet (Stewart, 2002). Additional information about Sarah Small can be found at http://www.pippinproperties.com/authill/stewart/.
─────────────── ❖

❖ ───────────────

Illustrator

David Small grew up in Detroit and now lives with his wife, Sarah Stewart, on several acres in Michigan. He began drawing when he was two, and at six years of age concentrated on drawing cats because he wanted one (Gauch, 2001). Both David and Sarah like silence and they work alone: he in a studio separate from their home and she in their library (Romano, 2003). Although he both writes and illustrates books, illustrating comes easier to him (Giorgis and Johnson, 2001/2002). As a child he drew cartoons and for a time he worked as an editorial artist for newspapers and magazines (Gauch, 2001). He received a Caldecott Medal for *So You Want to Be President?* (St. George, 2001). Additional information about David Small can be found at http://www .pippinproperties.com/authill/ small/.

───────────────

and we write about things of mutual interest. What did you learn about Lydia Grace from her letters? What did Lydia Grace write about that was of interest to her audience? You can ask the students to return to the text and find examples of when they knew how Lydia Grace was feeling and what she was thinking. What information did she provide to her family members in her letters? What did you learn about Lydia Grace's family in her letters?

WRITING

Mini-lesson—Letter Writing Conventions

- When we write personal letters we include the date, the greeting, the body, the closing, and our signature. To help the students understand these letter conventions, invite them to look carefully at the letters and determine the common parts of the letter.
- Project a copy of one of the letters using a document camera or by making a transparency of the letter. Label the parts of the letter for the students as you talk about them.
- Personal letters also contain information about things of mutual interest and questions for the recipient.
- Ask the students to locate sentences in the letter that reflect mutual interests and to locate questions Lydia Grace included in her letters.

❖ ### Modeling

- Before you model letter writing for the students share one of your letters with them. (See Figure 8-4.)

Figure 8-4. Letter to Grandmother

- Using a document camera or an overhead transparency, model writing a personal letter for the students.
- As you write ask the students to suggest sentences for your letter.

Writing Activity

- Start this activity by having the students decide who will be the recipient of their letter.
- The students could write a letter to a friend or relative or they could write to someone who is serving in the military.
- Remind the students that they need to write about things that will be of interest to both parties, and to ask questions.
- The letter in Figure 8-5 was written by a second grader to her cousin living in another state.

Conferencing

- As you conference with students or as they conference with each other have them point out the different parts of the letter.
- As you listen to their letters, ask questions about things you do not understand. Encourage the students to clarify their writing and to use the appropriate conventions so that the recipient will understand their writing.

Dear Josh I miss you when are you coming down here. are you having fun play, in the snow. dow you slide on the sled I hope you have fun.
Love Kathryn

Figure 8-5. Personal Letter

RESOURCES FOR LIBRARIANS AND TEACHERS

In this section are the books in the chapter and additional books written as letters and diaries that can serve as models for students' writing.

Ada, Alma Flor. 2001. *With Love, Little Red Hen.* New York: Atheneum.

Ahlberg, Janet. 1991. *The Jolly Christmas Postman.* Illustrated by Allan Ahlberg. Boston: Little, Brown.

———. 2001. *The Jolly Postman or Other People's Letters.* Illustrated by Allan Ahlberg. New York: Little, Brown.

Anderson, Laurie Halse. 2002. *Thank You, Sarah!!!: The Woman Who Saved Thanksgiving.* New York: Simon & Schuster.

Cronin, Doreen. 2000. *Click, Clack, Moo: Cows that Type.* Illustrated by Betsy Lewin. New York: Simon & Schuster.

———. 2002. *Giggle, Giggle, Quack.* Illustrated by Betsy Lewin. New York: Simon & Schuster.

———. 2003. *Diary of a Worm.* Illustrated by Harry Bliss. New York: HarperCollins.

Dewey, Jennifer Owings. 2001. *Antarctic Journal: Four Months at the Bottom of the World.* New York: HarperCollins.

Greenberg, Judith E. 1998. *Young People's Letters to the President.* New York: Franklin Watts.

Keats, Ezra Jack. 1998. *Letter to Amy.* New York: Viking.

Moss, Marissa. 1999. *Emma's Journal: The Story of a Colonial Girl.* San Diego, CA: Harcourt.

———. 2001. *Hannah's Journal: The Story of an Immigrant Girl.* San Diego, CA: Harcourt.

———. 2001. *Rose's Journal: The Story of a Girl in the Great Depression.* San Diego, CA: Harcourt.

Platt, Richard. 2001. *Pirate Diary: The Journal of Jake Carpenter.* Illustrated by Chris Riddell. Cambridge, MA: Candlewick.

Rakusin, Sudie. 2003. *Dear CALLA Roo . . . Love, Savannah Blue: A Letter about Getting Sick and Feeling Better.* Carrboro, NC: Winged Willow.

Sís, Peter. 1998. *Tibet: Through the Red Box.* New York: Farrar Straus Giroux.

Stewart, Sarah. 1997. *The Gardener.* Illustrated by David Small. New York: Farrar Straus Giroux.

Teague, Mark. 2002. *Dear Mrs. LaRue: Letters from Obedience School.* New York: Scholastic.

———. 2004. *Detective LaRue: Letters from the Investigation.* New York: Scholastic.

Williams, Vera B. 1988. *Stringbean's Trip to the Shining Sea.* New York: Greenwillow.

Winnick, Karen B. 1999. *Mr. Lincoln's Whiskers.* Honesdale, PA: Boyds Mills.

Other Resources

Berger, Barbara Helen. 2003. *All the Way to Lhasa: A Tale from Tibet.* New York: Philomel.

Kummer, Patricia K. 2003. *Tibet.* New York: Children's.

Leedy, Loreen. 1991. *Messages in the Mailbox: How to Write a Letter.* New York: Holiday House.

Roy, Jennifer Rozines, and Sherri Mabry Gordon. 2003. *You Can Write a Business Letter.* Berkeley Heights, NJ: Enslow.

RESOURCES FOR STUDENTS

In this section is a list of books by authors and illustrators whose works are highlighted in this chapter. Students who particularly enjoy a book by an author or illustrator may want to read other books they have written or illustrated.

Ashman, Linda. 2003. *The Essential Worldwide Monster Guide.* Illustrated by David Small. New York: Simon & Schuster Books for Young Readers.

Lewin, Ted, and Betsy Lewin. 1999. *Gorilla Walk.* New York: Lothrop, Lee & Shepard.

———. 2000. *Elephant Quest.* New York: HarperCollins.

Sís, Peter. 1996. *Starry Messenger.* New York: Farrar Straus Giroux.

Small, David. 1992. *Ruby Mae Has Something to Say.* New York: Crown.

Stewart, Sarah. 1991. *The Money Tree.* Illustrated by David Small. New York: Farrar Straus Giroux.

———. 1995. *The Library.* Illustrated by David Small. New York: Farrar Straus Giroux.

———. 2001. *The Journey.* Illustrated by David Small. New York: Farrar Straus Giroux.

St. George, Judith. 2000. *So You Want to Be President?* Illustrated by David Small. New York: Philomel.

———. 2002. *So You Want to Be an Inventor?* Illustrated by David Small. New York: Philomel.

———. 2005. *So You Want to Be an Explorer?* Illustrated by David Small. New York: Philomel.

IDEAS FOR PARENTS AND CAREGIVERS

To encourage children to write letters their parents and caregivers can provide them with stamps and stationery or pads of paper and envelopes to correspond with family and friends who do not live nearby. When they receive Christmas presents or birthday presents parents can help them write thank you notes. Young children and reluctant writers can draw pictures of the presents and sign their names. Children can also make greeting cards to send on special occasions. Author Richard Peck (1997) describes how he had a small table and chair in the kitchen where, under his mother's watchful eye, he composed thank you notes to his grandparents for gifts they gave him. These writing experiences provide students with authentic reasons for writing and audiences for their writing. Parents and caregivers can encourage children to keep journals and practice their writing by providing them with blank books or spiral notebooks. A kindergarten student used a small spiral notebook to practice his writing by composing notes to his family members. See Figure 8-6.

REFERENCES

Barlow, Bob. 2001. "Boost Writing Skills with Everyday Journaling." *Instructor* 111, no. 1 (August): 44.

Berrill, Deborah P., and Molly Gall. 1999. "On the Carpet: Emergent Writer/Readers' Letter Sharing in a Penpal Program. *Language Arts* 76, no. 6 (July): 470–478.

Bromley, Karen, and Penny Powell. 1999. "Interest Journals Motivate Student Writers." *The Reading Teacher* 53, no. 2 (October): 111–112.

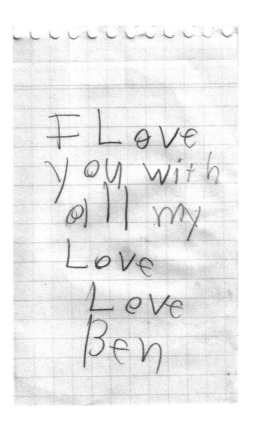

Figure 8-6. All My Love

Caggiano, Lynn Mondello. 2004. "The Writer Within." *Teaching PreK–8* 35, no. 3 (November/December): 54–55.

Gauch, Patricia Lee. 2001. "David Small." *Horn Book* 77, no. 4 (July/August): 421–423.

Giorgis, Cyndi, and Nancy J. Johnson. 2001/2002. "2001 Caldecott Medal Winner: A Glimpse into the Art of David Small." *The Reading Teacher* 55, no. 4 (December/January): 386–390.

Graves, Donald H. 1990. *Discover Your Own Literacy.* Portsmouth, NH: Heinemann.

Hannon, Jean. 1999. "Talking Back: Kindergarten Dialogue Journals." *The Reading Teacher* 53, no. 3 (November): 200–203.

Hostetter, Kristin. 2004. "Paper Trail." *Backpacker* 32, no. 8 (October): 43.

Johnson, Alexandra. 2002. "Golden Notebooks." *Writer* 115, no. 7 (July): 34–37.

Lemkuhl, Michelle. 2002. "Pen-Pal Letters: The Cross-Curricular Experience." *Reading Online* 55, no. 8 (September): 14–17. [Online] Available: http://www.readingonline.org/electronic/elec_index.asp?HREF=/electronic/RWT/lemkuhl/index.html [cited 5 March 2004].

Manning, Maryann, and Allen Raymond. 2001. "Journals and Diaries: How to Introduce these Valuable Tools for Classroom Response and Personal Reflection." *Teaching K–8* 31, no. 5 (February): 83–85.

Matthewson, Jennifer. 2004. "The Moments of Your Life: Journaling Is a Way to Record, Reflect, and Understand." *Writer* 117, no. 3 (March): 17–18.

McCaffrey, Meg, and Walter Minkel. 2002. "Net Gen Pen Pals." *School Library Journal* 48, no. 10 (October): 33.

Montgomery, Winifred. 2001. "Journal Writing: Connecting Reading and Writing in Mainstream Educational Settings." *Reading & Writing Quarterly* 17, no. 1 (January–March): 93–98.

Peck, Richard. 1997. *Love and Death at the Mall: Teaching and Writing for the Literate Young.* New York: Bantam Doubleday Dell Books for Young Readers.

Pitino, Donna Marie. 2004. "Healing through Writing." *NEA Today* 23, no. 1 (October): 64.

Romano, Katherine. 2003. "The Evolution of Sarah Stewart and David Small." *Teaching PreK–8* 33, no. 6 (March): 44–46.

Roy, Jennifer Rozines, and Sherri Mabry Gordon. 2003. *You Can Write a Business Letter.* Berkeley Heights, NJ: Enslow.

Sagan, Miriam. 2002. "Exercise Your Writing Muscle." *Writer* 115, no. 7 (July): 38–39.

Silvey, Anita, editor. 2002. *The Essential Guide to Children's Books and Their Creators.* Boston: Houghton Mifflin.

Sís, Peter. 2003. "From Behind the Iron Curtain to Tibet." *Chronicle of Higher Education* 49, no. 46 (25 July): B15.

Spandel, Vicki. 2001. *Creating Writers: Through 6-Trait Writing Assessment and Instruction,* 3rd ed. New York: Addison Wesley Longman.

Stewart, Sarah. 2002. "Authors/Illustrators: Biography." [Online] Available: http://www.pippinproperties.com/authill/stewart [cited 5 March 2004].

Wollman-Bonilla, Julie E. 2004. "Principled Teaching To(wards) the Test?: Persuasive Writing in Two Classrooms." *Language Arts* 81, no. 6 (July): 502–511.

USA Today. 2002. "Click, Clack, Giggle: Author Taps out 'Cows' Sequel." (16 April): Section Life, p. 4d.

———. 2004. "Why Not 'Duck for President'?" (15 March): Section Life, p. 4d.

Sources

SOURCE A: THE KEY COMPONENTS OF A WRITING WORKSHOP

❖ ———————————
Myrna Hynes (2000) recounts how one student's preference for nonfiction reading and writing alienated him from reading and writing in school where fiction was the predominant genre. Encouraging this student to read and write nonfiction helped him transition from being a nonreader to being a reader.
——————————— ❖

❖ ———————————
Lynda Graham (2001) describes how a reluctant writer maintained interest in his writing when he had multiple opportunities to read a book and saw books other students had written based on the book. These experiences gave him the confidence to write as an expert. Reluctant writers benefit from having books read aloud to them, mini-lessons showing them how the authors use different strategies, and collaborative writing experiences to help them gain confidence in their writing abilities (Robb, 1995).
❖

❖ ———————————
Peter Lancia's (1997) second-grade students' literary borrowing included borrowing characters, plot devices, setting, conflict, and language patterns from familiar books as well as borrowing ideas from their classmates. These second graders, immersed in a literature-rich environment, made connections between the books they read and their writing as they developed their own writing style.
——————————— ❖

TRY TO MAKE THE READING WRITING CONNECTION

Stephen D. Krashen (2004) notes that research strongly concludes that the only way to become good readers and writers is to read. Additional advantages of reading include developing an adequate vocabulary, a knowledge of grammar, and the ability to spell. Hearing books read aloud, reading books, and rereading books helps students internalize the grammatical features of the text and develop an appreciation of writing. Carefully examining the text in familiar picture books enables students to understand how writers incorporate literary elements and use grammatical concepts. Johnson and Giorgis (1999) advocate teaching students to read with a writer's eye so that they become aware of the structure of the text and how the author uses language. Thomason and York (2000) describe how teachers read books to their students, discussed the literary devices the authors used in the books, and during writing conferences they helped students determine ways to include the literary devices in their own writing. Rather than focusing on form or the direct teaching of grammatical features, teachers in Barrs's (2000) study provided students with opportunities to interact with text first through drama, then through reading, and lastly through writing. During the writing phase students were given time to read their writing to a partner who responded to their writing.

Exposing students to a wide variety of books written in different genres results in writing that is skillful and linguistically varied (Barrs, 2000). As students read and discuss books, they synthesize and analyze the information in the text. Discussions lead students to new understandings, and encourage them to think more deeply about their reading and critically analyze what they have read. Effective discussions include more student talk than teacher talk, students talking to one another, all students participating, and high-level questions (Asselin, 2000). After students have discussed the books, they need opportunities to write about the books. Writing about what they have read can give students an alternative perspective that clarifies their understanding (Shanahan, 1997). Writing to support a point of view helps students gain an in-depth understanding of the text's content that substantiates their view (Asselin, 2000).

Multiple opportunities to interact with texts of the same genre enables students to become familiar with the genre and provides them with feelings of expertise that assures them that they are capable of writing in that genre. Providing students with writing models enables them to conceptualize what their own writing should include. As students write they refer back to the books to determine the structure for their own writing. Working within a structure enables them to focus on their own thoughts and ideas. When librarians collaborate with teachers they can locate books in a particular genre written on the students' reading levels and that will appeal to the students. Caldecott books provide a variety of structures and genres for students to model.

❖

As a classroom teacher, I struggled with how to teach my students to write. Many of my students spoke English as a second language or had learning disabilities, which made teaching them to write even more challenging. The school librarian provided us with books to use as models for our writing and assisted us as we used the library computer lab. Collaborating with the librarian meant that my students had two adults to provide the support and guidance they needed as they wrote and published.

Prewriting may include discussion, thinking, planning, exploring, reading, brainstorming, sketches, lists, concept maps, observations, and charts. Prewriting is a time for students to explore ideas they have for their writing. These ideas may come to them at different times and during different activities. Encouraging students to collect writing ideas and to store them in a writing folder or a journal ensures that they have a variety of personally meaningful topics to explore through writing. They should also be encouraged to share their ideas with their classmates and their parents. With very young students, drawing and talking provides them with opportunities to explore and refine their understanding of the text (National Writing Project and Nagin, 2003). Prewriting takes time: time to think, time to talk, time to research, time to stare, time to gather ideas, and time to figure out what to write. It might be days, months, or even years before ideas develop into stories (Fisher, 1999).

Drafting includes students' attempts to put their thoughts in writing. This is a time to write without regard for the mechanics of writing, as the purpose is to get ideas on paper or on the computer.

Revising occurs throughout the writing process as writers rethink and reexamine their texts. As writers read their texts, they begin to see areas that *(continued)*

❖

WRITING ASSIGNMENTS

A careful examination of the classroom writing assignments gathered from the 1998 National Assessment for Educational Progress (NAEP) Special Study on Classroom Writing was conducted by National Writing Project teachers and Educational Testing Service researchers (Storms, Riazantseva, and Gentile, 2000). Results of this examination indicated that effective writing assignments involve more than the discrete steps of the writing process. Effective writing assignments include a balance of content and scope, organization and development, audience and communication, and engagement and choice. Effective writing assignments provide students with a real audience and a genuine need to communicate (Storms, Riazantseva, and Gentile, 2000). This need to communicate comes when students make connections between their lives and the lives of characters they encounter in books (Johnson and Giorgis, 1999). Students need writing assignments that include guidelines for organizing their writing and a scaffold for developing their thoughts (Storms, Riazantseva, and Gentile, 2000). They need writing assignments that require them to construct knowledge as they analyze, synthesize, and interpret information (National Writing Project and Nagin, 2003). When librarians and teachers collaborate, they create authentic assignments that result in significant achievement (Baskin, 2003).

The content and scope of the writing assignment should require students to interact with information they obtain through reading or personal experiences (Storms, Riazantseva, and Gentile, 2000). This interaction requires students to transform their knowledge by thinking deeply and critically about the information rather than to simply restate what they have learned. Writers need engaging contexts that allow them to explore ideas, discover their voice, and explore different ways of expressing their thoughts (Grainger, Goouch, and Lambirth, 2002). Emotionally powerful texts enthrall the students and help them make personal connections to the characters (Grainger, Goouch, and Lambirth, 2002), ensuring an engaging context for their writing. Engaging contexts and a range of choices in writing assignments motivates students (Storms, Riazantseva, and Gentile, 2000). They enjoy writing when they have the freedom to explore their own ideas and thoughts without impositions or limitations (Grainger, Goouch, and Lambirth, 2002). Students need opportunities for extended blocks of time to write, to play with the structure of the text, to explore using words to convey ideas, to not feel pressured, and to work in an atmosphere conducive to writing.

THE WRITING PROCESS

The writing process is ongoing and dynamic. It includes prewriting, drafting, revising, editing, and publishing. However, these steps are not linear; rather, they are interactive and may occur simultaneously (Pappas, Kiefer, and Levstik, 1999). Writing is a recursive process in which writers move back and forth across the steps or stages (Hillocks, 2002; National Writing Project and Nagin, 2003; Strickland et al., 2001). Writers' processes are all different; the amount of time they spend in each stage and the amount of interaction they require in each stage vary (Fisher, 1999). When librarians and teachers collaborate to teach writing, the students benefit from having two writing experts in the classroom to guide them through the writing process in whatever manner best suits the individual writers.

MINI-LESSONS

A mini-lesson is five to fifteen minutes of focused instruction that usually takes place at the beginning of the writing workshop (Routman, 2000). The curriculum, students' needs, and students' interests determine the content of the mini-lesson. Mini-lessons include modeling of a strategy, skill, or procedure followed by an opportunity for guided practice. At the conclusion of the mini-lesson, students practice what they learned in a writing assignment. Mini-lessons can be for small groups of students or for the entire class, and they offer opportunities to explore different aspects of the craft of writing found in the Caldecott medal and honor books presented in this text.

MODELING

To fully understand students' difficulties and concerns about their writing, librarians, teachers, and school administrators must be writers. Educators who write understand what it takes to write and know how it works (Richgels, 2002). They write with their students while their students are writing. Their writing successes and frustrations provide them with a knowledge base from which to work with students. As they conference with students about their writing they are able to conference as one writer to another writer. This enables them to develop empathy and respect for one another as writers. Teaching writing and modeling writing for students is not easy, but when librarians and teachers collaborate, they form a support system that makes the task less daunting.

CONFERENCING

Conferences are opportunities to listen, to value, to respect, to reinforce, to teach, and to assist writers (Routman, 2000). Conferences include asking questions, offering compliments, and making comments on the writing. A conference may be with one student, with pairs of students, or with small groups of students. The students bring their writing to the conference and talk about their writing. As the students read and talk about their writing, they need an attentive, silent audience who listens intently and offers thoughtful responses or asks clarifying questions. The audience gives the writer time to think and time to answer questions. Exactly what happens in the conference depends on the students' needs and their stage in the writing process.

A prewriting conference could include a discussion of writing topics or help with narrowing down a topic. A revision conference offers specific ideas for revising the piece. Students who are having similar problems may be involved in a mini-lesson conference that models a particular skill, strategy, or procedure. After meeting with a peer editor and reviewing the spelling, punctuation, and grammar in a piece of writing, the student may attend an editing conference with the teacher and the peer editor to determine if there are additional editorial changes that need to be made. At a publishing conference, students might celebrate their writing and consider what they will write next. This is an opportunity to encourage them to try new strategies or new genres.

PARENTS AND CAREGIVERS

Parents and caregivers are aware that their children are being required to write in order to pass standardized tests and they are concerned about how they can help support their children's efforts. Parents and caregivers can provide their children with a variety

need clarification, or they may find that the words they have written do not adequately convey what they are trying to say. Sharing their writing with partners or in small groups allows their peers to offer suggestions or to ask questions that cause the writers to pause and think about possible changes in their writing. Throughout the writing process writers think about what they have written and make changes.

Editing requires writers to examine the mechanics of their text. Whereas writers may automatically correct misspelled words or correct punctuation errors throughout the process, during the editing phase the particular emphasis is on working on the mechanics rather than the meaning of the text. Students who write regularly learn the conventions of language as they use them in their writing. They come to understand that by adhering to the conventions of language their writing becomes more readable (Thomason and York, 2000).

Publishing involves sharing writing with others in either a draft format or a final format. Publishing the final piece may involve writing it neatly, printing it from the computer, or creating books that are available for others to read. Publishing is the best motivation for revising, because if students know that their work is to be shared and to be read by others, they strive to make it the best that it can be. Power and Ohanian (1999) recognize the positive impact that publishing has on the writing program; however, they caution that over-publishing has a negative impact.

Throughout the writing process, students need to be in control of their writing and to maintain ownership of their writing (Pappas, Kiefer, and Levstik, 1999). Students need an environment that is conducive to writing and where writing is pleasurable (Thomason and York, 2000). This environment must include extended time for writing and a supportive environment that encourages risk taking.

❖ ——————————

Careful observations and studies of students throughout the writing process have shown that students' writing improved when they wrote about things that were important to them, wrote as experts, wrote with other children, read their writing aloud, and received genuine responses to their writing (Graham, 2001). These writing conditions led to improvements in both students' skills and the quality of their writing.

—————————— ❖

❖ ——————————

Students reported to their teacher that the most beneficial thing she did when teaching them to write was to write with them (Graves, 1990). Writing with and for students as they write is a valuable use of instructional time even when time is limited (Graves, 2004). Writing and sharing the writing with students demonstrates the importance and value of writing.

—————————— ❖

❖ ——————————

Conference Questions

What can I do to help you?

What is your writing about?

What will happen next in your story?

What do you need help with?

Why did you say it that way?

What will you write next?

How did you feel when that happened?

Can you think of another way to say that?

Can you think of something else to add?

What questions might your readers have about your writing?

How did you know you were finished with that piece?

—————————— ❖

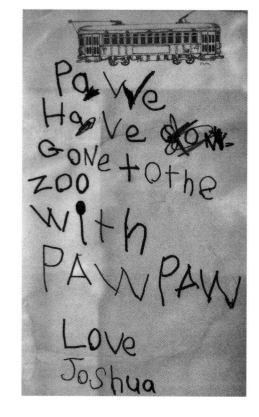

Figure A-1. Gone to the Zoo Note

of authentic writing opportunities, including writing items on a grocery list, writing down phone messages, and writing notes when they leave the house. (See Figure A-1.) Author Richard Peck (1997) describes how he had a small table and chair in the kitchen where, under his mother's watchful eye, he composed thank you notes to his grandparents for gifts they gave him. These writing experiences provide students with authentic reasons for writing and audiences for their writing.

REFERENCES

Asselin, Marlene. 2000. "Language for Learning." *Teacher Librarian* 27, no. 3 (February): 62–63.

Barrs, Myra. 2000. "The Reader in the Writer." *Reading* 34, no. 2 (July): 54–60.

Baskin, Kenda. 2003. "What Literature Has to Tell Us." *Library Media Connection* 21, no. 4 (January): 24–27.

Fisher, Bonnie E. 1999. "Social Influences on the Writing of Marion Dane Bauer and Katherine Paterson." *Language Arts* 76, no. 6 (July): 517–524.

Giorgis, Cyndi, and Nancy J. Johnson. 1999. "Children's Books: Visual Literacy." *The Reading Teacher* 53, no. 2 (October): 146–153.

Graham, Lynda. 2001. "From Tyrannosaurus to Pokemon: Autonomy in the Teaching of Writing." *Reading* 37, no. 1 (April): 18–26.

Grainger, Teresa, Kathy Goouch, and Andrew Lambirth. 2002. "The Voice of the Child: 'We're Writers' Project." *Reading Literacy and Language* 36, no. 3 (November): 135–139.

Graves, Donald H. 1990. *Discover Your Own Literacy.* Portsmouth, NH: Heinemann.
———. 2004. "What I've Learned from Teachers of Writing." *Language Arts* 82, no. 2 (November): 88–94.

Hynes, Myrna. 2000. " 'I Read for Facts': Reading Nonfiction in a Fictional World." *Language Arts* 77, no. 6 (July): 485–495.

Johnson, Nancy J., and Cyndi Giorgis. 1999. "Literature and Writing." *The Reading Teacher* 53, no. 3 (November): 234–244.

Krashen, Stephen D. 2004. *The Power of Reading: Insights from Research,* 2nd ed. Westport, CT: Libraries Unlimited.

Lancia, Peter J. 1997. "Literary Borrowing: The Effects of Literature on Children's Writing." *The Reading Teacher* 50, no. 6 (November): 470–475.

National Writing Project, and Carl Nagin. 2003. *Because Writing Matters: Improving Student Writing in Our Schools.* San Francisco: Jossey-Bass.

Pappas, Christine C., Barbara Z. Kiefer, and Linda S. Levstik. 1999. *An Integrated Language Perspective in the Elementary School: Theory into Action,* 3rd ed. White Plains, NY: Longman.

Peck, Richard. 1997. *Love and Death at the Mall: Teaching and Writing for the Literate Young.* New York: Bantam Doubleday Dell Books for Young Readers.

Power, Brenda, and Susan Ohanian. 1999. "Sacred Cows: Questioning Assumptions in Elementary Writing Programs." *Language Arts* 76, no. 3 (January): 249–257.

Richgels, Donald J. 2002. "Writing Instruction." *The Reading Teacher* 56, no. 4 (December): 364–368.

Robb, Laura. 1995. "A Workshop for Reluctant Writers." *Education Digest* 61, no. 4 (December): 65–68.

Routman, Regie. 2000. *Conversations: Strategies for Teaching, Learning, and Evaluation.* Portsmouth, NH: Heinemann.

Shanahan, Timothy. 1997. "Reading–Writing Relationships, Thematic Units, Inquiry Learning . . . In Pursuit of Effective Integrated Literacy Instruction." *The Reading Teacher* 51, no. 1 (September): 12–20.

Storms, Barbara A., Anastasia Riazantseva, and Claudia Gentile. 2000. "Focusing in on Content and Communication." *California English* 5, no. 4 (Summer). [Online] Available: http://www.cateweb.org/ce/cesu00.html.#Focus [cited 11 February 2004].

Strickland, Dorothy S., Angela Bodino, Kathy Buchan, Karen M. Jones, Audrey Nelson, and Michelle Rosen. 2001. "Teaching Writing in a Time of Reform." *Elementary School Journal* 101, no. 4 (March): 385–398.

Thomason, Tommy, and Carol York. 2000. *Write on Target: Preparing Young Writers to Succeed on State Writing Achievement Tests.* Norwood, MA: Christopher-Gordon.

SOURCE B: BLACKLINE MASTERS FOR ACTIVITIES

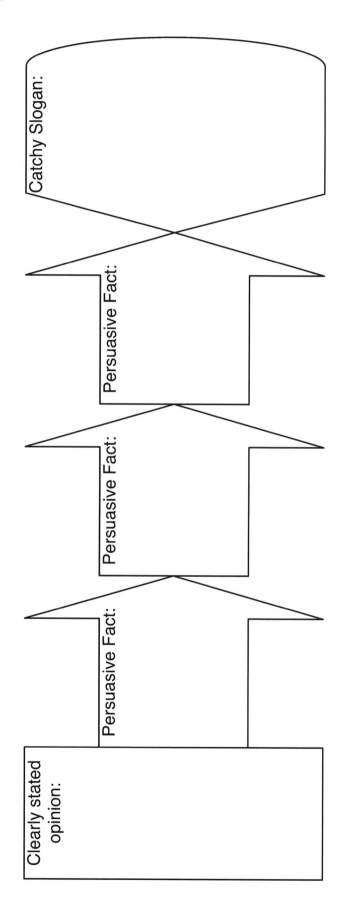

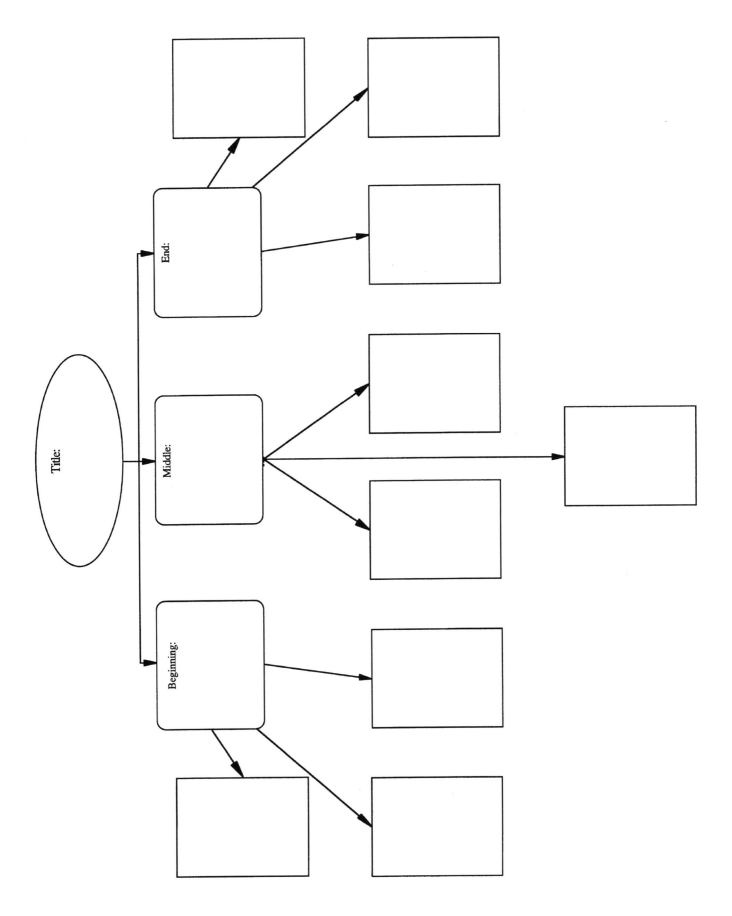

Title:

Beginning:

Middle:

End:

Ella Sarah's Family Members	Suggested Clothes	My Family Members	Suggested Clothes
Ella Sarah	pink polka-dot pants, dress with orange-and-green flowers, purple-and-blue striped socks, yellow shoes, red hat		
Mother	blue dress, matching socks, white sandals		
Father	yellow T-shirt, white shorts, tennis shoes		
Big Sister	overalls, old boots		

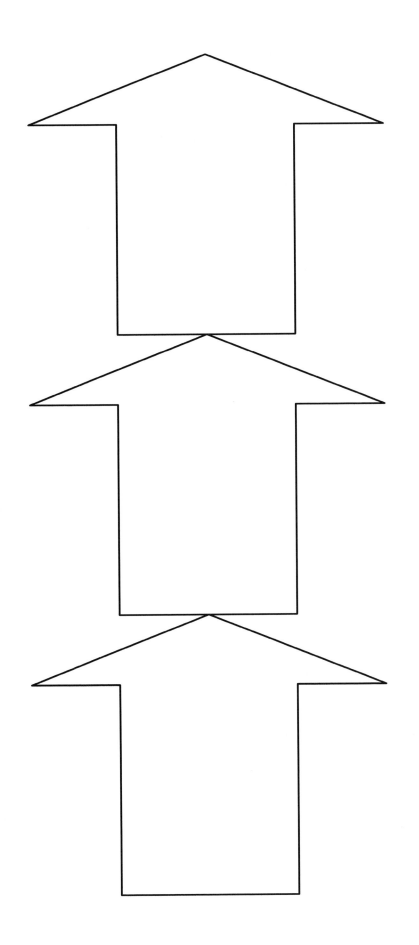

Name
Age
Sex
Hair color
Eye color
Height and weight
Favorite food
Favorite television show
Favorite singer
Favorite song
Number of brothers and sisters
What does the character like to do?
What makes the character angry?
What verbs describe how the character feels when angry?
How does the character deal with anger?

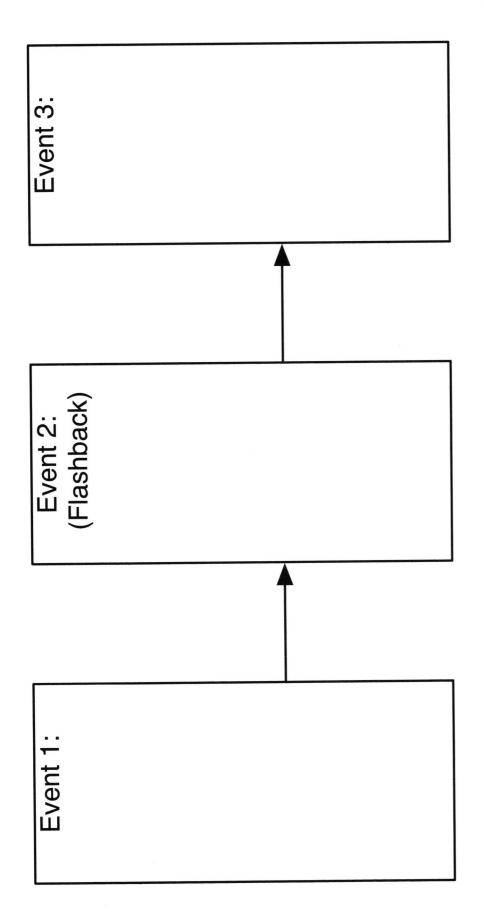

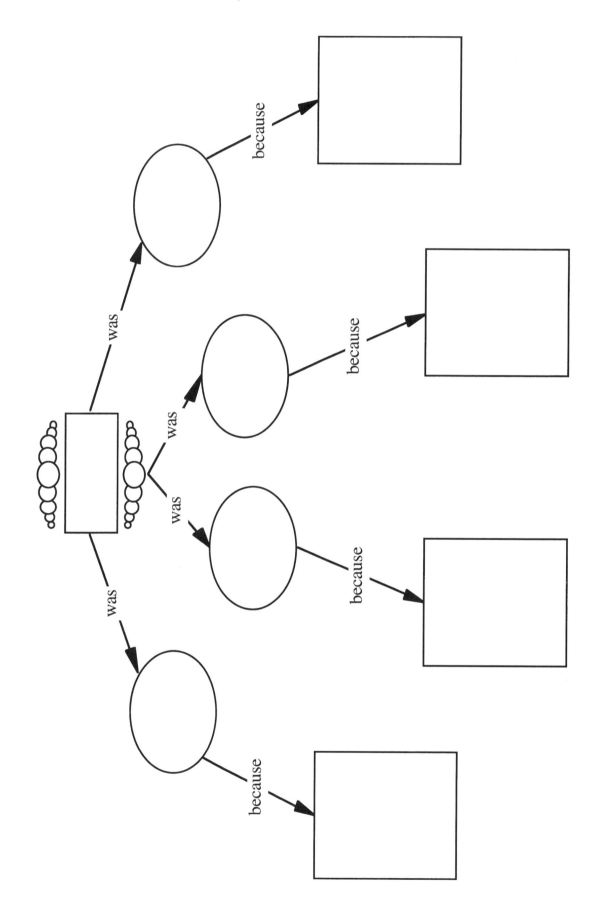

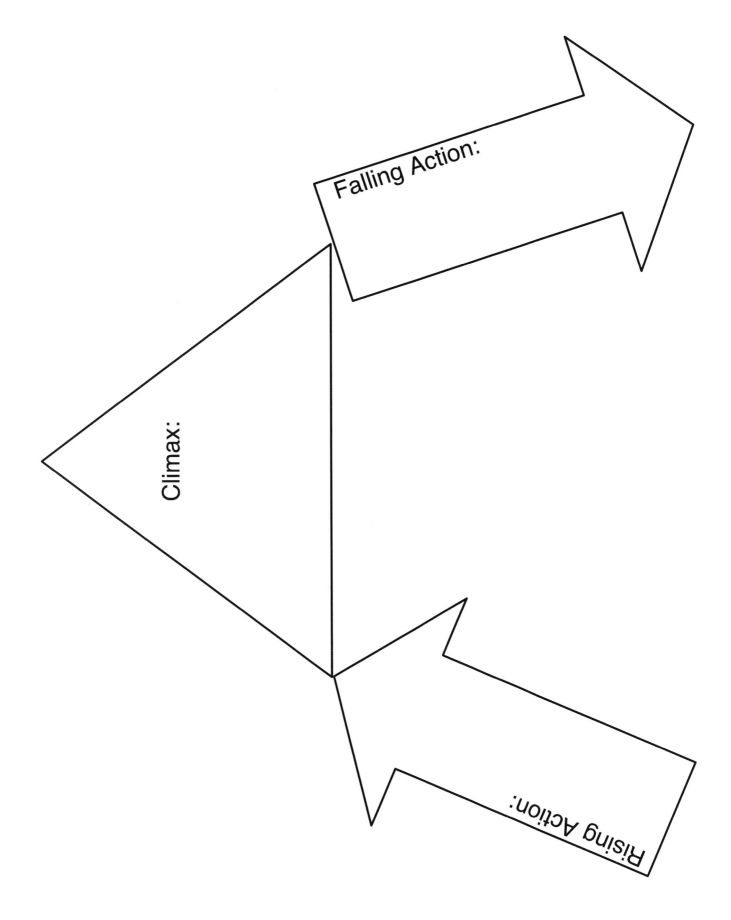

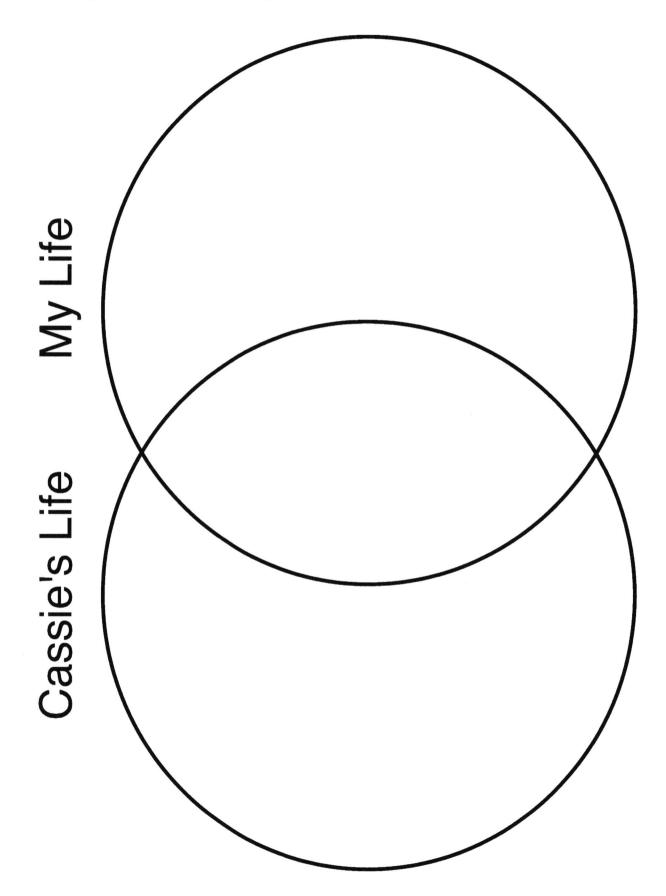

My Dreams

Why I Dream Them

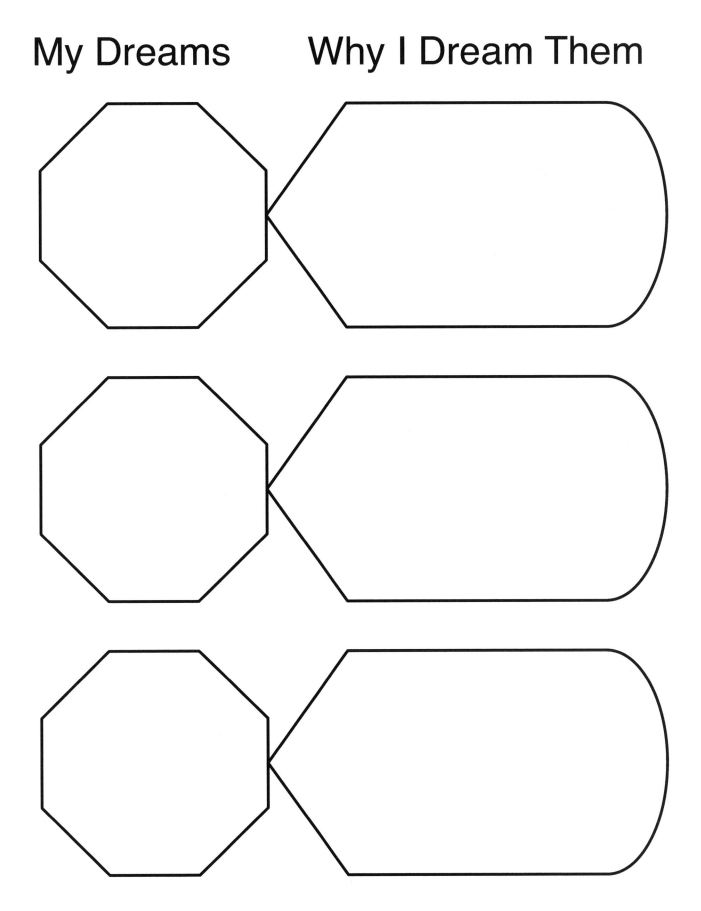

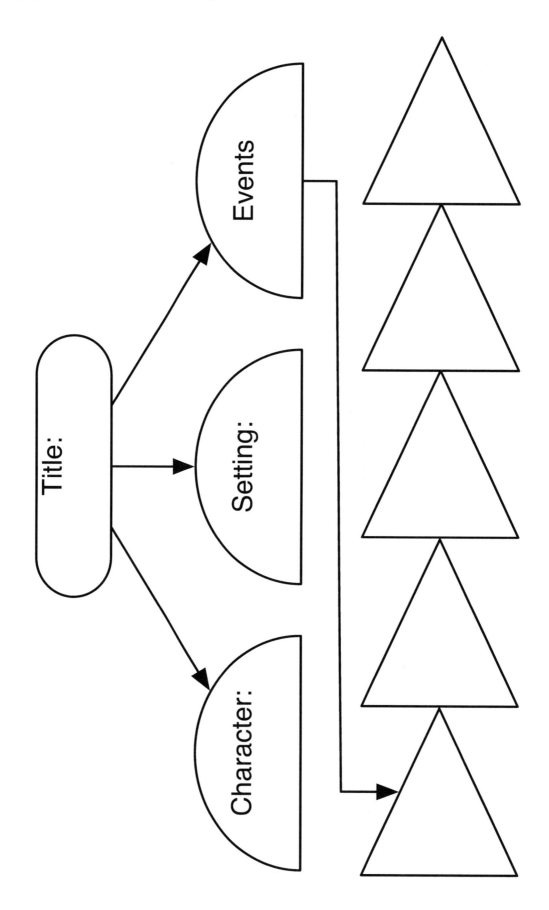

Common Characteristics of Fairy Tales	My Fairy Tale
Begin "Once upon time," or "A long time ago,"	
End "They lived happily ever after."	
Rural or forest setting	
Witches, ogres, giants, sorceresses, fairies	
Childless couple	
Time passes quickly	
Adventure, action, and drama	
Good overcomes evil	
Quest	
Abused and persecuted people	
Royalty and castles	
Number three	
Transformations	
Trials or tests	
Charms or magic	
Animal characters	

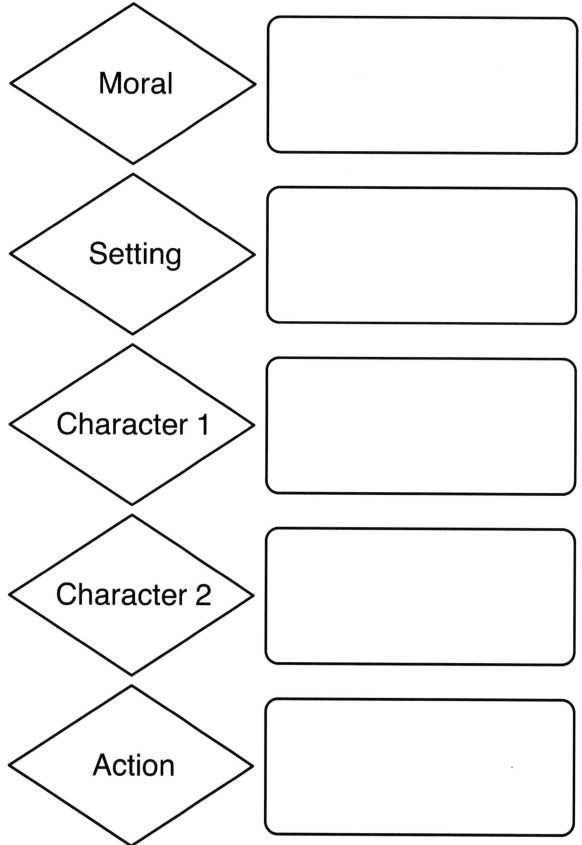

Name	
Description	
Superhuman Deeds as a Child (Hyperbole)	
Superhuman Deeds as an Adult (Hyperbole)	
Specific Job	
Powerful Object	
Companion	
Real Places	
Nature, People, or Progress impede them	
Dies or Disappears	

	Traditional Tale	My Parody
Title		
Characters		
Setting		
Beginning		
Middle		
End		

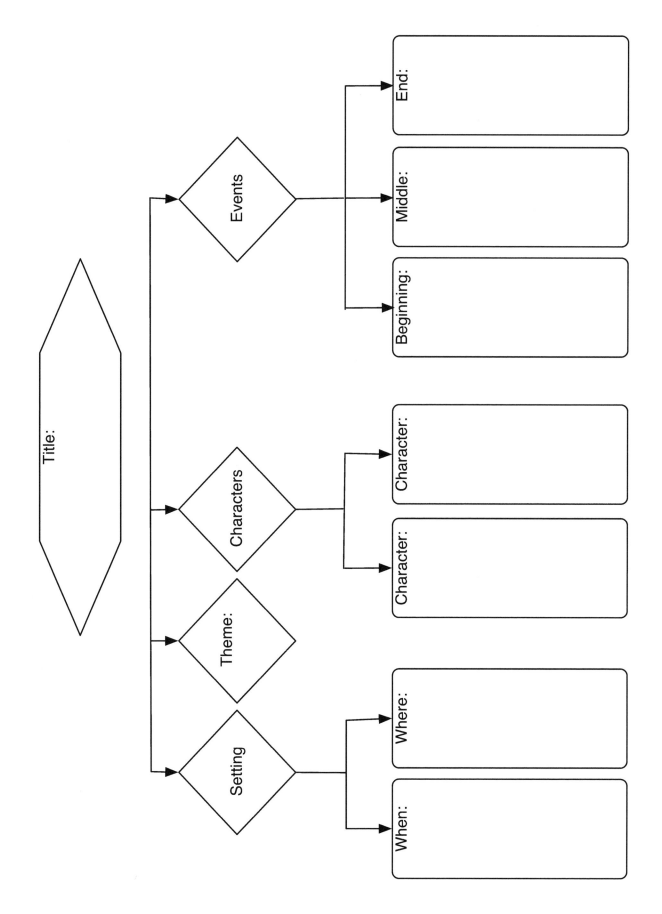

Birth: When and Where	
Places Lived or Visited	
Major Life Events	
Successes	
Obstacles	
Character Traits	
Why I Selected This Person	

Event	Feeling	Description

Early Years	
Preschool Years	
Elementary Years	
Middle School Years	

Objects	Ascribe human body parts	Verbs that depict human actions	Personal pronoun to refer to object

Terms and Definitions	Examples	Examples from the book
Onomatopoeia—makes the sound of an action	Pop!	
Alliteration—repetition of initial constants	slinky, slithering snakes	
Assonance—repetition of vowel sounds	bounce, trounce	

Cause   Effect

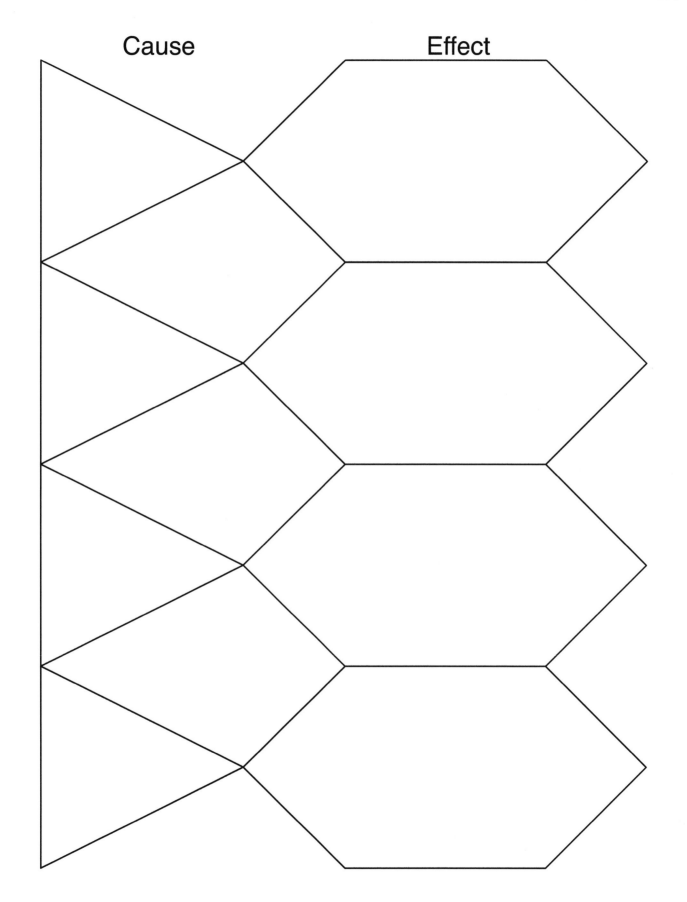

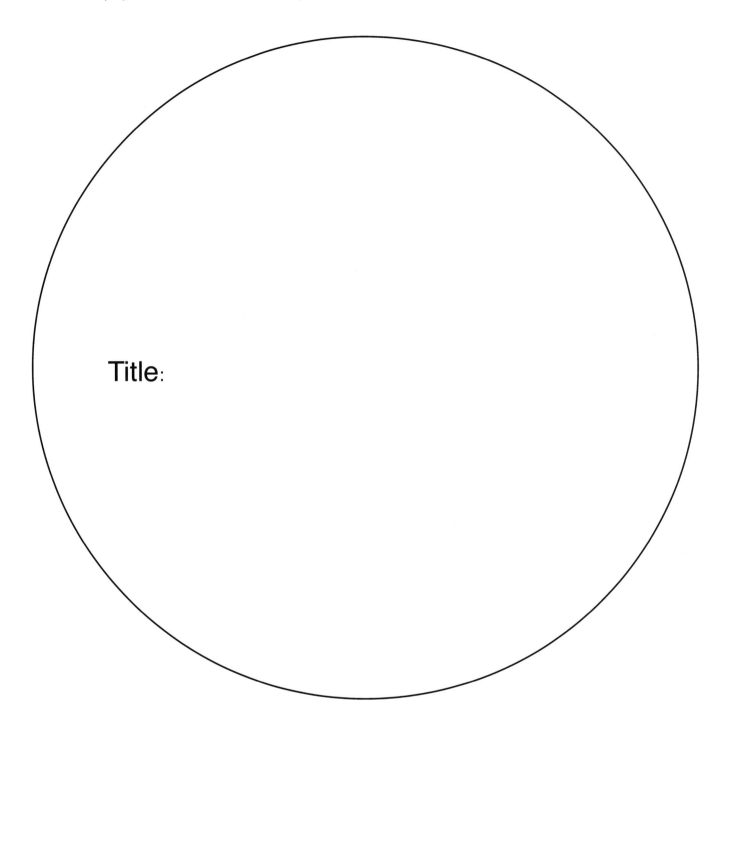

Title:

Title:

Beginning:

Event 1:

Event 2:

Event 3:

Event 4:

Event 5:

End:

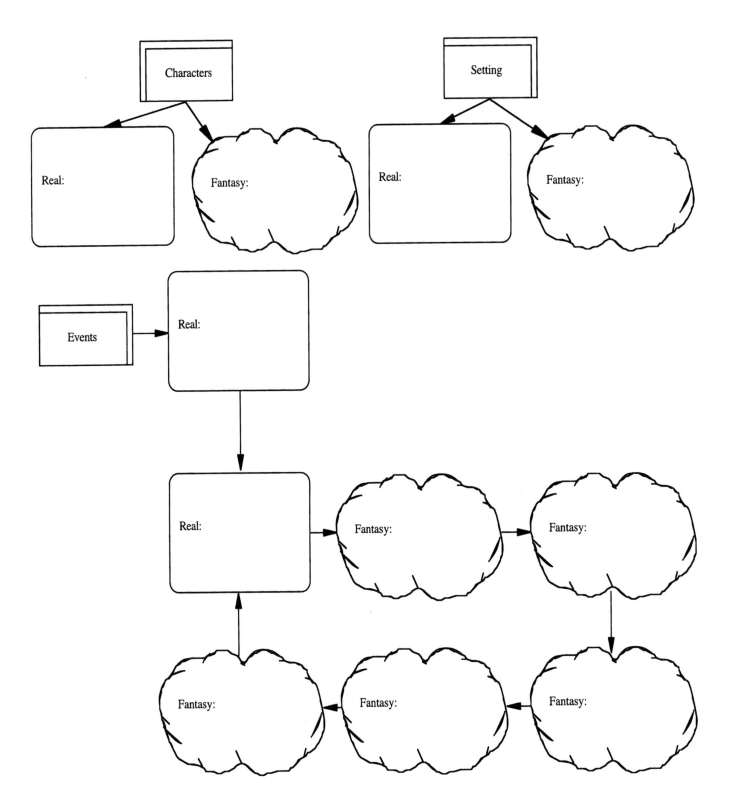

Visionary	Birthday	Birthplace	Company	Partners	Other Jobs

Cause   Effect

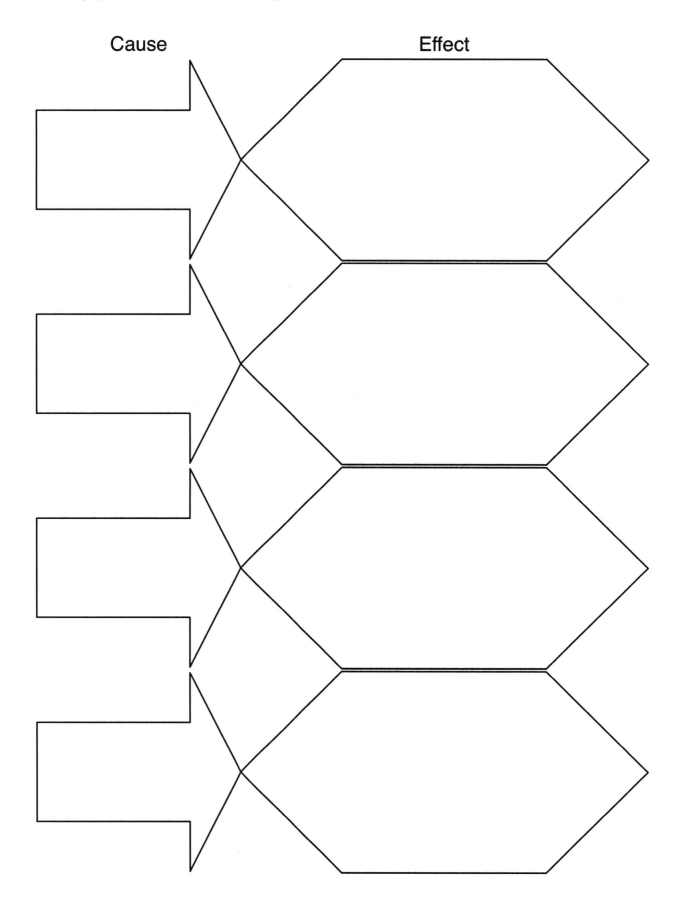

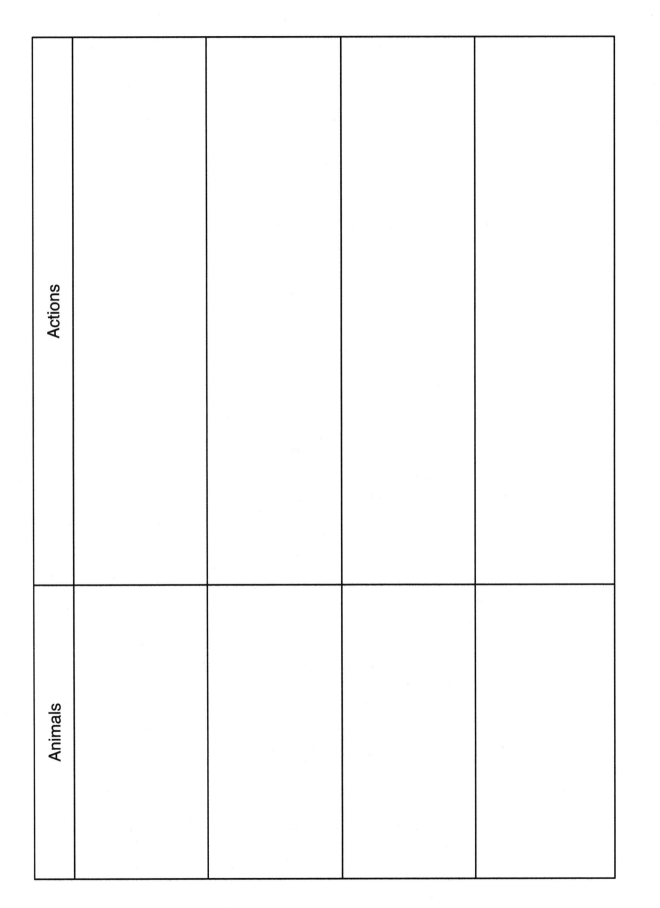

Opinion _____

Audience _____

Supporting Facts and Opinions	Possible Objections	Responses to Objections

	What I Saw	What I Tasted	What I Smelled	What I Heard	What I Felt
Day 1					
Day 2					
Day 3					
Day 4					
Day 5					

SOURCE C: AUTHOR AND ILLUSTRATOR INDEX

SOURCE D: TITLE INDEX

SOURCE E: SUBJECT INDEX

ABOUT THE AUTHOR

Kathryn I. Matthew received undergraduate and graduate degrees from the University of New Orleans. She received an Ed.D. in Curriculum and Instruction from the University of Houston. She has taught in elementary schools in Texas and Louisiana as a classroom teacher, English as a Second Language Specialist, and Technology Specialist. At the university level she has taught children's literature, reading, language arts, technology, and research classes. Kathryn co-authored the *Neal-Schuman Guide to Recommended Children's Books and Media for Use with Every Elementary Subject*; *Neal-Schuman Guide to Celebrations and Holidays*; *Reading Comprehension: Books and Strategies for the Elementary Curriculum*; and *Technology, Reading, and Language Arts*. She and her husband Chip live in Sugar Land, Texas.